LIVING IT UP

America's Love Affair with $\mathscr{L}$*uxury*

James B. Twitchell

SIMON & SCHUSTER

NEW YORK   LONDON   TORONTO   SYDNEY

For Liz

Simon & Schuster
Rockefeller Center
1230 Avenue of the Americas
New York, NY 10020

Copyright © 2002 by James B. Twitchell
All rights reserved, including the right of reproduction
in whole or in part in any form.

First Simon & Schuster Edition 2003
SIMON & SCHUSTER and colophon are registered trademarks
of Simon & Schuster, Inc.
Published by arrangement with Columbia University Press

For information regarding special discounts for bulk purchases,
please contact Simon & Schuster Special Sales at 1-800-456-6798
or business@simonandschuster.com
Manufactured in the United States of America
10 9 8 7 6 5 4
The Library of Congress Cataloging-in-Publication Data
Twitchell, James B.
   Living it up : our love affair with luxury/James B. Twitchell. —1st Simon
& Schuster ed.
      p.   cm.
   Includes bibliographical references and index.
      1. Affluent consumers — Psychology. 2. Luxuries — Marketing. I. Title.
   HF5415.32.T95   2003   306.3—dc21   2003041507
ISBN 0-7432-4506-7

Contents

Acknowledgments

This is not how I am supposed to be spending my time. I am supposed to be writing books on subjects like the curative powers of art. And I would be doing that had something not happened to me early in the 1990s. I was teaching a survey of English literature to undergraduates. I was explaining how knowing what people read in the past can be helpful in understanding who we are now. For instance, I moaned, it's almost impossible to make a literary allusion to anyone younger than thirty. A generation ago, had I recited what is arguably the best-known line in romanticism, "My heart leaps up when I behold a ____ in the sky," many educated people could have filled the blank in with *rainbow*. What a shame, I said to the class, that we have lost this once-shared culture.

A gangly kid in a baseball cap let loose from the back row, "*My* heart leaps up when I behold golden arches in the sky." The class roared in shared appreciation. As I remember, he never said another word all semester. He didn't need to.

Later, as I thought about it, Baseball Cap had a point. This generation really does have a shared culture, dreadful as it may be, a culture far more democratic and far more powerful than anything I ever experienced. It's not very deep and it's not very long lasting, but it's superpotent and increasingly understood all over the world. You need no formal education to participate; you're inducted from day one. To be sure, the members of this generation may have exchanged spirituality for materiality, landscape for brandscape, Giotto for Gucci, but they really do have something never seen before: a *Flashdance* culture that makes no distinctions (other than a willingness to spend) and is shared by front row and back row, all genders, all colors, all kinds, all at once.

Because part of my job, as I see it, is to explain the world around my students to the world around (and vice versa), I have pretty much left my post as gatekeeper to high culture and have gone native. I keep promising myself that I'll go back, but I suspect this is like the dean's saying that he can't wait to get back to his "real work." The commercial world has proved far more complex than I first thought. And far more alluring.

I have a number of people to thank for the fine mess I'm in. To my colleague Richard Brantley, who has shouldered my load as I started teaching courses for the advertising (!) department; to my editor, Jennifer Crewe, who has remained unfailingly polite and even went shopping with me; to my sister Mary, who can't believe what a turncoat I have become yet is still willing to proofread; to a captive (but not always captivated) audience at the Kellogg School of Management during the fall of 1999; and especially to my wife and daughters who . . . , well, you'll see: thanks.

Charlotte, Vermont

Introduction

At length I recollected the thoughtless saying of a great prince who, on being informed that the country had no bread, replied, "Let them eat cake."

—Jean-Jacques Rousseau, *Confessions*

Well, okay, so Marie Antoinette never said, "Let them eat cake." When Rousseau wrote these words, Marie was just eleven years old and living in Austria. But we know the words, and we like having her say them. She was a luxury junkie whose out-of-control spending grated on the poor and unfortunate French people. Americans especially like the story that, when she was told by an official that the people were angry because they had no bread, she responded, "Qu'ils mangent de la brioche." We fought a revolution to separate ourselves from exactly that kind of upper-crust insensitivity. She got her just deserts.

Now, however, two hundred years later, cake has become one of *our* favorite foods, part of the fifth food group: totally unnecessary luxury. And the great American revolution that is sweeping the world markets is how to get more and more of exactly those things that Marie also enjoyed. This is a revolution not of necessities but of wants. In fact, getting to cake has become one of the central unifying concerns of people around the globe. And one of the most disruptive.

I was thinking of Marie recently because I was invited to New York City to consult with an advertising agency. The agency folks were assembling a

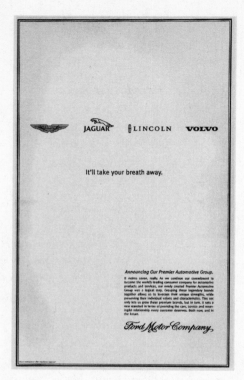

You don't need Sesame Street *to know that one of these things doesn't belong.*

video presentation on how well they understood how to sell luxury products. The multinational agency that hired me was trying to convince its client, Volvo, that the agency could reposition an upscale version of the sensible Swedish car as a luxury product. Ford had recently bought Volvo and was trying to *brand* it as a luxury automobile, to move it to where the profits are, from entrée to dessert.

My job, for which I was paid the equivalent of teaching many, many hours of Wordsworth, was to help the agency staff think about how to do it—not how to compose the ad but how to convince Ford that language and image could make Volvo sumptuous. What I thought was interesting, and what makes me think the subject is so central to our time, is that the agency people never seemed to question their ability to transform this pumpernickel of a car into a brioche. Sure, they seemed to say, we can do it. That's our job—piece of cake.

I asked my inquisitors—a roomful of late twentysomethings in the research department—does everything have to be luxurious? Aren't there enough luxury cars? From their horrified looks I realized that this was not an appropriate question. Volvo was going to be covered with frosting even though their slogan, "Luxury Inspired by Life," was, I thought, self-evidently ridiculous. Okay, I said, I'll help.

At one level, what the agency was doing is one of the central concerns of our commercial times. It was attempting to push a product up into a hitherto out-of-reach category: to *make* it a luxury object, an object of yearning, a badge of arrival. It is exactly this endeavor in any number of categories, in any number of markets all over the world, that seems to be linking us as One Nation Under Luxury.

Consuming cake, complete with its advertising, may in fact be doing what starry-eyed one-worlders have always dreamed of. It may be shrinking the world. How ironic that materialism may doing the work of idealism. Someone buying a Gucci-fied Volvo in Japan may well have more in com-

"Luxury Inspired by Life" — or by marketing?

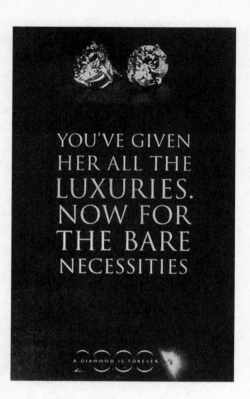

YOU'VE GIVEN
HER ALL THE
LUXURIES.
NOW FOR
THE BARE
NECESSITIES

A DIAMOND IS FOREVER
2000

The necessity of diamonds,
according to De Beers.

mon with his counterpart in Berlin, in Toronto, in Johannesburg than he
has with his own next-door neighbor precisely because of what he is buying. Prada, the Italian fashion concern, designs its store windows in Milan
and then sends that precise image to all its worldwide stores. A recent window treatment was simply called "Advertising Campaign."

Luxury spending in the United States has been growing more than four
times as fast as overall spending, and the rest of the West is not far behind.
And this spending is being done by younger and younger consumers. Take
a walk up Fifth Avenue in New York; at 58th, cross over and continue up
Madison. You'll see what I mean about who is swarming through these
stores. One of the most startling aspects of seeing the refugees streaming
from Kosovo was the number of adolescents dressed in Adidas, Nike, and
Tommy Hilfiger clothing. Others may pass judgment on this phenomenon,
many may be horrified by the waste and redundancy, but it is why so many
of us all over the world are becoming part of what, for lack of a better

phrase, is a mass class of upscale consumption. We understand each other not by sharing religion, politics, or ideas. We share branded things. We speak the Esperanto of advertising, *luxe populi*. Who knows? Perhaps we enter the global village by having dessert. To some people this is literally terrifying.

In the first part of this book I concentrate on some universally known things—I call them *opuluxe* objects—because the central movement in worldwide marketing since the 1980s has been to move more and more objects up into luxury brands. Think Prada, Montblanc, Mercedes, Ralph Lauren, Gucci, Evian, Starbucks, Rodeo Drive, Lexus, and the like. It's what Martha Stewart is doing at Kmart and why Shaft, the Harlem private eye of the early 1970s, is now wearing Armani. So many products are claiming luxury status that the credibility of the category is strained. Even poor De Beers seems flummoxed.

In the second part of this book I move to where luxury forms a coherent social pattern, a cake baked, if you will, by an industry. The industry is gambling, or *gaming*, as it is called in Las Vegas. Because the games are essentially the same, the frosting is what counts. What can you build over a collection of slot machines, roulette wheels, and card tables that will draw a huge crowd from all over the world? If you've been to Vegas recently, you know. You've seen the confections of opuluxe, the Bellagio and Venetian hotels and their waiting lists of eager attendees. These misnamed "hotels" are essentially self-contained city-states of sensational luxury, which may well presage the future of luxury not as objects but as linked experiences.

In fact, as I will argue, getting to these sensations may show the developing religious nature of modern luxury. For many shoppers consumption mimics epiphany, and luxury shopping becomes an almost transcendental experience. In other words, to mangle the analogy for the last time, for many millions of people all around the world the cake of luxury is becoming the wafer of presumed salvation. But before we get to this frightening consideration, let's back up a bit.

1.

Over the Top

AMERICANS IN THE LAP OF LUXURY

> *It is only shallow people who do not judge the world by appearances. The mystery of the world is the visible, not the invisible.*
>
> —Oscar Wilde, *The Picture of Dorian Gray*

If you want to understand material culture at the beginning of the twenty-first century, you must understand the overwhelming importance of unnecessary material. If you are looking for the one unambiguous result of modern capitalism, of the industrial revolution, and of marketing, here it is. In the way we live now, you are not what you make. You are what you consume. And outside of that which is found in a few aisles in the grocery and hardware stores, most of what you consume is *totally* unnecessary yet remarkably well made.

The most interesting of those superfluous objects belong in a socially constructed and ever-shifting class called luxury. Consuming those objects, objects as rich in meaning as they are low in utility, causes lots of happiness and distress. As well they should. For one can make the argument that until all necessities are had by all members of a community, no one should have luxury. More complex still is that, since the 1980s, the bulk consumers of luxury have not been the wealthy but the middle class, your next-door neighbors and their kids. And this is happening not just in the West but in many parts of the world.

When I was growing up in the middle class of the 1950s, luxury objects were lightly tainted with shame. You had to be a little cautious if you drove a Cadillac, wore a Rolex, or lived in a house with more than two columns out front. The rich could drip with diamonds, but you should stay dry. Movie stars could drive convertibles; you should keep your top up. If you've got it, don't flaunt it. Remember, the people surrounding you had lived through the Depression, a time that forever lit the bright line between have-to-have, don't-need-to-have, and have-in-order-to-show-off.

The best definition of this old-style off-limits luxury came to me from my dad. I was just a kid and it was my first trip to a cafeteria: Morrison's Cafeteria in Pompano Beach, Florida, February 1955. When I got to the desserts, I removed the main course from my tray and loaded up on cake and Jello. My dad told me to put all the desserts back but one. I said that wasn't fair. To me the whole idea of cafeteria was to have as much as you want of what you want. My dad said no, that was not the idea of cafeteria. The idea of cafeteria is that you can have just one of many choices.

The New Luxury, the Luxurification of the Commonplace

Look around American culture and you will see how wrong he was. Almost every set of consumables has a dessert at the top. And you can have as much of it as you can get on your plate or as much of it as your credit card will allow. This is true not just for expensive products like *town* cars and McMansions but for everyday objects. In bottled water, for instance, there is Evian, advertised as if it were a liquor. In coffee, there's Starbucks; in ice cream, Häagen-Dazs; in sneakers, Nike; in whiskey, Johnnie Walker Blue; in credit cards, American Express Centurian; in wine, Chateau Margaux; in cigars, Arturo Fuente Hemingway; and, well, you know the rest. Having a few TVs around the house is fine, but what you really need is a home entertainment center with a JBL Ultra Synthesis One audio system, a Vidikron Vision One front projector, a Stewart Ultramatte 150 screen, a Pioneer DV-09 DVD player, an AMX ViewPoint remote control. . . . Hungry for dinner with your entertainment? Wolfgang Puck has his own line of TV dinners . . . whoops, entrées.

Name the category, no matter how mundane, and you'll find a premium or, better yet, a super-premium brand at the top. And having more than you can conceivably use of such objects is not met with opprobrium but with genial acceptance. This pattern persists regardless of class: the average number of branded sneakers for adolescent males? 4.8 pairs. And regardless of culture: a favorite consumer product in China? Chanel lipstick dispensers sans lipstick.

What Every American Needs to Know

When I first started thinking about luxury, I took a list from the *Robb Report* of the "Best of the Best" (June 1999) to my upper-division class on advertising. The *Robb Report*, a "magazine for the luxury lifestyle," features "the best the good life has to offer," from luxury and exotic cars to yachts, high-tech equipment, dining, travel, aircraft, spirits, cigars, fashion, jewelry, art. Just a few minutes between its covers is enough to make even the most die-hard capitalist think that communism is not all that bad a way to distribute goods.

First, I asked my students to identify data from E. D. Hirsch's best-selling *Cultural Literacy: What Every American Needs to Know*—terms like *gross national product, Emancipation Proclamation, irony* . . . , listed in the appendix under the rubric "What Literate Americans Know." Naturally, they were abysmal, functionally illiterate. Then I gave them this list of the "best of the best," most of which I had never heard of, and asked them to identify. Here's just a bit of the list:

Men's wear designer: Armani	Sedan: Mercedes Benz S Class
Suit: Cesare Attolini	Sports car: Porsche 911
Shirt: Luigi Borrelli	Convertible: Ferrari F355 Spider
Tie: E. Marinella	Exotic car: Ferrari 456M GT
Formal wear: Giorgio Armani	Sports utility vehicle: Mercedes Benz
Casual wear: E. Zegna	Performance car: AMG CLK-GTR
Knitwear: Loro Piana	Sportfishing boat: Hines-Farley
Pants: Giorgio Armani	Sailing yacht: Alloy Yacht
Golf wear: Bobby Jones	Light jet: Cessna Citation Excel
Boating wear: Paul & Shark	Midsize jet: Cessna Citation X
Tennis wear: Lacoste	Heavy jet: Dassault Falcon 900EX
Eyewear: Silhouette Optical	Sport bike: Yamaha YZF-R1
Cuff links: Asprey & Garrard	Tour bike: BMW K1200LT Custom
Pen: Omas	Luxury hotel: Peninsula Hong Kong
Women's wear designer: Galliano	Golf irons: Ping
Evening wear: Oscar de la Renta	Putters: TearDrop

Casual wear: Helmut Lang

Shoes: Chanel

Handbags: Hermès

Lingerie: La Perla

Furs: Karl Lagerfeld for Fendi

Watchmaking: Patek Philippe

Jewelry: Harry Winston

Kitchen range: Le Chateau 147

Dishwasher: Miele 900 Series

Refrigerator: Sub-Zero

Spa/shower: Jacuzzi J-Allure

Outdoor grill: Lazy Man

Flat plasma TV: Pioneer

Desktop computer: Sony VAIO

Notebook computer: Toshiba

Golfwoods: Callaway

Casino: Caesars Palace

CD player: Krell KPS 25s

Tennis racket: Wilson Carbon

Ski resort: Vail

Skis: Volant Ti Power

Fishing rod: Thomas & Thomas

Airline: British Air

Spirit: Macallan Malt Whiskey

Aperitif: Cuvée Dom Perignon 1986

Cigar: A. Fuente

Humidor: Elie Bleu

DVD player: Pioneer DV-09

Personal organizer: Palm V

Cellular phone: Nokia

They know *these* names! I admit that this sampling is not very sophisticated. These are just college kids. But they are the tail of the tiger. They are relatively confined now but still very potent in the marketplace (about $20 billion a year and access to a whole lot more). What was interesting to me is that so much of their consumption knowledge is anticipatory, and some of it—like knowing the jet planes—is clearly never going to be realized. But don't tell them this. In a page one story on September 14, 1999, the *Wall Street Journal* reported that a KPMG International poll of college seniors found that fully 74 percent expect to become millionaires. No matter: They already know what some Americans need to know.

Basil Englis and Michael Solomon, professors of marketing in the School of Business at Rutgers University, were more sophisticated in their research. They wanted to show how tightly college students cluster around this kind of top-brand knowledge. They drew guinea pigs from undergraduate business majors at their institution and presented them with forty cards, each containing a description of different clusters of consumers.

The professors sifted the clusters to make four groups—lifestyles, if you will—representative of undergraduate society. They were Young Suburbia, Money & Brains, Smalltown Downtown, and Middle America. Then Englis and Solomon gathered images of objects from four product categories (automobiles, magazines/newspapers, toiletries, and alcoholic beverages) that fit into each group. The students were asked to put the various images together into coherent groups; they were also to state their current proximity to, or desire to be part of, each group in the future.

Next, they were asked to sort the cards into four piles, or categories, defined as

"These people are very similar to how I would like to be" (aspirational group).

"These people are very similar to how I currently see myself" (occupied group).

"These people are very similar to how I would not like to be" (avoidance group).

"These people have no meaning for me; I don't feel strongly about wanting to be like or not wanting to be like them" (irrelevant group).

As might be expected the Money & Brains cluster was the most popular aspirational niche. What Englis and Solomon did not expect was how specific and knowledgeable the students were about the possessions that they did not have but knew that members of that cluster needed. When asked what brand of automobile they would drive, here's what they said: BMWs (53.6 percent), Mercedes (50.7), Cadillacs (30.4), Volvos (23.2), Porsches (21.7), Acuras (17.4), and Jaguars (15.9). They knew what they wanted to read: travel magazines (21.7 percent), *Vogue* (21.7), *BusinessWeek* (20.3), *Fortune* (17.9), and *GQ* (15.9). Again, this is not what they did read but what they took to be the reading material of the desired group. What they were actually reading (or so they said) were *Forbes, Barron's,* the *New Yorker,* and *Gourmet.* No mention of *Rolling Stone, Playboy, Spin,* or *Maxim* for this group. They certainly knew what to drink: Heineken beer (33.3 percent), expensive wines (26.1), scotch (18.8), champagne (17.4), and Beck's beer (15). They also knew what to sprinkle on their bodies: Polo (27.5 percent), Obsession (15.9), and Drakkar (15.9).

What the professors found was not just that birds of a feather had started to flock together but that these young birds already knew what flock to shy away from. They were not ashamed of smoking, for instance, but of smoking the wrong brand. Their prime avoidance group corresponded to the Smalltown Downtown cluster. The Money & Brainers knew a lot about the Smalltowners. They knew about favored pickup trucks, Chevys (23.2 percent) and Fords (18.8). They knew that this group reads *People* (30.4 percent), *Sports Illustrated* (26.1), *TV Guide* (24.6), *Wrestling* (21.7), fishing magazines (20.3), and the *National Enquirer* (18.8). They assumed that

Smalltowners preferred Budweiser (59.4 percent), followed by Miller (24.6) and Coors (18.8). Essentially, the Money & Brainers had learned not just what to buy but what to avoid (or at least what to say to avoid). As chefs say, what is sent back to the kitchen is often more important than what is eaten.

Such shared knowledge, as Professor Hirsch knows well, is the basis of culture. This insight was, after all, the rationale behind a liberal arts education. John Henry Newman and Matthew Arnold argued for state-supported education in the nineteenth century precisely because cultural literacy meant social cohesion. No one argued that it was important to know algebraic functions or Latin etymologies or what constitutes a sonnet because such knowledge allows us to solve important social problems. We learn such matters because it is the basis of how to speak to each other, how we develop a bond of shared history and commonality. This is the secular religion of the liberal arts and sciences, what Pierre Bourdieu calls cultural capital.

In our postmodern world we have, it seems, exchanged knowledge of history and science (a knowledge of production) for knowledge of products and how such products interlock to form coherent social patterns (a knowledge of consumption). Buy this *and* don't buy that has replaced make/learn this, *don't* make/learn that. After all, in the way we live now, everyone is a consumer, but not everyone is a worker. As Marcel Duchamp, sly observer of the changing scene, said, "Living is more a question of what one spends than what one makes" (quoted in "Thoughts":160). Thus a new denomination of cultural capital.

A shift in currency has clear ramifications. A producer culture focuses on the independent self of the worker: *self*-help, *self*-discipline, *self*-respect, *self*-control, *self*-reliance, *self*-interest. Responsibility is situated in the individual. Can she get work? A consumer culture, however, focuses on community. Fit in, don't stand out. Be cool. The standard of judgment becomes the ability to interact effectively with others, to win their affection and admiration—to merge with others of the same lifestyle. Can he consume the right brands?

The Message of Massage

When consumption is triumphant, one witnesses an almost universal sense of entitlement to the supposed sensations of luxury. "Pamper yourself" is no longer a rallying cry for the rich or for Leona Helmsley's bridge club. Now it's for the rest of us. Day spas that offer a full menu of massages, pedicures, and wraps jumped to three thousand in 1998 from fewer than one hundred in 1988, according to *Dayspa* magazine. In 1998 J.C. Penney opened day spas at nineteen of its stores and expected to add five to ten new ones each year (Springen 1999:12).

Not surprisingly, given all these pampered people, the U.S. Department of Labor has projected a 44.7 percent increase in job openings for manicurists between 1996 and 2006. Massage is now for the masses too. Thirteen percent of Americans received at least one rub from a massage therapist in 1999—up from only 8 percent in 1997, according to the American Massage Therapy Association. Today the bashful don't even need to disrobe. Places like Minute Massage near the Chicago Board of Trade offer ten-minute chair massages for $12.50 (Springen 1999:12). In Las Vegas I saw a blue hair getting a massage as she was pulling the arm of a slot machine. And just look at the Sharper Image catalog and you see the eruption of the minispas and such gadgets as the Private Masseuse back massager ($249).

In the older culture, my dad's culture, the limited production capacity of the economy sharply reduced aspirations to material comfort. In the modern world, my culture, much greater material satisfactions lie within the reach of even those of modest means. Thus a producer culture becomes a consumer culture, a hoarding culture becomes a surplus culture, a work culture becomes a therapeutic culture. Because what you buy becomes more important than what you make, luxury is not a goal; for many it is a necessity.

Michael J. Apter, a psychologist at Northwestern University, has studied why we do things and, by extension, why we buy things. In *The Experience of Motivation: The Theory of Psychological Reversals,* he divides general orientations into *telic* (arousal reducing) and *paratelic* (arousal seeking). A telic motivation starts with isolating a need and then feeling anxious about resolving it. The experience ends, if successful, with a feeling of relaxation. If the ending does not satisfy the need (postdecision dissonance), the anxiety continues, and the process is repeated until it abates. A paratelic tendency, however, begins in a state of well-being that edges over into boredom. The person seeks excitement and judges the act by the experience. Does it resolve boredom? Not to put too fine a point on it, but consuming luxury for many Americans has gone from telic to paratelic, from product to process, from problem resolution to emotion seeking, from object to experience.

Letting Go

And there is something else, uniformly neglected by commentators, that needs to be acknowledged, at least in passing. The act of luxury spending is often pleasurable irrespective of the object. Sometimes we spend so that we will *not* save. Spending for many is power, intoxication, conquest, even sexual. It's the letting go, the relaxing part of getting and spending, what the French call *jouissance,* releasing restraint, just pissing it away. The "urge to splurge" is no haphazard trope. I once asked my students what *disposable* meant in the economic term *disposable income.* You can guess what some of them said.

The pleasure of spending just to spend is the dirty little secret of affluence. The rich used to do it; now the rest of us are having a go at it. A sign of the time, perhaps, is a recent book by David Brancaccio, genial host of public radio's "Marketplace," called *Squandering Aimlessly: My Adventures in the American Marketplace.* The shtick: What would you do with a windfall of money? The choices: a shopping spree, doing good, starting a business, gambling, giving it away, investing in the markets, buying a house, going back to school, retiring early, or saving for a rainy day. What was interesting was not that the first choice was far more popular than the last; it was that none of his respondents was dumbfounded that indeed found money would be coming her or his way. In fact, many had already seriously contemplated this question.

Little wonder that *Who Wants to Be a Millionaire?* in which riches come to you for answering questions of no special importance, has replaced *The Millionaire* of the 1950s, in which riches come to you because J. Bereford Tipton has learned of your special qualities. Now you get riches by following *wants.* It used to be by following *deeds.*

This is all quite glib, to be sure, but it is already part of what we take for granted. Gross generalization that it is, we have gone from an "ought" culture where superego was central—where we had rules for everything from how to commence courtship to how to tip the porter—to a "want" culture—where entitlement to branded objects, or at least the wherewithal to buy such objects, is a given. At the center of this consumer-based world is always the luxury object, the object known to us by the brand, years and years before we ever come close to purchase.

In a world informed by marketing, the shame of consuming too much has been reconfigured into the shame of not consuming the proper stuff. We don't scoff at having children out of wedlock, but please don't dress the baby in mismatched outfits from Baby Gap. We don't glower at the Wall Street banker filing for bankruptcy, but don't let him be seen in an Armani suit and Weejuns. And, please, let his second wife, the trophy wife, be smart enough not to wear silver with gold. Don't mix Tommy Hilfiger with Gucci, don't get your SUV dirty, don't wear your cell phone on your belt. . . .

New Luxury: Think Cashmere — Whoops! — Pashmina

This powerful desire to associate with recognized objects of little intrinsic but high positional value is at the heart of Luxe Americana. It is what Martha Stewart is doing down at Kmart introducing her Silver Label goods. Of her many endorsed products, one is of special interest: her line of matelassé coverlets and shams—really, just bedcovers. They are available in yellow, white, and multicolored stripes and come in silk, linen, crushed velvet, Egyptian cotton, cotton sateens, and even . . . cashmere. Remember three things: This is Kmart, a bedspread is something you buy not to show off to others but to please yourself, and cashmere is, well, supposed to be something really special.

So here is the *Cashmere* Company hawking something it calls *pashmina*. The word is a linguistic trick. Cashmere is goat hair from Kashmir, an area between India and Pakistan, whereas *pashmina* is simply the Persian word for the same goat in the same area. In other words, it's the same stuff. But that's not what is interesting. It is that pashmina has been introduced precisely because places like Kmart have too much cashmere. So what we have is a top-of-the-line product topped because too many people were in the checkout line.

But then again what of Michael Graves–designed toasters for Target (pronounced by wits like the French but with ironic flair—tar-ZHAY), Ralph Lauren house paint, and Ernest Hemingway– and Cole Porter–brand furniture at Ethan Allen Furniture stores? This tectonic shift in consumption is why the designer Lynette Jennings, host of the Discovery

Channel's *Lynette Jennings Design* and *HouseSmart*, is peddling door-knobs at Home Depot.

To capture this luxe-lite market is also why some one-time high-end stores are moving down-market. Abercrombie & Fitch and Neiman Marcus have had to lose a bit of stiffness to survive. They have not lost their affectionate sobriquets, however. They are still known as "Abergrabbie and Snitch" and "Needless Mark-Up."

But if you want to see how varied the consumer for the new luxury is, just take a tour of your local Costco or Sam's Club parking lot. Observe the shiny new imported sedans and SUVs alongside aging subcompacts. Or spend an hour watching what is being sold on the Home Shopping Network, a televised flea market for impulse buyers. The system now has twenty-three thousand incoming phone lines capable of handling up to

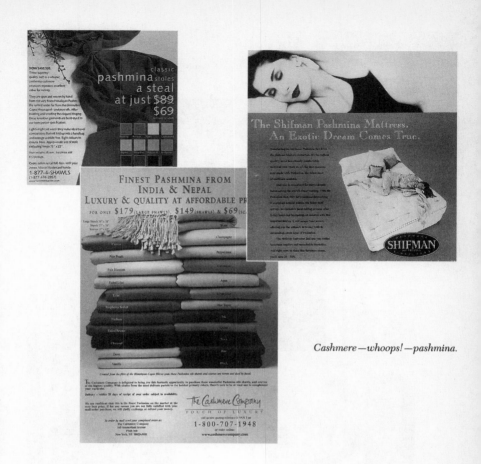

Cashmere—whoops!—pashmina.

twenty thousand calls a minute. Home Shopping no longer sells just cubic zirconium rings. Not when the real money is in designer handbags.

As rapidly as boomers are moving up to luxury, so luxury is moving down into hitherto common grounds. Just try having a normal cup of coffee and you'll see what I mean. Bad enough that Starbucks should have colonized almost ever street corner, just go into the 7-Eleven. The convenience store chain, that most fundamental of all modern on-the-go stores, is still the retail leader in fresh-brewed coffee-to-go. Now inching over from latteland is French roast, whole-bean gourmet coffee, served in a special vacuum container with a hand pump. It's only a matter of time before the QuikStop starts selling croissants and microbrewed beer.

But is having 7-Eleven in the $3 cuppa-joe business any different than having Staples, the discount office supply store, selling $185 Montblanc ball-

point pens, or having Wal-Mart, the discount chain, selling designer products like Dooney & Bourke's $300 drawstring handbags or Ray-Ban sunglasses for $99? Sam's Club, Wal-Mart's "let's pretend" warehouse unit, recently began installing prefabricated humidors to sell premium cigars. The one characteristic of modern luxe is its profound oxymoronic nature: If everyone can have it, is it still luxury?

You can see this wonderful mix-up almost everywhere in current American commercial culture. It's why rappers are draped in oversized Tommy Hilfiger shirts and shod in Nike swooshes. It's why music videos

feature such groups as Wu-Tang Clan performing their popular song "Wu Wear." The song is entirely about what to wear. As the lyrics make clear, "It ain't what you want, baby, it's what you need, baby." And just what is it that you need? The rap artists (who have their own clothing line) explain:

> *Went through a garment renaissance*
> *And stopped wearing Benetton, Tommy Hill*
> *Perry Ellis, Nautica, or Liz Claiborne,*

Ocean Pacific, Fila, Bill Blass and leave fitted.
Quit the Armani sweaters with the Gucci wool knitted
Now all he buys Kani's, Cross Colors, Shabazz Brothers,
Mecca, Pelly Pell, 88 North Q and a few others.

The entire song is telling fans (mostly suburban teenagers) what to wear and what to avoid. What they are avoiding is startling because it shows how deeply the brand names of luxury have penetrated. These kids are moving through luxury brands as if they were clicking through television channels.

This phenomenon explains why companies like Starbucks and Ben & Jerry's are appearing on street corners in poor urban neighborhoods; why Gen Y-ers are clutching bottled water with French names and cigars with Cuban wrappers; why cars like *Lexus* (get it?) have elbowed aside cars like Cadillac; why Calvin Klein jeans gave the heebie-jeebies to Levi Strauss and are now getting the heebie-jeebies from Diesel; why fake Rolex watches are sold on street corners and on the Internet; why R. J. Reynolds is touting its Winston S2 brand of "100 % first cut tobacco"; why Mattel makes Ralph Lauren Barbie, Bob Mackie Barbie, and Donna Karan Barbie; why Las Vegas casinos like the Bellagio and the Venetian have impressive art collections right next to gaming rooms and adjacent to Rodeo Drive shops that are selling stuff from Tiffany and Chanel; why Ferrari makes a golf bag and Porsche makes watches; why Brooks Brothers has a line of wine and Jack Daniels sells barbecue sauce and clothes; why Ralph Lauren puts his name on eyeglasses and bras; why Toyota's motto of a few years ago was "Affordable Luxury" and Buick advertises its Century as "a luxury car for everyone," while Pontiac claims its Bonneville is "luxury with attitude"; why Cape Cod Potato Chips, a thick and very crisp potato chip, have risen from the ranks of junk food to the status of "gourmet" treats, just like David's cookies and Dove Bars.

Where Do You Put All This Stuff?

Look at any house-as-self magazine and you will see how important the closet has become. It should be central. We have to put all this unnecessary stuff somewhere. In fact, the closet itself has become a marker of luxury consumption. It has gone from storage, to walk-in, to live in. "Internal storage systems" have developed as a way not to contain your stuff but to show it off.

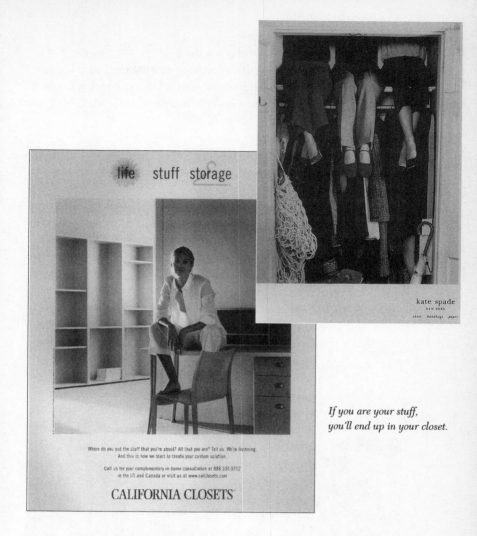

If you want to see the importance of the luxury closet, ponder this recent television ad from Nordstrom, the high-end retailer. The commercial never mentions a single object that the store sells. Instead we follow a young woman carrying an armful of bags up into her apartment. She opens the door, barely able to get her stuff in, it's so cramped. She has to close the door using her backside. She drops some of her booty and barely squeezes into her kitchen and from there into her tiny bedroom. The bed takes up most of the space. The entire apartment is claustrophobic. She even has to step on the bed to get to her closet to put her purchases away. But when she opens the closet door and flips on the light, we see that the room is massive, huge, never ending. It's clear from the way the camera lovingly pans and the music surges that this is her reward, the safe harbor in a troubled world. Her cat meows and scurries in as she walks over to one wall and hangs up the clothes that she has just bought.

On-line luxe
from pre-dot.com crash days.

The Internet Only Speeds up the Process of Loading up on Stuff

What is the great promise of the World Wide Web? Take a look. Because there are so many, I've chosen just those luxury sites advertised in the February 2000 issue of the vade mecum of luxe lite, *Vanity Fair* magazine.

Now, admittedly, these sites are mostly for jewelry, watches, rings, and the like. But if you really want at see the audience for such stuff as satin sheets, glass vitrines, ready-made monogrammed heirlooms, canopied four-poster beds, embossed stationery, kilim pillows, linen shirts, Verona stemware, copper pots, signature underwear, chemically distressed furniture with machine-made patina, remote-control CD players for the shower, and stainless steel portable gas grills, just log on.

When LuxuryFinder.com, an Internet shopping site, went on line in October 1999 ("Where generation luxe shops the Web"), it exploded. In its first week of operation the service sold, inter alia, one hundred Asprey & Garrard travel bags at $575 each. Visitors to the site are advised, "For purchases over $50,000, please call a customer service representative to make special delivery arrangements." Customer services include personal cybershoppers and cybersecretaries.

Luxury shopping on the Web has since collapsed. But over time it will become a venue for certain specialized stuff. For instance, want a family crest? You can buy one on the Web. Want a ring with your family crest? Get that too. Want a painting of your children looking as though they belong next to Little Lord Fauntleroy? Just download the photo to a dot-com service, and a computer-generated "oil" painting arrives by FedEx in a few days.

The Vocabulary of Consumption

Here's another word that has moved in tandem with luxury: *trophy*. A trophy used to be a shiny object that you won for distinction in some endeavor. The name of the event was engraved on the trophy and *then* your name was added. Often trophies were circulated so that you only held the vaunted object for a short time. Then you returned it so that others could compete for it. Your name remained but grew dimmer and dimmer with time. Tarnish, like patina, only made it more precious.

Now trophies have become a standard way of giving and publicly displaying acknowledgment. Look in the Yellow Pages of almost any town and you will see that "Trophies, Medals and Awards" has its own section. At the same time *trophy* has become an adjective for luxury consumption, as in a

You're a winner. Now design your own trophy.

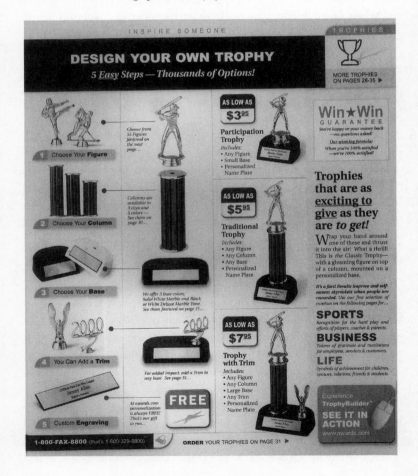

18

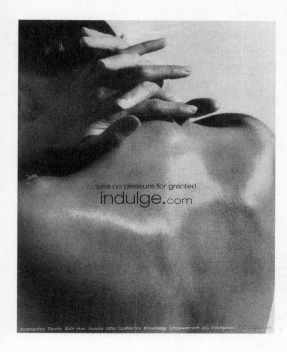

take no pleasure for granted
indulge.com

Accessories Beauty Bath Hair Jewelry Gifts Confidence Knowledge Empowerment Joy Indulgence

*Take no pleasure for granted
that you can't buy on-line.*

trophy car, trophy house, trophy wife, or, most recently, with the selling of reproductive material, trophy sperm or trophy egg.

And another word that charts this same course is *indulgence*. An indulgence was once a business deal struck with the church in which the penitent exchanged something of worth, usually money, for either partial forgiveness (partial) or full forgiveness (plenary). The transaction was so powerful that not only did the de Medicis make part of their fortune converting indulgence monies into florins but innovations such as the printing press were soon being used to codify the process. Certificates of indulgence were some of the first printed matter to be produced, well before the Bible.

The misuse of this system of trading lucre for grace was what upset Martin Luther and brought on the Reformation. The word *indulgence* had a pejorative note until recently. But if advertising is to be believed, the bargain implicit in indulgence has just been reformatted. Now you exchange money not for grace in the next world but for satisfaction in this world. "Indulge Yourself" is the implicit promise of modern luxury goods. You deserve a break today. You are worth it. We're here to help you indulge.

The Penalty of Leadership

IN EVERY field of human endeavor, he that is first must perpetually live in the white light of publicity.

Whether the leadership be vested in a man or in a manufactured product, emulation and envy are ever at work.

In art, in literature, in music, in industry, the reward and the punishment are always the same.

The reward is widespread recognition; the punishment, fierce denial and detraction.

When a man's work becomes a standard for the whole world, it also becomes a target for the shafts of the envious few.

If his work be merely mediocre, he will be left severely alone—if he achieves a masterpiece, it will set a million tongues a-wagging.

Jealousy does not protrude its forked tongue at the artist who produces a commonplace painting.

Whatsoever you write, or paint, or play, or sing, or build, no one will strive to surpass or to slander you unless your work be stamped with the seal of genius.

Long, long after a great work or a good work has been done, those who are disappointed or envious, continue to cry out that it cannot be done.

Spiteful little voices in the domain of art were raised against our own Whistler as a mountebank, long after the big world had acclaimed him its greatest artistic genius.

Multitudes flocked to Bayreuth to worship at the musical shrine of Wagner, while the little group of those whom he had dethroned and displaced argued angrily that he was no musician at all.

The little world continued to protest that Fulton could never build a steamboat, while the big world flocked to the river banks to see his boat steam by.

The leader is assailed because he is a leader, and the effort to equal him is merely added proof of that leadership.

Failing to equal or to excel, the follower seeks to depreciate and to destroy—but only confirms once more the superiority of that which he strives to supplant.

There is nothing new in this.

It is as old as the world and as old as the human passions—envy, fear, greed, ambition, and the desire to surpass.

And it all avails nothing.

If the leader truly leads, he remains—the leader.

Master-poet, master-painter, master-workman, each in his turn is assailed, and each holds his laurels through the ages.

That which is good or great makes itself known, no matter how loud the clamor of denial.

That which deserves to live—lives.

What a difference a few generations make— penalty becomes reward (Cadillac at the beginning of the twentieth century, Lincoln at the end).

This should finally put an end to all that "less is more" nonsense.

LINCOLN

The new Town Car from Lincoln. What a luxury car should be.

Defining Luxury Down: The Example of Prestige Cars

If you want to see the difference that a generation makes in downshifting luxury, just look at how top-of-the-line domestic automobiles are advertised. Compare Cadillac in the early part of the twentieth century with Lincoln at the end of the century, and you'll get the idea.

Cadillac's pitch in 1915 was that luxury comes at a price and that price includes humility, even mild mortification. You buy this car and you take responsibility for sharing excellence. The true price of luxury is not cheap. In fact, you will be reviled, assailed, and envied. This car is a laurel. Be careful how you wear it. The real headline is not just "The Penalty of Leadership," it is "The Penalty of Luxury."

By contrast, Lincoln's current pitch is pure indulgence. Buy this object and let your lust for comfort run wild. Lincoln is "what a luxury object should be." And after all you've been through, you deserve it. If not to own, then to lease.

Needless to say, as the twentieth century faded into oblivion, Cadillac, which had a history of "owning" the luxury category, lost its vaunted place as the best-selling domestic luxury car to Lincoln. The Lincoln division of the Ford Motor Car Company has a single-word advertising motto: "Luxury."

Incidentally, Ford also owns the prestigious English car company Jaguar. Lest anyone doubt how powerful the modern claim on luxury is— the company also owns Aston Martin, which really *is* a luxury car—just look at how the company couches the appeal.

The refreshing candor of Jaguar.

Perhaps the best example of what I call luxury creep, in which a down-market product comes uptown solely on the basis of advertising, is Buick Century. Buick has had a history of being a car for strivers who have not quite made it. Just look back on Buick advertising in the sixties and you can see the company's typical reticence. In 1965 Buick advertising carried the tag line, "Wouldn't you really rather have a Buick?" which survived through the 1980s. In 1980 the company added a second theme: "The great American road belongs to Buick." Then in 1986 McCann-Erickson, the ad agency, positioned Buicks as "premium American motorcars."

Saying it doesn't necessarily make it so: luxury by proclamation.

Now Buick does have a luxury car, the Park Avenue. But the Century is an underling, now positioned as "A luxury car for everyone." The TV ad reinforces this positioning. In one commercial we see scenes of family bliss, as the voice-over by the actor Willem Dafoe asks: "Are rich people taller than the rest of us? Are their loved ones more deserving of an air bag? Was the sun created solely for their enjoyment?" Cut to the "beauty shot" of the car. And what is this car? It's just a regular bucket of pig iron and plastic from Detroit, a standard 3.1-liter V-6.

Never mind the oxymoron and tautology of "a luxury car for everyone." The problem is more fundamental. This car is just a standard Buick, which is just a jazzed-up Chevy, which is just a dumbed-down Cadillac, which is just an Oldsmobile, which is just like tons of Fords and Chryslers, as well as most Japanese midrange cars. The only luxury about it is the pretension of saying this is luxurious.

A Personal Note in Passing

You can already tell by my tone that part of me is a little wary of the eruption of opuluxe. In the last few years I have spent hours flipping through a new genre of magazine—the *Robb Report, Millionaire, Indulgence, Flaunt, Luxe, Icon, Self: The Best of Everything, Ornament: The Art of Personal Adornment,* or *Cigar Aficionado* (with the "cigar" now lowercased and "The Good Life Magazine for Men" added as a subtitle), as well as standard glossy pulp from Condé Nast like *GQ, Vogue, Vanity Fair,* and, most recently, *Lucky.* I have trolled Rodeo Drive, Worth Avenue, and upper Madison Avenue and traveled to Las Vegas where I stood agog for hours in the Bellagio and Venetian hotels.

I admit from the start that you could argue that this is not real luxury that I am studying but a kind of ersatz variety, punk luxe, and maybe you would be correct. My father would have argued that real luxury is characterized not by shine but by patina, that its allure comes from inborn aesthetics, not from glitzy advertising, that it is passed from generation to generation and cannot be bought at the mall, and, most of all, that its consumption is private, not conspicuous. His words for modern luxury would have included *gauche, vulgar, nouveau, tasteless,* and, most interestingly, *offensive.*

In fact, maybe the rich have only two genuine luxury items left: time and philanthropy. As the old paradox goes, the rich share the luxury of too

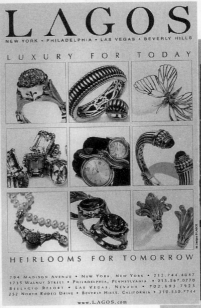

*The appeal of old-style,
pass-it-down luxury.*

much time on their hands with the very people with whom they often share
their philanthropy. For sure, the rest of us are having a go at all their stuff,
albeit for a knockoff to be held only a short time. I can't afford a casita on
Bermuda, but my timeshare can get it for me at least for a week. I can't
own a limo, but I can rent one. If I can't fly on the Concorde, I can upgrade
to first class with the miles I "earn" by using my American Express card. I
can lease a Lexus.

In a sense luxury objects don't exist anymore as they used to because
"real" luxury used to be for the "happy few," and in the world of the jubi-
lant Dow there is no more "happy *few*." Sudden Wealth Syndrome, as the
Los Angeles Times called it, is not just for dot-com innovators or contest-
ants on *Who Wants to Be a Millionaire?* but for a generation whose wealth

is being transferred to it by the steady demise of the Generation That Fought the War. The "wealth effect," as Federal Reserve Chairman Alan Greenspan calls it, drives more and more money to chase after goods whose production can hardly be called beneficial.

To be sure, in a world in which so many different brands compete for our attention, the prestige of one seemingly overnight luxury soon cancels out another, and "the best" is simply the latest, the hottest, the most talked about. The world of new luxury is the world of "butterfly economics," a world in which every Christmas must have a sold-out toy, every summer a movie too crowded to see, each year a car with a six-month backlog, a baguette handbag almost impossible to own.

The world that we live in, as John Seabrook recently argued in *Nobrow: The Marketing of Culture and the Culture of Marketing,* and as David Brooks explored in *Bobos in Paradise: The New Upper Class and How They Got There,* no longer easily fits into intellectual classes. It now fits into consumption communities. So, for instance, we don't talk about high class, upper middle class, and middle class. Instead we talk about boomers, yuppies, Generation X, echo-boomers, nobrows, bobos (short for bourgeois bohemians), and the rest, who show what they are buying for themselves, not what they do for a living. And that's why each of these groups has its own luxury markers—positional goods, in marketing jargon—to be bought, not made.

The Concept of Brow

In a way, the new luxury is the ineluctable result of a market economy and a democratic political system. As Thomas Beer wrote, "Money does not rule democracy. Money is democracy" (in Lapham 2000:8). Back in the late 1940s Russell Lynes, editor of *Harper's,* concocted a taxonomy of taste: high-brow, upper middle-brow, lower middle-brow, and low-brow. His system, as gleefully celebrated in the April 11, 1949, issue of *Life* magazine, was scandalous when published, the topic of much cocktail party concern.

Lynes knew even then that Americans were no longer divided by "wealth, birth, or political eminence" but by consumption. These material distinctions were further explored in the 1980s in Paul Fussell's *Class: A Guide Through the American Status System.* Tongue almost in cheek, Fussell even proposed a new class, what he called "category X people," to

Everyday tastes from highbrow to lowbrow.
Russell Lynes, "High Brow, Middle Brow, Low Brow,"
Life, April 11, 1949, 100–101.

EVERYDAY TASTES FROM HIGH-BROW

	CLOTHES	FURNITURE	USEFUL OBJECTS	ENTERTAINMENT	SALA
HIGH-BROW	TOWN Fuzzy Harris tweed suit, no hat — COUNTRY Fuzzy Harris tweed suit, no hat	Eames chair, Kurt Versen lamp	Decanter and ash tray from chemical supply company	Ballet	Greens, oli wine vine ground salt, pepper, g unwash salad be
UPPER MIDDLE-BROW	TOWN Brooks suit, regimental tie, felt hat — COUNTRY Quiet tweed jacket, knitted tie	Empire chair, converted sculpture lamp	Silver cigaret box with wedding ushers' signatures	Theater	Same as hig but with to avocado, Ra cheese a
LOWER MIDDLE-BROW	TOWN Splashy necktie, double-breasted suit — COUNTRY Sport shirt, colored slacks	Grand Rapids Chippendale chair, bridge lamp	His and Hers towels	Musical extravaganza films	Quartered lettuce store dre
LOW-BROW	TOWN Loafer jacket, woven shoes — COUNTRY Old Army clothes	Mail order overstuffed chair, fringed lamp	Balsam-stuffed pillow	Western movies	Coles

RINKS	READING	SCULPTURE	RECORDS	GAMES	CAUSES
glass of quate little" ed wine	"Little magazines," criticism of criticism, avant garde literature	Calder	Bach and before, Ives and after	Go	Art
y dry Martini lemon peel	Solid nonfiction, the better novels, quality magazines	Maillol	Symphonies, concertos, operas	The Game	Planned parenthood
rbon and nger ale	Book club selections, mass circulation magazines	Front yard sculpture	Light opera, popular favorites	Bridge	P. T. A.
Beer	Pulps, comic books	Parlor sculpture	Jukebox	Craps	The Lodge

27

be based not on material consumption but on a shared taste for the better life. Fussell got the phenomenon of the "massification" of the upper class correct, and he certainly understood how the democratizing of luxury was a mixed blessing, but he missed the materiality of this confluence. Instead of superfluous stuff being pushed aside, it became even more central. You had to *buy* your way out, one Volvo, one glass of merlot, one bow tie, one Sub-Zero refrigerator, one granite countertop at a time.

A Kind Word for Opuluxe—The United Colors of Benetton?

I must say that I found most of the luxury objects that I looked at, from Patek Philippe watches to Porsche Turbos with giant spoilers on their heinie (presumably to keep them earthbound) to the men's room of the Bellagio Hotel to be a little . . . over the top. But I am not so oblivious to the world around me that I can't appreciate how important the new luxury has become. And I can't overlook how high-end consumption promises to do exactly what critics of the stuff have always yearned for, namely, to bring us together, often traumatically. Yes, indeed, the transgenerational poor are excluded, as the bottom fifth of our population has not budged an inch in the luxe explosion. Absent the poor, more people than ever are entering the much-vaunted global village *because* of consumption, not despite it.

Yes, the poor are looped-out in such a materialistic system. But the de-moralized destitute do not wage wars. Terrorism is their métier. As the *Wall Street Journal* reported on its front page (Zachary 2000:A1), the Swedes, who keep up on this kind of data, report that the world seems, and is, relatively peaceful. One reason: Robust economies have given prospective foot soldiers something better to do: go shopping. Russell Belk has even coined a term for this version of pax Americana: *Pax McDonald's*.

Not all would agree, of course. In *A Nation of Salesmen* Earl Shorris, reformed ad man and now contributing editor of *Harper's,* believes that commercialism has drained humanity of its get-up-and-go: "It may be a lack of imagination on my part, but I cannot conceive of a great host of people trudging across all of Europe, willing to fight and die in a crusade on behalf of the videocassette player. Nor does it seem likely to me that any-one would be willing to die on the cross for the suits of Giorgio Armani or the scents of Chanel" (12). Yet, when you think of the role that religious terrorism has played in building a deep and loving relationship between peoples, perhaps mindless materialism doesn't seem so bad.

As for the well-meaning critics who never tire of reminding us how wasteful and unnecessary empty-calorie consumption can be, remind them that a few hours of high-altitude bombing does more environmental damage than an autobahn full of SUVs.

In fact, one could argue, as Dinesh D'Souza, Virginia Postrel, and Michael Cox and Richard Alm have recently done, that the aspiration of the poor to get at these unnecessary goods has done more than any social program to motivate some of the disenchanted to become enfranchised. While one may be distressed at seeing a dish antenna atop a ramshackle house or a Caddie out front, the yearning to have superfluous badges of affluence may promise a more lasting peace around the world than any religion or political system has ever delivered. I don't mean to overlook the complexities here. This is *not* a universal phenomenon, as al Qaeda have wickedly demonstrated. Part of the world's poor are most certainly *not* becoming better off in absolute or relative terms. But I only want to say that, given a choice between being mugged for your sneakers or having your ethnic or religious heritage cleansed, the lust for sneakers may prove a more lasting way to improve the general lot of humanity.

Let's face it. In the world that I grew up in, your religion, your family name, the color of your skin, your language skills, your gender, where you went to school, your accent, and your marriage partner were doing the work that luxury consumption does now. My dad went to Exeter, Williams, and Harvard Med, and he never drove anything fancier than a Plymouth. He never had to. Today I wouldn't go to a doctor who drove a Plymouth. I would figure that if she doesn't drive a Lexus, she is having trouble with her practice.

So I admit the ugly truth. After spending the last few years trying to understand the pull of the material world, I am far more sympathetic to its blandishments and far more forgiving of its excesses. The democratization of luxury has been the single most important marketing phenomenon of modern times. And it has profound *political* implications. It may not be as bad as some lifestyle scolds make it out to be. In its own way it is a fair, albeit often wasteful, system, not just of objects but of meaning. Don't get me wrong: It's not that I came to mock and stayed to pray, but I do feel that getting and *spending* has some actual worth. Nobody checks the number of vowels in your name, or the color of your skin, or whether you know the difference between *like* and *as* when you are buying your Prada parka—that's got to mean something.

Current Criticism on a Thumbnail

I mention my confusion because from time to time in Western history there is vociferous antipathy toward high-end consumption. From Plato to the early Christians to the Renaissance, luxury (from *luxus*—sensuality, splendor, pomp—and its derivative *luxuria*—excess extravagance, riot) was thought to effeminize and weaken. But this was hardly a pressing problem, because just getting to the necessities of life was a full-time job for most (Berry 1994).

With increasing affluence this view shifted. Luxury became dangerous not because of debasement but because it was a sign of overreaching, of getting out of place. An interesting transformation begins that shows how fluid this category can be. In the Renaissance luxury objects became those things thought worthy of being painted. Such objects were called objets d'art. Now, of course, the luxury object is the painting itself. But you can see that even before the industrial revolution there was a growing desire to show stuff off, to use the material world as marker of social dominance, to strut, to flaunt.

By the eighteenth century, social critics like Bernard Mandeville and economists like Adam Smith were beginning to suggest that, for improving the weal of humanity, the promise of consuming luxury might be a better

William Hogarth, The Rake's Progress
British Museum; Sean Shesgreen, ed., *Engravings by Hogarth*
(New York: Dover, 1973), plates 1, 2, 3, and 8.

carrot than the stick of shame. Yet there was still deep resentment for consuming out of your class, beyond your means. Have a look at Hogarth's
Rake's Progress, Marriage à la Mode, or *Harlot's Progress,* and you will see
how the path of luxe consumption leads to no good end. These cartoons of
consumption need no gloss; the message is writ large. Observe the young
rake debauched by the blandishments of luxury.

This suspicion about consuming beyond your class continued well into
the nineteenth century. In fact, ancient sumptuary laws, explaining exactly
what objects were forbidden by church and state, were read from the An-
glican pulpit until the 1860s. Reading these laws took two hours of church
time to complete, and the laws kept people in their places, if only to have
to listen to them.

Clerics, clearly supported by the aristocracy, were not alone in stiff-
arming luxury. With the onset of industrial surpluses, secular pundits like
Henry David Thoreau railed against what they took to be the excesses of
mass production. "Most of the luxuries, and many of the so-called comforts, of life are not only indispensable, but positive hindrances to the elevation of mankind," he pointed out in *Walden* (14).

By the fin de siècle this view of high-end consumption had so exploded
that Thorstein Veblen unloosed the first modern sustained attack on luxury in his thoroughly entertaining *Theory of the Leisure Class* (1899). Coin-

ing all manner of nifty concepts like conspicuous consumption, invidious comparison, bandwagon effect, symbolic pantomime, vicarious leisure, and parodic display, Veblen had at the excesses of robber-baron shopping.

Thorstein Veblen

In fact, one might say that Veblen enjoyed it rather too much and succeeded only too well. When he formulated his theory of the leisure class at the turn of the century, ostentation in dress was at its full plumage, not least because new money was desperate to prove that it had made it to high society. Veblen's argument was so simple that it cut like Occam's razor. It has proved so powerful that it has achieved the status of unquestioned truism.

Here is Veblen's argument: As wealth spreads, what drives consumers' behavior is increasingly neither subsistence nor comfort but the attainment of "the esteem and envy of fellow men" (32). Because male wage earners are too circumspect to indulge themselves, they deposit consumption on surrogates, on loved ones. Vicarious ostentation—the way that plainly dressed Victorian men encouraged their wives and daughters (not to mention their mistresses) to wear complicated trappings of wealth—is how this unfolds. Ditto their servants, horses, and even house pets.

All you have to do to see how right Veblen was is to look at photos of the early robber barons. Notice how they are always in black suits, scuffing the ground with their black boots, while their women, their livery, their carriages, their houses, and their dogs are decked out to the nines. You can still see how powerful this myth is in this recent advertising send-up from a money-management firm.

In retrospect, Veblen was too successful, too neat, too sharp. Veblen thought that the purpose of acquisition was public consumption of esteem, status anxiety resolved by material display. Not much more. Wealth, he argued, confers honor; it suggests prowess and achievement. Not just muscular Christianity but muscular materialism. But wealth would have no social meaning were it simply consumed or possessed. "In order to gain and to hold the esteem of men," he wrote, "it is not sufficient merely to possess wealth or power. The wealth or power must be put in evidence, for esteem is awarded only on evidence" (36).

Thus the absolute centrality of conspicuous consumption. In what Veblen called "barbarian culture," trophies such as property or slaves were signs of successful aggression. But in modern societies luxury is a sign of

Money.

It's just not what it used to be

Today the barriers to
making it have fallen.
Once and for all.

A new generation of entrepreneurs
have already made an indelible
mark on American business. But
where do they go from here?
Phoenix has been offering
innovative new suggestions
for nearly 150 years. We
understand that making
money—and keeping it far
to do with it—are two different
skills. It's one reason high
net-worth people and their
advisors turn to Phoenix for help.
To learn more about how Phoenix
could be helping you, contact
your financial advisor or visit
www.phoenixwm.com.

PHOENIX WEALTH MANAGEMENT

*Veblen is made modern
to sell insurance.*

status and class. It's what we have for harems. But only certain sorts of
goods work this magic. There is no rational system. The only constant is
that consumers seek the luxurious object for two reasons: to show that they
are members of the classes above and to distinguish themselves from those
below. Veblen calls the first motive "pecuniary emulation"; the second, "invidious comparison."

From this comes the economic irrationality of the Veblen effect, namely,
that the value of a luxury object is in direct proportion to its cost. Raise the
price of certain luxe objects and you increase their value. The Veblen effect
is why a T-shirt sold at Sears costs less than the same T-shirt at the Gap,
which costs less than the same T-shirt at Hugo Boss, and so forth. Could you
sell Evian water if it were priced *below* a generic? What about Ben & Jerry's
ice cream? The *Robb Report*? A Lexus? An Ivy League education? It is not
enough for me to know what I paid for opuluxe. *You* have to know.

Today these products, which are no more (and maybe less) useful than
their functional equivalents, are sometimes called positional goods, goods

that are valued not despite their expense but because of it. Indeed, Veblen argued that since the reasons for buying such goods are pecuniary emulation and invidious comparison, their utility rises as their prices go up. With insights like this, Veblen proved himself to be too strong a critic to dismiss. You don't need to have read a word he wrote to know him. He set the tone of modern criticism.

Veblen's Successors

The second modern attack on luxury came in the 1950s with John Kenneth Galbraith's *The Affluent Society* and, to a lesser degree, the popularizing work of Vance Packard in *The Hidden Persuaders, The Status Seekers*, and *The Pyramid Climbers*. Veblenism is all over these books. Galbraith had read Veblen, if not wisely, then too well. In fact, he had edited the *Theory of the Leisure Class* with all kinds of approving nods and winks. Packard and his snappy titles went along for the ride. To these critics high-end consumption is against our "better nature"; we are duped into consuming by advertisers; consumers are dolts who should be doing other things; luxury is consumption run amok.

The usual suspects for Galbraith had changed from being the captains of industry to the Joneses across the street. Keeping up with them was every bit as dangerous as it had been for a Carnegie to keep up with a Vanderbilt, a Morgan with a Gould. Perhaps even more dangerous because these Joneses now are so numerous. And, as opposed to the robber barons who were outfitting family members, this new solipsistic breed of showoff was outfitting himself.

The peacetime economy after the Second World War had let loose a flood of populuxe items, most notably kitchen appliances and outrageous cars. And we were gobbling them up, heedless of the economic tummy ache to come. But that tummy ache has still not come. The economy for unnecessary objects is still booming, and the descendants of the dour Norwegian and his avuncular popularizers are still at it.

The Third Generation of Veblenites
A central irony of a robust consuming culture is that it affords the supreme luxury of criticizing it. And academics, a group that has the added (and not

entirely deserved) luxury of outrageous job security and controllable work time, has not been slow to rise to the task.

Following in the footsteps of Galbraith have been two moralists passing as economists: Juliet Schor, a lecturer at Harvard, who has published *The Overspent American: Why We Want What We Don't Need*, and Robert Frank, a professor at Cornell, who contributed *Luxury Fever: Why Money Fails to Satisfy in an Era of Excess*. Just read the subtitles.

The modern attack from the lush groves of academe usually centers around discussing one specific object as an exemplum. While Galbraith disliked Cadillac tail fins, Schor disdains granite countertops in the kitchen, and Frank holds up expensive watches as symptomatic of bad habits. On the surface they have such good points: How do those fins help the car move, are those stone countertops better than Formica, does a Lucian Picard keep better time than a Timex?

But here's the problem. The 1958 Cadillac has been featured in the Museum of Modern Art's retrospective show celebrating industrial design as art, and if you now want to buy one in mint condition, you'll pay about twenty times the purchase price. The granite countertop really makes more sense as a cutting surface than as a slab to lay down over the dead body of Uncle Louie, and—who knows?—it might even be passed from generation to generation, while the sensible Formica is carted out to the dump. And had Frank invested in Lucian Picard watches at the beginning of the bull market, he would have made more on his watch investment than on the S&P 500. Drats! That this stuff could have *increased* in value tells us how slippery these slopes can be.

No matter. Critics of consumption love to point out that people with these things are no *happier* than people without them. Ergo, why buy extra stuff? But people who can't buy unnecessary opuluxe are definitely unhappier for not being let into the cycle; *buying* this notational stuff and *having* such stuff are different experiences; consumers move in definite stages, from adolescence, where consumption is central, to middle age, where it ceases to be so important, to old age, where having things is positively a hindrance; and religious fanatics invariably rank highest on happiness scales, irrespective of culture or religion. Let's give happiness a rest. Consumption of the new luxury is about far more interesting sensations.

Whereas Veblen contended that male aggression caused the crazed consumption of deluxe items at the end of his century, these modern critics are more au courant in putting forth their etiology. They medicalize consumption, in large part because the bulk consumers of luxe are now young women. The diagnosis, although they would never use this precise term, is addiction. We are addicted to luxury. That's what causes the *fever*. That's why we yearn for what we don't want. Diagnosis from the National Public Radio crowd: not just Sudden Wealth Syndrome but . . . the dreaded *affluenza*.

Affluenza

Addiction has become one of the cant terms to explain less-desired behavior of all sorts. In the 1950s, when I was growing up, addiction meant horrible obsession and dealt almost exclusively with drugs, usually alcohol. With the rise of the self-help movement addiction has come to describe a less-pleasing behavior than one might like. You now can be addicted to chocolate, video games, procrastination, late night TV, sex, eating and/or not eating, and buying expensive things you don't need, in other words, the dreaded luxury *fever*.

As addiction has become part of the lexicon of everyday life, it has become interchangeable with another casual coinage, *inappropriate behavior*. The assumption is that appropriate behavior is the nonconsumption of some dangerous material. Thus *affluenza* describes the hunger not just for stuff but for top-of-the-line stuff. In putting forward this "hypodermic" theory of behavior (the injection of advertising/jealousy/greed creates a craving for, a desire for, some poison), these critics form the last bastion of romanticism. Like Rousseau and Wordsworth, they assume the *natural* condition of humans is to live apart from manufactured things.

How to cure ourselves of luxe addiction? Groups of Voluntary Simplifiers often invoke the twelve-step method of renunciation developed by Alcoholics Anonymous; these are the people who announce themselves in the daily newspaper under the rubric "support groups." Or if not in the newspaper, then in books (Sarah Ban Breathnach's *Simple Abundance* industry) or, most recently, in magazines. What could be more telling than that Time Warner, incubator of such advertising-rich magazines as *Southern Living, Entertainment Weekly,* and *People,* as well as Breathnach's own Simple Abundance book series, has launched a startlingly successful magazine, *Real Simple,* dedicated to battling overconsumption by yet more consumption? Major advertisers in the first issue? De Beers, Baby Gap, Polo by Ralph Lauren, and many of the usual suspects.

The Academic Bandwagon

Railing against the consumption habits of others does have a kind of self-satisfied allure. In 1999 Roger Rosenblatt, commentator for the Public Broadcasting System and an editor at *Time,* corralled a herd of academic types and collected their views in *Consuming Desires: Consumption, Culture, and the Pursuit of Happiness.* Almost without fail the scolds put forward their examples of inappropriate consumption. Their view in a sentence? Immature people are *desiring* the wrong stuff, thanks to the interventions of greedy capitalists and their accomplices on Madison Avenue. Rosenblatt's consensus: we (but thankfully not the authors) are buying things we don't need. Take your pick: cars too fancy, houses too big, vacations too far away, television with too many channels, food too fast, too much entertainment.

In some ways the piece by Stephanie Mills called "Can't Get That Extinction Crisis out of My Mind" is a typical bit of agonized hand-wringing. We are consuming ourselves to death—that's the "extinction crisis" of the title. We are going to die from consumption, the modern tuberculosis. This is so serious that Mills left the I-want-it-now world of California and headed to the Waldenesque ponds of Michigan. Still not safe, however, for there in the bosky dells she observes the steady influx of summer people with their second houses, blaring boom boxes, and hideous jet skis. Noisy people with power boats, dish antennae, and too many children are all over the place. Michigan is being Californicated and Mills is distraught.

So, as luck would have it, when "there came a windfall just when my neighbor wanted to sell thirty of his acres, I bought them because I could. I didn't want to see the smoke coming from my neighbor's cabin." Mills more than doubles her estate. "The only thing I do with my land is inhabit it," she says proudly of her own savvy consumption.

Now, of course, it's nifty that she can live on a big chunk of land where all she does is "inhabit." I too don't like jet skis, SUVs, and barking dogs. But would we all be better off if each of us exchanged our noisy toys and pets for more than thirty acres? Especially when fierce environmentalists tell us that we really only *need* a dwelling of less than 10 by 16 feet?

A More Sympathetic View

Clearly, what is going on is that *luxury* has become a mallet with which one pounds the taste of others. In the chapters that follow I am going to put forward a different view of modern luxury. My view will be based on these assumptions:

1. Humans are consumers by nature. We are tool users because we like to use what tool using can produce. In other words, tools are not the ends but the means. So too materialism does not crowd out spiritualism; spiritualism is more likely a substitute when objects are scarce. When we have few things, we make the next world luxurious. When we have plenty, we enchant the objects around us. The hereafter becomes the here and now.

2. Consumers are rational. They are often fully aware that they are more interested in consuming aura than objects, sizzle than steak, meaning than material. In fact, if you ask them—as academic critics are usually loath to do—they are quite candid in explaining that the Nike swoosh, the Polo pony, the Guess? label, the DKNY logo are what they are after. They are not duped by advertising, packaging, branding, fashion, and merchandising. They actively seek and enjoy the status that surrounds the object, especially when they are young.

3. As opposed to buying turnips and aspirin, consuming top-of-the-line stuff stimulates the neurotransmitters that send waves of self-satisfaction coursing around our bodies (Finnerty 1997:30). Consuming luxe is consuming a feeling, maybe even, as I will finally suggest, a religious one, an epiphany. To admit that we enjoy this sensation isn't to declare that I live to shop, or, to borrow a line from Barbara Kruger, that "I shop therefore I am." But it does mean that most of us can distinguish between the pleasure of a healthy spree and a desperate addiction, between the "happy shopper" and the junkie.

4. We need to question the criticism that consumption of opuluxe almost always leads to disappointment. Admittedly, the circular route from desire to purchase to disappointment to renewed desire is never-ending, but we may follow it because the other route—from melancholy to angst—is worse. In other words, in a world emptied of inherited values, consuming what looks to be overpriced fripperies may be preferable to consuming nothing.

5. We need to rethink the separation between production and consumption, for they are more alike than separate and occur not at different times and places but simultaneously. Instead of wanting less luxury, we might find that just the opposite—the paradoxical luxury for all—is a suitable goal of communal aspiration.

But before we get to the ramifications of these assumptions I need to reassert what is so obvious that it is often overlooked: Before all else, luxury is a social construction. Starting here, belaboring the obvious, may pave the way for a new appreciation of what has become a characteristic contradiction of our time, the necessary consumption of the unnecessary.

2.

The Social Construction of Luxury

A TAXONOMY OF TASTE

*When scissors, which surely do not date from remote
antiquity, were invented, what wasn't said against the
first people who clipped their nails? They were doubtless called dandies and squanderers, who bought an
expensive instrument of vanity to mar the work of the
Creator. What an enormous sin to shorten the horny
matter which God created at the end of our fingers! It
was much worse when shirts and socks were invented. It
is well known how furiously the old councilors, who had
never worn them, clamored against the young magis-
trates who showed themselves in this wicked luxury.*

—Voltaire, *Philosophical Dictionary*

Voltaire has never been more modern. For he saw in the eighteenth century what we are still either unwilling to confront or are overly eager to
admit, namely, the social construction of taste. Such a paradox! If we dis-
like what is being produced, we refer to it as the ineluctable result of hegemony, the browbeating of consumers by producers, the infantalizing of our
natural desires by the crafty manipulators of fad and fashion.

But if we do like it, we say it's socially constructed, which exchanges the
sense of oppression for the allure of cooperation. In the academy today no
one blanches when someone asserts that authorship, gender, literacy,

Getting there is half the fun, or it used to be: luxury transportation.

THE *New* KIND OF
LOW COST LUXURY TRAVEL
TRAILWAYS
THRU-BUS SERVICE

MORE LUXURY FLIGHTS TO FLORIDA!

This Winter National Doubles Its Luxury Fleet With New DC 5B's!

There'll be more Stars in the sky to Florida this winter! Yes, the nation's newest fleet of DC-6B's joins National's luxurious DC-6's. Every day 1000 *more* Florida vacationists will enjoy world-famed Star service at standard fare...

Make Your Reservation Now!

Finest Aircraft! A wide variety of agents...berthight Lounge...air-conditioned, pressurized cabin for above-weather flying...individual seats for greatest comfort.

Finest Service! Fine engines dinners...snacks, flowers...5-abreast seating...radi-carpet spaciousness, smooth...refreshments and relaxation in the Starlight Lounge.

THE *Star*
MIAMI
JACKSONVILLE   TAMPA
HAVANA
PALM BEACH

Get The NATIONAL Habit—FLY!

NATIONAL Airlines
Airline of the Stars

MOORE-McCORMACK LINES

RESUMES LUXURY CRUISE SERVICE TO
South America

The World's Most
CHEVROLET
for Economical Transportation

Luxurious
Low-Priced Automobile

Never before has a low-priced automobile exhibited such marvelous beauty, such interior smartness and completeness of appointment, as the Bigger and Better Chevrolet.

Built on a 107-inch wheelbase—4 inches longer than before—equipped with non-locking 4-wheel brakes and incorporating scores of vital contributions to every phase of motoring enjoyment, this great new car completely revolutionizes every existing standard of luxury in the low-price field.

You will be delighted with a ride in this beautiful car. Your Chevrolet dealer will be glad to arrange a demonstration.

CHEVROLET MOTOR COMPANY, DETROIT, MICHIGAN
Division of General Motors Corporation

The Roadster, $495; The Touring, $495; The Coach, $585; The Coupe, $595; The 4-Door Sedan, $675; The Sport Cabriolet, $665; The Imperial Landau, $715; Utility Truck (Chassis only) $495; Light Delivery (Chassis only) $375. All prices f. o. b. Flint, Mich.

Chevrolet Enclosed Cars with Bodies by FISHER

The COACH $585
f. o. b. Flint, Mich.

Q U A L I T Y   A T   L O W   C O S T

NEW YORK CENTRAL'S
NEW Luxury Coaches—
adding enchantment
to your first post-war
vacation!

FIVE solid gleaming miles of luxury coaches are rolling off the production lines. They're alive with the up-to-the-minute features for which thousands of New York Central passengers voted. And many of these cars of tomorrow are ready today for your first post-war vacation. Ready to carry you, at low coach fares, on your way to the Adirondacks, New England, Niagara Falls, Canada, the Great Lakes or the Western Wonderlands.

motherhood, history, nature, law, or even reality is "socially constructed." If you want to talk about race, gender, culture, literature, or even science and sound as if you've thought a lot, this is where you start.

That said, here, in a nutshell, is the problem. Although we like to pretend that our desires to consume are foisted upon us and that luxury is just the excess of these desires, luxury is *always* a social construct. We have always had it; we need it; if we didn't have it, we'd create it. Yet it doesn't really exist. Like weeds or predators, there is no such thing as luxury other than what we declare it to be.

Like the classic Victorian definition of dirt ("matter out of place"), luxury has tended to be covertly defined as those things that you have that I think you shouldn't have. In this sense luxury is rather like Justice Potter Stewart's definition of pornography. Hard to define, but you know it when you see it—especially when you see it being consumed by people you know.

What makes matters more complex is that, almost without fail, one generation's indulgence becomes the next generation's necessity. Think buttons, window glass, rugs, fermented juice, the color purple, door handles, lace, enamel, candles, pillows, mirrors, combs, umbrellas. . . . As the nineteenth century gave way to the twentieth, indoor plumbing was thought a horrible waste of living space and an environmental hazard. Our government now considers its lack to be one of the markers of poverty. If you don't have it, you're considered destitute.

Before World War II a large house was a necessity. Generations lived together. Now it is a luxury. Saucers were a luxury until Wedgwood mass-produced them. Consider for a moment how we move around. First shoes were a luxury, then horses, bicycles, then cars, ships, trains, buses, airplanes.

A Quick Trip to the Pottery Barn

I am holding in my hand the most recent catalog for Pottery Barn. Like Crate & Barrel or even Restoration Hardware, Pottery Barn sells midlevel versions of simple objects. I am leafing through the pages. Here's what I see: glass vitrines, sisal rugs, napkins, mirrors, slipcovers, duvets, hand towels, scissors, sconces, armoires, kilim and pillows, shams, sheets, torchères, placemats, drapes, bed skirts, and lots of stuff covered in velvet. Now *each* of these objects entered the marketplace, and was doubtless condemned, as a luxury. Velvet was not so long ago what cashmere—whoops, pashmina—is today.

A terrible and awesome welfare system is at work here in this down-streaming of luxury. We need to pay attention to it. Once people want something that makes life more comfortable, only the rich buy it. At this stage it is a luxury. As more and more people buy it, the price drops, the item becomes less of a luxury and more of a want-to-have. The Victorians even had a name for this type of object. They called such objects expectancies. Soon, as production increases, the price falls, and it becomes a-need-to-have.

Econ 101, Argh

Capitalism is, for better and worse, the most efficient way to turbocharge this process of transforming luxuries into necessities. Harvesting the economies of mass production of erstwhile luxury is also known as "the good life," the putative goal of every cultured society. The road of excess may not lead to the palace of wisdom, as William Blake predicted at the beginning of the industrial revolution, but, as the economist Friedrich Hayek showed in the mid-1970s in *The Road to Serfdom*, it leads to a better life for more people than any other road. And, ironically, while upper-level consumption does not contribute to increased happiness for those who can afford it, such spending often makes it easier for those at entry levels to buy what was previously out of reach.

Often what looks like a "winner-take-all" society is really one in which the rest of us take lots precisely because someone gets there first. Sure, the "upfronters" get HDTV, digital cameras, laser eye surgery, Palm Pilots, and superfast Internet connections before the rest of us. They are willing and able to pay the high first costs. They also get first crack at Edsels, the Betamax, eight-track stereo, and Corfam shoes.

In *Luxury Fever* Robert Frank says that luxury needs to be contained because it aggravates a deep paradox that informs our market. Here it is in a sentence: What's smart for each individual may not make sense for the group. He believes that we must be made to stop "piling on." Here are some of his examples. At crowded rock concerts everyone feels compelled to stand. If everyone would just sit down, we could all see. But, oh noooo, those morons in the third row jump up and everyone else must follow. The upfronters should be tamped down, Frank argues. Or it would be okay if only a few people wanted a big house, but now everybody has to have a McMansion. What a waste of space. Or if competitors are wearing $1,500 suits to job interviews, you need to do the same thing. Not fair. Once the

They'll know you've *arrived*

when you drive up in an Edsel

Unfortunately, they will know when you've arrived.

Joneses get an SUV, you'll have to trade in your economical environmentally friendly Honda Civic. Well, maybe he has a point here.

Assuming all this is true and we are indeed so lemminglike, how dangerous is this piling on that Professor Frank says is the basis of hyperconsumption? Isn't it exactly the same piling on that has made cell phones affordable, allowed television to come into almost every home, and accounts for boom boxes on the street corner? Whoops, sorry, wrong examples.

Here are some better ones. While it would seem sensible to wait your turn for indoor plumbing, sewing machines, air bags, dishwashers, college educations, videocassettes of foreign films, air-conditioning, photocopies of Milton's *Comus,* antibiotics, microwave ovens, classical music CDs, refrigerators, coronary bypasses, disk brakes, power steering, birth control, coaxial cable, hip replacements, air travel . . . it's a demonstrable fact that the market does indeed extend at progressively lower prices exactly those products precisely because the dummies in the third row jump up on their chairs.

Piling on is at the base of the incredible explosion of the Internet. Moore's Law, namely, that the memory capacity of computer chips doubles every eighteen months, is based on the "I want it and I want it now!" behavior of those who cannot repress desire. Often the rest of us benefit.

This is not an easy irony to grasp. Plus, it seems to violate principles of fair play and equitable distribution. Peter Singer, the lightning rod for rad-

Luxuries No More

Average number of hours' labor needed
to purchase various products

EARLY YEAR	PRODUCT	EARLY COST	1970 COST	1997 COST
1908	Automobile	4,696	1,397	1,365
1915	Refrigerator	3,162	112	68
1915	Long-distance call	90	0.4	0.03
1917	Movie ticket	.48	0.47	0.32
1919	Air travel, 1,000 mi.	221	18	11
1919	Chicken, 3 lb fryer	2.6	0.4	0.2
1947	Microwave oven	2,467	176	15
1954	Color television	562	174	23
1971	Soft contact lenses	95	n/a	4
1972	VCR	365	n/a	15
1984	Cellular phone	456	n/a	9
1984	Computing*	57	n/a	0.4

*Million instructions per second

Source: Federal Reserve Bank of Dallas

W. Michael Cox, "The Low Cost of Living." *The Wall Street Journal*,
April 9, 1998, A22.

Luxuries No More.

ical utilitarianism, has continually argued—since "Famine, Affluence, and Morality" in 1972—for confiscatory policies against luxury consumption so long as one hungry mouth remains open. Why should a single soul suffer while the masses thrive, and some positively glut themselves? Here's Singer's firebrand analogy: You must decide whether to drive your totally unnecessary luxury automobile into the path of a train in order to save the life of a child. You don't have to be a philosopher to tackle the dilemma, but the extension of the typical response—adios, Lexus—leads to a sourball of a paradox. Here, if you really want to bite down on this, listen to T. J. Rogers, CEO of Cypress Semiconductor:

> I keep hearing, "Feed the poor, clothe the hungry, give shelter to those who don't have it." The bozos that say this don't recognize that capitalism and technology have done more to feed and clothe and shelter and heal people than all the charity and church programs in history. So they preach about it, and we are the ones doing it. They rob Peter to pay Paul, but they always forget that Peter is the one that is creating the wealth in the first place.
>
> (Goodman 2001:3)

True, what's good for the individual may not be good for the group. But as Bernard Mandeville pointed out three centuries ago in *The Fable of the Bees* (1714), what benefits the hive may not be good for the individual bee. It works both ways. Without sounding too much like Pangloss or, worse, like Gordon Gekko's infamous "greed is good" speech in the film *Wall Street*, individual greed may indeed promote the general weal. And often does. Who among us, aside from Ayn Rand enthusiasts, wants to admit that the private vices of the rich often build more hospitals, endow more schools, and extend more help to the needy than the public virtues of the poor? Not me.

It is shocking and *not fair*. It is profoundly immoral. I remember how I felt when I first encountered a shard of this nasty truth. It was as a freshman in Econ 101. We were reading the still-canonical textbook *Economics* by Paul Samuelson. He was discussing the Paradox of Thrift: "High consumption and high investment . . . go hand in hand rather than competing. What is true for the individual—that extra thriftiness means increased savings and wealth—may then become completely untrue for the community as a whole" (238).

What a wicked irony for a young Puritan, raised to trust *Poor Richard's Almanac* that "a penny saved is a penny earned." That profligacy should breed growth, that the gourmand should feed the hungry, that the competitive, endless, mindless desire of the haves should promote the betterment of current have-nots. That the relative disparity between rich and poor should have something (anything!) to do with the absolute improvement of conditions of the poor is . . . obscene.

Should you ever wonder why the critics of consumption, invariably in their middle age, are so brittle and unforgiving in their censure of the spending habits of the young, it is partly because they were raised, as was I, believing in the unquestioned moral value of equality. They rarely countenance the idea that disparity might contribute to the "good of all."

The Good Life Pictured

Thanks to exactly the kind of "mindless" consumption that critics abhor, we now have what the cultural analyst David Frum has dubbed a "mass upper class" and *Money* magazine calls the "ultra class" (December 2000). This is the 1 in 7 American families that earns more than $100,000 a year and is raising all the hubbub. This is the 1 in 14 households that has a net worth of

"LIVING IT UP"
Percentage Identifying Item As Part of "The Good Life"

	1975	1991
Vacation home	19	35
Swimming pool	14	29
Color TV	46	55
Second color TV	10	28
Travel abroad	30	39
Really nice clothes	36	44
Car	71	75
Second car	30	41
Home you own	85	87

SOURCE: Roper Center, University of Connecticut; published in *American Enterprise* (May-June 1993), p.87.

What constitutes the "good life."

more than $1 million—four times as many as a decade ago. These are the "affluentials" (Gertner 2000:94). If you want to see where their good life has come from, just look at what the Roper polling service found out about how we used to identify what constitutes acceptable *and* expected objects. First in 1975 and then in 1991, Roper asked Americans at random to identify objects as belonging to "the good life." Remember, this was being generated just as the baby boom wave was cresting. Now it's a veritable tsunami.

And if you want to know where this comes from, look at the graph from the National Bureau of Economic Research, an independent think tank.

As an English professor with a bad case of innumeracy, I have trouble understanding such data. If you want to *see* the change in the accumulation of luxury goods during the last half of the twentieth century, there are no better images to contemplate than a recent American Express ad and the cover of the the now-defunct *Saturday Evening Post* for August 15, 1959.

First, the cover. In the foreground of an evening scene by a lake are two young lovers. A brilliant full moon casts an eerie shade of blue light. The youngsters are recumbent in the crook of a magical tree that has a vine of starry moss creeping up into the heavens. The lovers are looking up into those heavens.

Let's call them Missy and Buck or, if you prefer, Adam and Eve. Beside Missy on the ground are her white gloves and, interestingly, her purse. She looks rather like Debbie Reynolds of the Tammy movies, and her eyes are now dreamily shut in reverie. Presumably, she's already seen what is be-

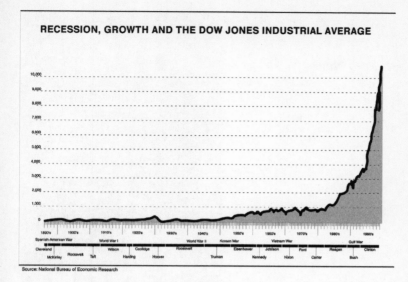

Recession, Growth, and the Dow Jones Industrial Average. Adapted from Associated Press and National Bureau of Economic Research.

tween her and the moon. Next to her sits her beau, himself looking a bit like Tab Hunter. Earnest, crew cut, paying attention, he is still focused on what is in the sky.

And well he should. For in the blue sky, drawn in what looks like white lines on a blueprint, are the objects that we easily recognize. We see them as if they were the outlines of star clusters like Leo the Lion or the Big Dipper. In pagan times the sky might have been filled with the imaginary connect-the-star images of the constellations, and in the Renaissance these heavens might have been peopled with the saints and divinities of Christianity, but in the modern world the heavenly host is composed mostly of machine-made stuff.

Heaven on earth? Or materialistic blasphemy? Who cares? The point is that each and every one of these objects, even the piano, was considered a luxury. A few generations earlier, having a piano *in the home* was most certainly an indulgence. As well, recall the peculiar appearance of the parlor organ and the player piano at the beginning of the twentieth century—a regal event.

*If it's good enough for the king, it's good
enough for your music room.*

Readers of the *Saturday Evening Post*, who saw this Edenic view as the cover art, must have been a little concerned about the overreaching of their trusty midcult magazine. For at one level this is a sacrilegious vision, to be sure. This is the stuff of heaven?! An unnamed editor even took time to note that this aerial view, painted by Constantin Alajalov, an emigré from Russia, had originally been planned as castles in air. But the painter changed his mind, the editor explained in a note about the cover, not out of "cynicism" but because it "takes as much magic to create a two-car domicile as it does to whip up an air castle. In essence, what the young romantics want is happiness; and since they have each other, their dream will come true. And to whatever extent they amass worldly goods, they'll share their happiness with the manufacturers and distributors of same."

All it takes to make this scene modern is to freshen the inventory. In the update the split-level ranch is now a McMansion, the cars are an SUV and a Beemer, the pool is covered and air-conditioned, the fridge is a Sub-Zero,

The American Dream à la the Saturday Evening Post *of*
August 15, 1959.

the stove is Vulcan, the rotisserie is a stainless steel Weber, there is a big
screen TV and, well, let's face it, you know the rest. Time to move to the
lake country of Michigan and buy those thirty acres? Perhaps. But for
some, especially the have-nots, this view still makes sense.

People and Their Stuff

Now have a look at a recent advertising campaign for American Express. The
campaign was called "People & Their Stuff" and featured occasional celebrities and common people standing in front of their possessions. Credit cards

How political strategists and lovebirds go nesting with the American Express card.

are notoriously hard to advertise because the service that they offer is almost totally interchangeable. After all, a dollar of debt is a dollar of debt.

Here is one of the ads, typical of the campaign in that while we may know the foregrounded characters, we do not know them because they are rich. We know these two people because they are in politics. They are a particularly modern kind of professional worker; they are spin doctors.

On first view we see Mary Matalin and James Carville on their lawn surrounded by their favorite things. This stuff is not above them in heaven, as it was for Missy and Buck. It is in the here and now. In the foreground are two spaniels and a fax machine; in the background, a Viking stove. In the middle, next to a wine rack, is a baby. The arrangement is not random, although it is tongue-in-cheek: Children seem just part of the inventory of a well-equipped life. There is some truth in advertising, for the couple really does have a Virginia farm (ninety-four acres, twenty-seven cows), and the barn in the background is theirs. However, the rest of their stuff can be on your front lawn too. Just use the card.

Matalin and Carville are presented as Grant Woods's *American Gothic* made modern—he with pitchfork, she slightly behind to his left. For the political cognoscenti there is a frisson of recognition. For these spin doctors are not just in a state of attraction but in positive unity. These two have clearly put aside their political differences (she a Republican operative, he a Democratic insider) in order to use the card and consume expensive stuff. Although they may find themselves on opposite sides of the partisan divide, the ad says that Carville and Matalin clearly share a conception of the good life. Love conquers politics, and top-of-the-line appliances trump squabbles.

The ad subtly implies that in consumption we resolve differences. By getting and spending we are held together. The family that pays together stays together. In fact, in the upper right-hand box of the ad we see those things drawn in outline and glossed at the bottom. What are they? They are metonymies of the good life. Stuff to garden with, flowers to court with, riding mower to farm with, books (nonfiction) to spend time with, pots and pans to cook and entertain with, Maalox to recuperate with, and fax and paper shredder to practice their trade with.

To sound like a college professor, I might also say that, at a slightly deeper level, the American Express ad is a nice illustration of the failures of both liberals and conservatives to address questions of political meaning, letting things carry the day. In a sense this is the message of the *Saturday Evening Post* cover as well. In the AmEx ad meaning is suspended. Things do the work of conversation. Carville, famous for his 1992 campaign motto, "It's the economy, stupid," stands for the liberal preoccupation with issues of material well-being at the expense of any concern for matters-of-meaning. Matalin, on the other hand, is more likely to handle clients on the Right who would speak about the collapse of families, the difficulty of teaching good values to children, the fear of crime, and the absence of spirituality. Out on the lawn amid her latest purchases from Williams-Sonoma and F.A.O. Schwarz, she signifies the failure of the American Right to understand the contradiction between its defense of "traditional values" and its promotion of the market economy that has done much to undermine those values. And he, surrounded by his tools and toys from Jim's Appliance and Sports Depot, mutely acknowledges that government interference or the redistribution of wealth cannot control the inequitable distribution of wealth. O tempora, O mores.

The Taste for Luxury

I am not trying to play the village idiot who has read too much Baudrillard but only to state what will be an endless series of paradoxes. The new luxury, while it is often everything critics say it is—wasteful, unaesthetic, overbearing—is also more complex. Sometimes it is the exact opposite of what it is calumnized for. It is not meaningless; if anything, it's *too* meaningful. In addition, often what we find is that what is passed off as unnecessary waste is really just a matter of learned preferences. What counts as luxury often depends on who's doing the counting.

Look, can we get a little personal? John Kenneth Galbraith spends the summer just to the south of me in Vermont. He has a huge spread and a beautiful house, nice stone fences, ancient oaks. He stays there for only part of the summer. He takes jet planes to Switzerland to his digs in Gstaad, great skiing. He stays there for only part of the winter. Okay, okay, he may drive an old Volvo, wear the same suit for years, and have sensible tie-up shoes when he's in Cambridge.

Ask the professor if it's okay to buy a Steinway baby grand, take a trip to the south of France to attend a kaffeeklatch on the plight of the Etruscans, or send your kid to Harvard at 30K a year, and you will be greeted with a wink and a nod. Now say that you are going to buy a Les Paul signature electric guitar, spend the week in Las Vegas at the Bellagio, or send your kid to State U at 10K a year, and you will be met with a gentle tsk, tsk.

Just for the thrill of doing some actual fieldwork, I told some colleagues in my department that I was planning to buy a rare copy of Wordsworth's 1850 *Prelude* for $6,000. I teach the English romantic poets. Without exception, they told me that this was a capital idea, even though they all knew that this book had absolutely no scholarly value. Since the advent of the photocopy the only research value of a rare book is either in physical description or as an example of book making. For twenty bucks you can buy a paperback edition of *The Prelude* that has all the variant lines glossed for you. Or you can go to the library and borrow it for free. (Why public universities still own, and add to, huge collections of rare books from the twentieth century is such a blatant . . . luxury. You won't hear a peep from academic scolds about this, however.)

So later that week I told them that I was reconsidering. I was now contemplating buying a used BMW. I could have said that I was investing in a collection of Beanie Babies comics or a diamond pinky ring for the shocked response that I got.

While this is a difficult concept for academics, the rest of the world seems to easily understand it. Here are two journalists having at it. I admit they are writing in suspicious venues, but they do have a point worth considering. In the *Wall Street Journal* Daniel Akst takes issue with critics like Schor, Frank, et al.:

> America's frenzy of consumption poses ideological problems on all sides. Liberals worry about an ecological meltdown when the Chinese and Indians take up our ways, and complain of "faceless suburbs," sport utility vehicles, and big-screen TVs. Yet they're strangely untroubled by apartments on the Upper West Side, country houses in Vermont, and Volvo station wagons. The message, apparently, is Le Corbusier good, La-Z-Boy bad. (W17)

And writing in *Worth* magazine, Richard Todd comments in "Spending It: The New American High": "Thus the person who mocks 'consumers' for trying to meet their needs for status or self-esteem through buying a new car or remodeling a kitchen—such a person goes to the antique shop to try to satisfy his own, more basic (more desperate!) hungers, yet again through things" (72).

All this is not to say that new luxury can be passed off as de gustibus non est disputandum but only that one needs to be eternally cautious and perpetually wary about what it is, what it does, and who should have it. Often what is condemned as luxury is really just a matter of taste. And of permitted social order.

Prohibitions of Luxe

One can see this anxiety about overreaching consumption by looking briefly at how we attempt to control the habits of others less enlightened than we. Whereas we once used the law to prohibit certain consumption, we now use taxes. For instance, in 1990 we tried taxing private transport such as planes, certain cars, and boats, as well as standard luxury items such as jewels and furs valued at more than $30,000. Three years later the tax was gradually repealed as it became clear that those hurt most by the tax were thousands of low- and middle-income workers who lost their jobs when the luxury goods and recreational boating industries suffered a severe loss of revenue.

Professor Frank now proposes a variant of this: Tax the difference between income and savings—the smaller the difference, the smaller the tax. Although his progressive consumption tax seems a contradiction, he maintains that by exempting all savings while imposing steeply progressive marginal rates on all income that is not saved, we could raise the necessary amounts of capital and not impose burdens on lower-income families. Better yet, such a tax on extraneous consumption will encourage the haves to stay away from what the professor thinks they don't need. Best yet, we will spend the extra money on the general weal. In a *New York Times* op-ed piece he delivers the coup de maître under this headline: "Which Do We Need More, Bigger Cars or Better Schools?" How about this one: "Which Do We Need More, People Using Cell Phones in Public or Money for AIDS Research?" If only it were so simple.

Earlier cultures often enacted sumptuary laws to remove exactly these experiences from circulation, except that the laws were designed to control the desires of the have-nots and not the haves. Certain kinds of meats like the king's deer, exotic beverages like teas and coffee, styles of fashionable livery and particular fabrics, rare spices and sweeteners, chocolate, styles of wigs, places to live, playing cards, hair powder, clocks, armorial bearings, even colors like Prussian blue and royal purple were placed off-limits to the hoi polloi. The ecclesiastical courts administered these laws against consuming what was called luxuria. This was because luxury was defined as living above one's station, a form of insubordination against the concept of copia—the idea that God's world is already full and complete.

While the proffered sins behind such laws were gluttony and greed—luxury objects were by definition sumptuous—in truth, the prohibitions were social. Sumptuary laws were part of an elaborate symbolic system designed to keep class demarcations in place. They are interesting to consider for this reason: Is there any possibility that the same unarticulated human anxieties that generated these laws are still at work in our tax code? Of course, instead of invoking religious humility, we act in the name of cleansing the environment, the equitable redistribution of wealth, and building better schools. Wonderful idea, good motives, difficult reality.

The promise of buying a Bentley is that shopping can stop—there is nowhere left to go, nothing left to buy.

Just bear in mind that you'll never be able to upgrade from here.

Luxury as the Top of Materialism

The social construction of luxury always depends on your tools of definition. While modern moralists call luxury an indulgence, economists say that the value of luxury goods results from inelastic demand, stoics claim that it results from abhorring simplicity, socialists say that it happens when the wrong class consumes it, clerics say that it comes from pride and ends in gluttony, liberals say that false needs are the problem, Marxists say that it comes from reified consciousness, and semioticians contend that it is material oversignified with meaning.

Whatever it is, luxury is the allure of getting to the edge, getting to the top, maybe even going just beyond the margin. Cynics like John Motley, the nineteenth-century U.S. diplomat, get to the heart of the matter: "Give us the luxuries of life, and we will dispense with the necessaries." And Coco Chanel continues, "Luxury is the necessity that begins where necessity ends." The appeal of luxury is that nothing is higher.

So let's leave aside the complexities of defining luxury as an aesthetic or a moral category and just look at the world of material objects. Why? First, the obvious: Modern culture is a material culture, a culture in which machine-made objects are not only produced in great profusion but are rapidly used, exchanged, discarded, shown off, stolen, and reused. Ours is a culture of downtown shops, of suburban strip malls, of massive enclosed malls, of discount malls, of independent big-box stores, of e-tailing, in which buying and selling objects of little discernible difference consumes much of the time and dream life of consumers.

It is tempting to say that we have this "mallcondo" culture because we are uniquely materialistic. But what we find by looking around the world and by looking into the past is that everyone else seems to want, and have wanted, to do the same thing: to have quality things, to hold *goods*. Berlin Walls fall, ayatollahs step aside, indigenous cultures crumble, as people, mostly young people, struggle to hold and use and show off these things deluxe.° We are not just tool-using animals. First, we like the stuff that tools make. Second, the better the items are made, the better we like them. And,

---

°North Korean officials had better watch out. They are allowing shopping tours to South Korea. In 1989 East Germany's Egon Krenz did the same. He thought that by allowing his people to visit West German stores and collect the 100-mark shopping allowance given by the West Germans, he could delay reunification. His logic: After a day of shopping East Germans would return home eager to get back to work.

third, we often want the meaning of such objects, which resides not *in* the objects but in the language surrounding them.

Of all the "isms" coming out of the twentieth century, none has been more misunderstood, more criticized, more slandered, and more important than the steady erosion of other systems by materialism. Who but fools, toadies, hacks, and occasional loopy Libertarians have ever risen to its defense? Yet while materialism may be the most shallow of the century's various isms, it has triumphed. The world of commodities seems so antithetical to the world of ideas that it is almost heresy to point out the obvious: Most of the world most of the time spends most of its energy producing and consuming more and more unnecessary stuff.

If you think about it, the yearning for luxury does not mean that we are too materialistic but perhaps that we are not materialistic enough. By that I mean that if we knew what these machine-made objects meant, if we had a language of things that we all understood, we would all cluster around certain things like bees around sugar. If we knew what objects meant, we would gather and hoard, use and discard, steal and donate, based on some inner principle that we all understood. But we don't. We *learn* what objects mean. And during certain times of our lives we pay rapt attention to learning the meaning of things.

If we knew the worth of the material world, advertising would not exist. This is what Raymond Williams meant when he spoke of advertising as being the central part of a magical system (1960). This is the invisible web between us and objects. Without it the market in gold would not exist, we would not be able to choose from among thirty-two different brands of sport utility vehicles, we wouldn't be wearing diamonds or even deciding among eight different kinds of Crest toothpaste. In addition, the value of different materials would not change. A century ago people prized white bread as a luxury and disdained brown bread. Not so today. Two centuries ago buttons were trifles for the rich. Three centuries ago forks were unnecessary.

My definition of the new luxury, at least for the time being, is going to be tied to this perplexity. Most new luxury is material that is super-rich in meaning, and this meaning is almost totally attributed—through labeling, branding, licensing, packaging, and especially through advertising. But note: The meaning of objects is not just attributed; it's attributed with quicksilver fluidity. That's why, if you want to study luxury at the beginning of the twenty-first century, don't ask moralistic economists like professors

Galbraith, Schor, and Frank or a righteous philosopher like Professor Singer. Ask a cultural anthropologist. Or better yet, ask someone in the marketing department of a soap, beer, blue jeans, automobile, bottled water, or even computer company. And if you want to see how luxury is *made*, just pick up any magazine with more than two hundred pages of advertising, the ones that go "thud" when you put them down.

A Taxonomy of Modern Luxe

So far I have talked about luxury as if it were a coherent body of objects whose only characteristic is that its attributed value is greater than that of other similar objects in the same class. And I want to stay with this definition because it shows how the process of commercial speech, the process of advertising, is responsible for adding this admittedly bogus value.

Luxury objects fall into four obvious categories. The first is sustenance, food and drink. In a sense this is where luxury begins and ends . . . in the mouth, with literal tastes. The second is shelter, which historically was probably the first site of separation via luxury. One place is more comfortable than another. The third is clothing, still a central concern of elevated consumption. Think logos. And the last is the most modern, and in many ways the most perplexing, in that it separates us from what has come before, the luxury of sufficient leisure to consume such objects. Or criticize them.

Each category has gradations of refinement. In sustenance, the levels of luxury are usually covered in the concept of "gourmet," that sense of elevated taste. Think only of how complex the tasting of wine has become. Or the appearance of stores like Zabar's or Dean & DeLuca. Or how the grocery store has exploded. In the area of shelter there is not just magnitude—square footage—but greater and greater softness, *luxuria*, really, in various rooms of the house. Whereas the parlor used to be the place to show off stuff, we have moved luxury deeper into the house. The luxury bathroom, the luxury kitchen, and especially the "master" bedroom have displaced the "living" room. Again, think of how the bed became an important marker in the 1960s, complete with such variations as the "king" and "queen" sizes. In the 1990s the sheeting took over the role of signifier. Count the number of threads. The Company Store, a catalog of home furnishings, sells an eiderdown pillow (king size) for $230.

The luxurification of clothing is fashion. If you want to see this process, observe how the label has gone from inside the collar or the waistband to outside, across the chest, down the side, hidden in plain sight in logos, buttons, crests, initials, and whatnot. You are not *what* you wear but *who* you wear.

The Leisure to Consume

The final luxury category is leisure time, such matters as recreational travel, the weekend trip, luxury liners on Cruises to Nowhere, and the rise of vacation timeshares. *Time* itself is at the essence of luxury leisure—saving it, wasting it, or sharing it. Thanks to the timeshare, you can vacation in luxury. You just can't stay too long.

"Excite her senses this weekend." Take her shopping in Short Hills, New Jersey.

A favorite way of using leisure time is to go recreational shopping. The massive Mall of America, or the even more massive Edmonton Mall, are advertised as tourist destinations. A popular vacation for time-starved couples is a night at a mall motel or a city hotel followed by weekend shopping. Called a spree in the trade, it's a package deal with the discounted rooms bundled in with retail discounts at local stores. The Maxwell Hotel in San Francisco even features a spree with free $25 gift certificates on the pillow instead of mints, free foot massages for weary shoppers, and a bronze statue of a female shopper in the lobby to make it all seem elegant and a little (wink-wink) ironic.

Obviously, the reason that these categories have exploded is because, in the felicitous phrase of the Harvard sociologist Lee Rainwater, "creature needs" have become easier and easier to satisfy. Why? Ironically, because of the churning and downstreaming of luxury items. Whereas in 1918 food took fully 40 percent of urban spending and consisted of a rather monotonous diet of bread, hot cereal, potatoes, beans, and rice, with meat appearing only at dinner and fruits (other than apples) a rarity, today's percentage is closer to 9. And the choices have multiplied. Housing took a quarter of the household budget after World War I with the average urban household of five members living in about the same number of rooms, only half of which had indoor plumbing and not all of which had hot water. Clothing took another 15 percent, leaving not much for transportation, education, and medical care. Food, shelter, and clothing now account for about half of a typical family's expenditures, compared to 80 percent in 1918 (Katz 1997).

Luxury Objects

Inside these general categories—sustenance, shelter, and clothing—are the specific objects. Here is an admittedly crude taxonomy of these objects in no special order but only to show how different they can be. I call them technoluxe, populuxe, and opuluxe.

• *Technoluxe*. Almost every labor-saving device enters culture as a luxury. From plumbing to electricity to the washing machine to the telephone to radio to the personal computer . . . the initial response to technical innovation is "it's a luxury." We don't need it. While the rich may pay the high introduction costs of technoluxe, the rest of us soon benefit. While it's happening it may look like the "winner" (aka the rich) is taking all, but what he

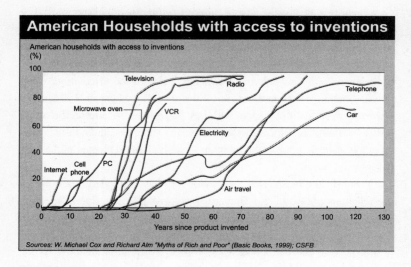

How luxury becomes necessity: access to inventions. W. Michael Cox and Richard Alm, *Myths of Rich and Poor: Why We're Better off Than We Think* (New York: Basic, 1999), 162.

in fact is taking is the product at the top of its price curve—he is paying the "first-unit costs." This consumption starts what often turns out to be a boon to the rest of us—heartless capitalism's welfare system.

• *Populuxe*. The word *populuxe* is a mixture of the words *populism, popularity,* and *luxury* (with an unnecessary *e* tacked on to give it a little class) and was coined in the 1980s by the architecture critic Thomas Hine. Populuxe is the stuff that came flooding into the marketplace after World War II, a result of two separate developments: the ability to mass-produce highly sculptural pieces of metal and plastic and a venue in which to display their use, namely, the movies. For it was the movies, not the little sputtering black-and-white television tube, that furnished the dreams of consumers. And in buying those bulbous two-toned autos and colorful opened-up kitchens consumers aspired to a vision of Hollywood glamour and grandeur—the good life for the average Joe.

The eruption of populuxe was all over the homes of the 1950s and 1960s. The lifestyles of the rich and famous were purchased cut-rate by means of Naugahyde furniture, plastic laminate kitchens, and a truly awful vinyl substance called Con-Tact, which was applied to walls in dens and living rooms to give a look of marble or brick. In these products can be found the optimism and innocence, the hunger for speed, and an eager embracing of the polychromatic future that Americans shared as a vision of the good life.

Soon populuxe spilled out into all manner of secondary stuff like hula hoops, crinolines, boomerangs, push buttons everywhere (most shockingly on the transmissions of Chrysler Corporation cars), Formica, electric hot-dog cookers, blob-shaped coffee tables, Sugar Pops, lots of knotty pine, pointy-toed shoes with spike heels, and Lipton onion soup mix out of which one might make a dip for corrugated potato chips ("extra strength allowed for heavy-duty dipping").

If you want to observe populuxe in architecture, where it gets blown up to Brobdingnagian scale, just think of Morris Lapidus and his Miami hotels, or hurry and take a trip to modern-day Las Vegas and look at the old hotels like the Dunes and the Sands that are being imploded to make way for the modern opuluxe variety like the Bellagio or the Venetian. Or go to Disneyland. This is the stuff of the movies—grandiose, elegant, pompous, and, thankfully, ephemeral. Seeing it once is exciting, seeing it twice is interesting, seeing it a third time is a chore.

• *Opuluxe*. This is the stuff that gives luxury its current reputation. And therefore the stuff most interesting to study. Opuluxe is frippery, from Old French, where it means ruffled, as in the feathers of a bird or the wrinkling around the edge of a collar. This is downstream couture, conspicuous display, top of the line, what in ad lingo is "premium" and what salespeople describe to me as an "instant classic." And, as such, opuluxe plays the role of heraldic crests, self-applied badges, what are called in Marketing 101 "bridge goods" or "positional goods." Opuluxe gets you somewhere. Or is supposed to. It is a shortcut to some consumers, the goal of consumption to others. It is easy to criticize because it is so low in utility, but it has become more and more necessary to more and more people.

A precursor for opuluxe is what used to be called objects of virtu. Of all the objects of virtu, none was more popular, or more revealing, than the ornamented snuff box. Like all good opuluxe objects, it was easy to ornament and, better yet, easy to display to others. You took it out, you held it up to your face, you took a pinch, and everyone around you had a good look as you inhaled.

Such virtu is all over the place: the Gucci slippers worn at work, the $80 sunglasses, the Fendi baguette purse, the three-hundred-thread cotton sheet, Tiffany key chain, cashmere socks, Armani suit. . . . The sense of "here, have a look" motivates purchase, "you shouldn't have" is the viewer's response, and "I'm worth it" concludes the process. A golfer buys the Big Bertha golf club because he thinks it will help him, yes, but also because it looks snappy in the golf bag covered up with a huge sock that spells the brand name in capital letters.

Like populuxe, opuluxe can explode to gargantuan size. In a few chapters we will go out to Las Vegas, the "new" Vegas, the Vegas of such themed opulence as the Bellagio and the Venetian hotels. These hotels are beautifully made snuff boxes. Their utility is that they sit atop casinos promising what an association with luxury always promises: safe passage to the next world or at least a momentary reprieve from this one. Come here, they say, strike it rich. In Vegas one can see the metaphysical purpose of top of the line, the sublime sensation of transcendence, the promise of luxury. Modern luxury is, at its peak, a liminal experience, a lifting up and out of the dreary and vulgar world.

Who Is Buying Virtu Today?

Most opuluxe is not being consumed by the rich but by the rest of us. Ponder this: The duke and duchess of Windsor surrounded themselves with the world's finest goods—from jewelry to bed linens to flatware, virtu galore. The duchess, the twice-divorced American Wallis Simpson, would never be queen, but she never let it prevent her from living like one. In their household the coasters came from Cartier, the placemats from Porthault, and their dogs ate from silver-plated Tiffany bowls. When Sotheby's auctioned more than forty thousand items from their Paris home in 1997, the remnants of their royal life went up for grabs.

But those who missed out on the bidding or prefer their own monograms needn't worry. Quite a number of the same suppliers of life's little luxuries remain open for business. Take a look at some of the auction items in the Sotheby's catalog. Most are still being made, either in the same form or in an updated version.

- Kenneth Jay Lane enamel bracelet tipped with faux pearls and a faux onyx-and-diamond ring can be had for $125 and $90, respectively, at Saks Fifth Avenue stores.

- Chanel faux-pearl earrings that the duke gave to the duchess cost about $360 at Chanel stores.

- The duchess's Cartier "Love Bracelet" in eighteen-karat gold with screw closure, which was presented by the president of Cartier to the Windsors and other "great lovers" in 1970 (among the recipients: Elizabeth Taylor and Richard Burton, Sophia Loren and Carlo Ponti), is yours for $3,625 at Cartier boutiques.

- T. Anthony luggage, the Windsors' favorite (they owned 118 such trunks), is still being made and is available in Manhattan.

- Porthault linens complete with hand embroidery are available at your local mall.

- The duke's velvet slippers now are sold at Brooks Brothers, which owns the London company that made them. Instead of getting an *E* for "Edward" below the embroidered crown, the slippers are monogrammed *BB* ($188).

- The Windsors' stationery from the Mrs. John L. Strong Company, pure cotton paper with hand-engraved monograms, can be yours for $80 to $750, depending on the ornamentation.

- Okay, okay, you'll never have as many scarves and gloves as the duchess, but Hermès and Balenciaga sell exactly the same ones for more than $300 a pop.

Now, admittedly, most of us cannot afford the entire ensemble of opuluxe that surrounded Wallis Simpson. But we can buy it piecemeal. In fact, it is the act of buying that seems so important. She had it. I can get it. But since we can't peek into the royal closet, how do we know *what* belongs there?

The Importance of Print Media

Buying social place *and* feeling good about it may seem hopelessly vulgar, but that is precisely what characterizes the new luxury. Knowing what to buy, and where to buy it, therefore becomes a central act of adaptation. And if advertising is what adds luxury to a product, then how to read advertising is crucial to understanding. Although most critics who come to

Who will you be? and who will drive off with your personality? The dilemma of Things 'R' Us.

this subject are forever pointing to television and the movies as the place where we learn consumption, opuluxe is different. We learn luxe consumption from the slowest-moving medium: print.

Although I will concentrate on the importance of the Condé Nast magazines (the *New Yorker, Vanity Fair, House & Garden* . . .) and their central role in teaching luxe consumption, they are by no means alone. In fact, you can't find a better introduction to luxury consumption than by looking at the "Styles" section of the *New York Times* each Sunday or the box ads that border the first few inside pages of the daily *Times.* The *Wall Street Journal,* which usually is more focused on getting than on spending, has a special Friday section called "Weekend Journal," which makes a regular roundup of stuff to buy, be it the "House of the Week" or the "Object of the Week." Needless to say, the ads are in keeping with the text, with the word *luxury* featured in almost every ad. For slow learners the *Daily News* even has an occasional column under the rubric "Tastes," called "Little Luxuries," in which the paper spotlights a gourmet treat or a small indulgence.

The role of print can't be overestimated in selling opuluxe. Modern lux-

Lest there be any doubt, De Beers answers a man's question.

ury is the result of too much money chasing not too many things but too many similar things. Machines make fungible things. To maximize profits they have to be distinguished. Marketing attempts to make similar things different. More than anything, marketing creates luxury by branding it with a story, a myth. Magazines, and to a lesser degree newspapers, are where this happens. In print tap water gets bottled; purses become billboards; ensembles are put together. Print advertising holds the object still, fills it with meaning, and tells you how to consume it.

Why does this work? Why do we accept a system carried by advertising that is so patently irrational? At one level the answer is simple. Because you cannot differentiate yourself from others with claims of family heritage, religious affiliation, job title, educational vitae, marriage partner, and the like, you must differentiate yourself with something that shows that you know how to consume. The label moves from the inside of the garment to the outside. Displaying connoisseurship becomes central. You separate yourself not by buying things but by buying meaning and then by knowing how to display that meaning. Knowing where that meaning is has become the quest of modern life, and the glossy ads of magazines tell us where to find it.

Why Now? Why Us?

Henry James was not far off when he predicted that the United States was to become an "empire of goods." For most of the twentieth century the rich consumed "wants," while the rest of us consumed "needs." The times have changed; in fact, as a recent Goldman Sachs report on retailing points out, those earning less than $50,000 a year are experiencing the great burst in the consumption of upmarket branded products (Kaufman 1999:A1).

About 40 percent of the U.S. population—or more than one hundred million people—live in households earning $35,000 to $75,000 a year. Of course, consumers in all income brackets continue to crave a little luxury in their lives, but the great bursts in new luxury are occurring at lower and lower income levels. Savvy marketers are figuring out ways to provide it— or at least a close facsimile—for a lower and lower price.

It stands to reason that the most startling opuluxe transformations are being made with ordinary consumables. One of the first to see this coming was Peter Drucker, the wizard of predictive marketing. In 1969 he saw what is moving through the market like the proverbial rabbit in the python:

> A universal appetite for small luxuries has emerged. They signify a little independence, a little control over economic destiny. They are a badge of freedom. Where the means are very limited—among the poor or among teenagers without much income of their own—the small luxury may be a soft drink, a lipstick, a movie magazine or a candy bar. For the emerging middle class, it may be the appliance in the kitchen. For the truly affluent it may be the advanced degree. That one can do without it makes the small luxury into a psychological necessity. (97)

Ernst and Young, the accounting and consulting firm, points to these

Be all that you can buy.

affordable luxuries as one of the six big consumer trends at the beginning of the new century. And McKinsey and Company, which tracks this kind of consumption, estimated in 1992 that spending on the fourteen main categories of luxury goods—fashion and fashion accessories, cars, leather goods, perfumes, cosmetics, shoes, watches, jewelry, champagne, wine, spirits, crystal, silverware, and china—in their seven biggest markets would total almost $50 billion. Similarly, the members of the Comité Colbert, a trade association for seventy big French luxury-goods firms, predicted their sales would grow by an average of 20 percent a year (Upmarket 1992:95). LVMH, the largest French conglomerate, has gone from $4 billion in sales in 1992 to almost $12 billion in 2000 (Tagliabue and Horyn 2001:1).

In this context Moët & Chandon, the champagne company has created what it calls the "luxury index," or "the cost of *really* living." Admittedly, the index includes such items as Rolls-Royces and full-length mink coats. But it also includes such items as chocolate truffles; a day of maid service; a wash, cut, and blow dry at an upscale New York City hair salon; and a one-hour limousine rental. Along with round-trip fares on the Concorde to Paris, it records such good-life items as champagne, caviar, and Broadway theater tickets. In fact, the construction of the index gives disproportionate weight to luxury food stuffs like champagne and caviar. Clearly, the people who are counted in the index are not the wealthy but the middle class (Kleinfield 1991:D8).

As Debora Silverman has argued in *Selling Culture,* the luxurification of the middle class is the great legacy of Reaganomics. Trickle-down did indeed work. Trickle-down luxury, bubble-up status. While the working affluent may not be able to assemble the entire constellation of deluxe lite, this group can come close. Thanks to the credit card and boilerplate leases on big-ticket items, you can have just what that millionaire next door has. Not the money but the stuff.

Since the early 1980s, for the first time in Western culture (and, I hasten to add, in many Asian cultures as well), middle economic classes have had access to objects previously in the domain of the well-to-do. To be sure, we can't all have the same brands. We can't all have '57 T-Birds, we can't all go off hiking in Nepal; we can't all afford to send our kids to Princeton. But play by a few economic rules—finish high school, don't start parenting too soon, hold a steady job for four years, don't experiment with addictive drugs until you are thirty years old—and chances are you can have a car and weeks of leisure time as well as a five-day workweek and access to a good education and medical care. Plus a lot of unnecessary stuff.

The language of the middle class reflects this luxurification of ordinary stuff. Words like *gourmet, premium, boutique, chic, accessory, classic,* and *gated community* have jumped loose from their elite moorings and now describe such top-of-category items as popcorn, hamburgers, discount brokers, shampoo, scarves, ice cream, and trailer parks. "Luxury for all" is an oxymoron all right, but it's the aspirational goal of modern culture, at least as perceived by marketers.

This psychological phenomenon, which economists call the wealth effect, has driven the down-marketing of high-end objects with a vengeance. When stock prices rise and when people observe the spending of others, consumers feel rich and go shopping, often consuming such positional goods as those sold at Cartier, Louis Vuitton, and Bulgari while redoing their bathrooms or adding an entertainment center or a home gym. Thus in a generation the garbage can with briquettes at the bottom becomes the chrome flamethrower on wheels. How else to explain the Viking Grill?

The transformation of a simple tool like the barbecue is typical. And its mutation into opuluxe shows the rising role of men. *Esquire* recently completed a two-year study of its readership to learn how men view consumption. According to Jason Lundy, executive director of marketing and strate-

Luxury for men: the ultimate grill.

Samuel L. Jackson as a more elegant version of Shaft, thanks to
TAG Heuer, Armani, and Reebok.

gic planning for *Esquire,* the luxury market and men's views of luxury have changed dramatically since the early 1980s. In his words,

> Men today think of luxury in terms of accessibility and not exclusivity. People no longer feel that Neiman Marcus or Brioni are things for rich people. The feeling is that if you can afford it, you deserve it. And that's new, because what's happened is that today's luxury customer did not grow up rich, but middle class. They're buying luxury products to reward themselves for working hard, and as investments. (Mui 2000:30)

In this context one can understand why the designer Giorgio Armani has aligned himself with Paramount Pictures' remake of *Shaft* and the Guggenheim Museum. At first glance one might wonder what the connection is between the gritty urban detective and a $1,300 knee-length black leather coat. But the copy makes it clear: "Attitude by Shaft/Clothing by Giorgio Armani." And the movie explains the *attitude.* In one scene a tough guy shoves Detective Shaft. Mr. Shaft doesn't like it. "Get your hands off my Armani," he barks. (Ditto his TAG Heuer watch and Reebok sneakers.) Meanwhile, the Guggenheim, erstwhile arbiter of highcult, gives over almost all its space to highlight Armani as major artist ("An Exhibition of Visionary Works" was the show's title) at about the same time that the major artist makes a sizable contribution to the museum's endowment (Klebnikov 2001:68).

Why We Want What We Don't Need

How did we get to this? Why do some things mean so much that they can only be explained as meaning too much? One explanation comes from Philip Cushman, a psychologist, who argued in the *American Psychologist* in 1990 that the filling of the modern self with meanings from the material world is one of the central endeavors of our industrial culture. While the Victorians had attempted to shrink the self by controlling and repressing excess, in the twentieth century we tried expanding and extending it into the world of things.

In "Why the Self Is Empty" Cushman points to an interesting development that parallels the rise of modern consumption: the unfolding of a professional therapeutic culture. Oddly enough, while they seem oppositional, idealism and commercialism do converge at points. For instance, much is made in therapeutic culture of enlarging lifestyle choices, elevating consciousness, and finding the "true self." And indeed, if you look at the *therapeutic* ethos of modern life, it is all about buying into a secular personality, a coherent lifestyle. While the Greatest Generation was more inner directed and self-reliant, we have become more outer directed and socially sensitive in the modern world. In fact, as Cushman cannily observes, the rise of consumer culture parallels the rise of two newly recognized psychological "disorders": narcissism and borderline personality.

The solution to modern angst, to filling up the self, happens both at the psychologist's office and down at the mall. In the office you are offered a choice of therapeutic personalities, and at the store you are offered an equally varied choice of adaptive lifestyles. As Cushman concludes, "The great beneficiaries of this narcissistic dynamic are the modern state, the advertising industry, and the self-improvement industries (including psychotherapy). All three perpetuate the ideology of the empty self, and all three profit from it" (608). From this, of course, comes the irony that foreigners never tire of observing, namely, that the wealthiest nation on earth is also one of the emptiest. This irony is no longer limited to North America.

How to Fit in? Join a Consumption Community

Once consumption is sprung loose from concerns of social class and made part of a lifelong attempt at creating meaning, we can finally appreciate why the new luxury has proved to be so powerful. The object of self-realization via consumption is no longer preordained by heritage but results from a never-ending shifting of individual choice. We have moved the word *class* from inherited social position to a quality of an object. So the Armani suit has "class," not someone whose family has kept the same pew in the Episcopal church for generations. A house in the Hamptons carries the weight of ancestors arriving on the *Mayflower.* A Gulfstream jet does the work of four years at Groton.

The study of consumption clusters goes by any number of names: psychographics, ethnographics, macrosegmentation, to name a few, but they are all based on the ineluctable principle that birds of a feather flock together. As one might imagine, the keenest knowledge of these groups comes from those who have the most to gain by understanding and selling such information, namely, marketing specialists. Tell a savvy marketing analyst your most recent purchase, and she will tell you with amazing detail what you'll buy next.

Take zip codes, for instance. Marketing firms have separated neighborhoods into about forty designations called PRIZM (Potential Rating Index for Zip Markets) clusters. So at one end of the residential microgeography are consumption communities like Blue Blood Estates, Money and Brains, Furs and Station Wagons, which buy predictable expensive stuff. Then in the middle are clusters like Pools and Patios, Two More Rungs, Black Enterprise, New Beginnings, New Melting Pot, Towns and Gowns, Rank and File, Old Yankee Rows, Bohemian Mix, Gray Power, Young Influentials, Young Suburbia, and Blue-Chip Blues. Off to the side are Shotguns and Pickups; Levittown, U.S.A.; Public Assistance; and the newest category, Old-Old.

Each of the forty clusters is defined by detailed demographic, lifestyle, and consumption information, often including brand-level data. For example, the Shotguns and Pickups cluster is partly defined by high usage of chainsaws, snuff, canning jars, frozen potato products, and whipped

It's not what you just bought that matters, it's what you are going to buy next.

toppings. Members of this cluster are exceptionally unlikely to use car rental services, belong to country clubs, read *Gourmet* magazine, or drink Irish whiskey. By contrast, members of the Furs and Station Wagons cluster are much more likely than the typical consumer to have a second mortgage, buy wine by the case, read *Architectural Digest*, drive BMW 5–series cars, eat natural cold cereal and pumpernickel bread, and watch the *Tonight Show*. Members of this cluster are unlikely to chew tobacco, hunt, drive a Chevette, use nondairy creamers, eat canned stews, or watch *Wheel of Fortune*.

You immediately get the point of this data because observing stuff is the way we understand each other. What you may not appreciate is that each of these groups has more in common with a zip code thousands of miles away than with one a few digits off. For instance, parts of Palo Alto, California, can be exchanged with parts of Princeton, New Jersey (both are dominant in the Money and Brains category), and no one would know the difference. Marketers can predict with eerie accuracy not just the kind of automobile but the specific brands of luxury items, like cameras, television sets, toilet paper, and deodorant, for specific zip codes in Beverly Hills, California; Scarsdale, New York; Bloomfield Hills, Michigan; McLean, Virginia; and Lake Forest, Illinois.

Marketers can also chart your passage through life by using not zip codes but shifting purchases of desired goods. Give a consumer specialist an optical reader, a computer, and all your bar-coded purchases for the past week and he will tell you not only what you bought last year but what you will consume next week. Taking this into consideration, *tribes* would be a better descriptive term than *class* to describe the way we live now, and the tribe with which you affiliate yourself probably has more to do with the brand of bottled water you bought last Tuesday than with your income, age, education, job, bloodline, religion, or country club (Maffesoli 1996).

Luxe Is the Lifestyle of the Yuppie

One reason that terms like *yuppie, baby boomer, bobo, thirtysomething, echo-boomer,* and *Gen X* have elbowed aside such older designations as *upper-middle class* is that we can't understand class as well as we can understand lifestyle. *Lifestyle* came in with the 1960s for a reason. The post–World War II generation was becoming unhinged from traditional markers and affiliations. Also, the word *upscale* had become common parlance by 1966. In 1983 *yuppie* would catch hold.

Even if no one knows exactly how much money it takes to be a yuppie, or how young you have to be, or how upwardly aspiring, everybody knows where yuppies gather, how they dress, what they play, what they drive, what they eat—and that they hate to be called yuppies. They are instantly recognizable in movies. Everybody knows that they were the first ones to serve goat cheese, that they tend to drink spritzers, and that they populate 90 percent of all ads and almost all the ads for opuluxe products.

The original definition was a young urban professional, but at some point this became corrupted to young upwardly mobile professional. Demographically, yuppies were part of the seventy-six million people born between 1946 and 1964. Their number was small—the only definitive estimate of the yuppie population found just four million of them, representing a mere 5 percent of late baby boomers—but their influence on the rest of us has been huge (Leiby 1994:D1).

With respect to the explosion of luxury goods, the yuppie stands front and center. Yuppies were one of the first communities since the Renaissance known almost entirely through their display of goods. Here are just a few from the late 1970s: yellow ties and red suspenders, merlot, marinated salmon steaks, green-bottled beer, Club Med vacations, stuff with ducks on it, Gaggenau stoves, clothing from Ann Taylor or Ralph Lauren, designer water, Filofax binders, Cuisinarts, kiwifruit, Ben & Jerry's ice cream, ventless Italian suits, pasta makers, bread makers, espresso-cappuccino makers, cell phones, home fax machines, air and water cleaners, laptop computers, exercise machines, massage tables, and remote controls for the television, VCR, CD player, stereo receiver, and garage door. Of course, the car—especially the BMW, the infamous Beemer—was the yuppie badge nonpareil.

Yuppies were unique in that they had no spokesmen. No one like Marlon Brando, Abbie Hoffman, John Wayne, or Elton John came forward to personify the group. Richard Gere laying out his clothes on the bed in the movie *American Gigolo* (1980) might have been the yuppie archetype, but he seemed a little too moody about his Armani outfits. So, rather like Eagle Scouts, yuppies had no distinct personality other than their merit (or demerit, it's up to you) badges, worn almost Pancho Villa–style around their "lifestyles."

Perhaps the only person who really qualifies as the Ur-yuppie is a superannuated one, Donald Trump. The Donald has become an eidolon of

The Donald flaunts it on the cover of the Times Literary Supplement for July 10, 1998, and in various other places.

DONALD J. TRUMP
PROUDLY PRESENTS:

BREATHTAKING
LUXURY AT THE
WORLD'S MOST
INTERNATIONAL
ADDRESS.

Rising above Manhattan and the East River, and
overlooking the U.N. The Trump World Tower
at United Nations Plaza is one of the most
luxurious residential towers anywhere in the world.
This stunning new landmark offers elegantly
oversized condominium residences that range from
superb two bedrooms to sumptuous penthouses with
four bedrooms, formal dining rooms, maids rooms
and wood burning fireplaces. Every home also offers
ten to sixteen foot ceiling heights, extraordinary
room proportions and spectacular River or City
views. Designed to rival the world's five-star hotels,
amenities and services include a private spa and
health club with a 60-foot swimming pool,
a world-class restaurant, a private wine cellar,
a landscaped garden, around-the-clock concierges,
doormen, security and extensive service staff, even
valet parking in the garage. Spectacular two, three
and four-bedroom condominium residences are
priced from the $700,000's to over $10,000,000.
For sales information, please call (212) 247-7000.

THE TRUMP WORLD TOWER
UNITED NATIONS PLAZA

Beluga chilling in the fridge.
Frette linen in the bath.
Slippers and robe by the chaise.

Luxury is liberating.

TRUMP
INTERNATIONAL
HOTEL & TOWER
ONE CENTRAL PARK WEST

opuluxe on steroids. Not only has he moved through serial marriages complete with fathering a daughter named after a store (Tiffany), not only has he demonstrated his unflagging interest in pimping objects brandishing his name, but he has remained unrepentantly materialistic. It's me, me, me. If old-style luxury was about subtly advertising that you had money, Trump has removed all the subtlety. Trump is a gleeful, literal luxurist. His buildings, with all the polished brass and gold reflective glass, actually look like money.

In a way, the Donald is almost a modern *humour* character. You are what you have, and what you have is what you buy, and what you buy is only as good as what you can show. Not for nothing did Donald Trump almost run for president. As he himself said, whom do you trust? A politician or a man who has "great stuff"? Little wonder he became such rich grist for Garry Trudeau's mill.

Dreadful as it may be, such a system of ordering experience with someone like Trump at the top may be a far more equitable and democratic process than what most of us have experienced in the past. As Trump likes to point out, he has fallen into legal, if not literal, bankruptcy on a number of occasions. He has worked his way back. Trusting pocketbooks over prayer books may make the world safer and even more humane. After all, the only things that separate us are . . . things. And you can buy things. You can't buy ancestry, religious affiliation, or the number of vowels in your name. Consuming status at the cash register is vulgar, to be sure, but the alternatives have often been worse. So let's give it a try. Let's go shopping!

3.

Let's Go Shopping

THE STREETS OF MATERIAL DREAMS

*[The department stores] were handsome, bustling,
successful affairs, with a host of clerks and a swarm
of patrons. Carrie passed along the busy aisles, much
affected by the remarkable displays of trinkets, dress
goods, stationery, and jewelry. Each separate counter
was a show place of dazzling interest and attraction.
She could not help feeling the claim of each trinket and
valuable upon her personally, and yet she did not stop.
There was nothing there which she could not have
used—nothing which she did not long to own. The
dainty slippers and stockings, the delicately frilled
skirts and petticoats, the laces, ribbons, haircomb,
purses, all touched her with individual desire, and she
felt keenly the fact that not any of these things were
in the range of her purchase.*

—Theodore Dreiser, *Sister Carrie*

At the end of the nineteenth century Sister Carrie passes a department
store window. Theodore Dreiser describes what she sees. A century later
her not-so-fictional granddaughter passes through the mall, sees the same
scene, pulls out her charge card, makes the transactions, gathers up her
booty, tosses it into her leased SUV, and goes home to her condo inside the
gated community.

Meet Modern Carrie

To pass the time on the way home between cell phone calls, she reads bumper stickers celebrating her recent act. "Shop 'til you drop," "People who say money can't buy happiness don't know where to shop," "When the going gets tough, the tough go shopping," "But I can't be overdrawn! I still have some checks left!" "If I'm walking, I'm shopping," "I'm spending my grandchildren's inheritance," "Nouveau riche is better than no riche at all," "A woman's place is in the mall," "Work to live, live to love, love to shop, so you see . . . if I buy enough things I'll never have to work at love again."

As our modern Carrie pulls off the interstate, she passes a billboard for Diesel clothing. It pictures a young woman in the arms of a man. The tag line at the bottom reads, "He came at me with a whole load of charm, but after a while I decided to go shopping." Carrie remembers other quotes from the same campaign: "People say love is a great experience. I prefer shopping" and "They all wanted an answer, I just wanted to go shopping." What she may not know is that another version of this ad appears in men's magazines. Under the rubric of "The Luxury of Dirt," the young woman is now holding the man and *he* is saying, "She kept telling me about the importance of love, but I couldn't wait to go shopping."

Students of materialism have never paid enough attention to shopping: the anticipation of, the trip to the streets, the search, the hands on the mer-

What the hell is the "luxury of dirt"? Is this why men shop?

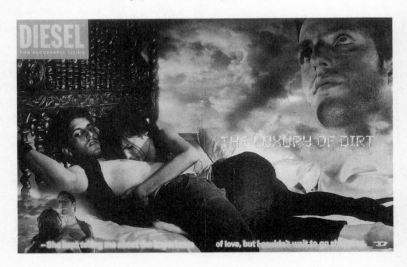

chandise, the take-it-to-the-register, the pay-for-it, and the cart-it-home. And they have never paid enough attention to the deep preparation for shopping: seeing the ad, dreaming of having the product, harboring the abiding faith that having it will prove meaningful.

Matters are changing. When a book like Paco Underhill's *Why We Buy: The Science of Shopping* becomes a best-seller, when the *New York Times* dedicates an entire issue of its Sunday magazine to "Spending: How Americans Part with Their Money" (October 15, 2000), and *Money* magazine does the same with "Here Comes the Ultra Class" (December 2000), when the Victoria and Albert Museum has a show dedicated to consumer brands ("Brand.new," 2000), when the *New Yorker* issues a special book of its pieces on consumption called *The New Gilded Age: The "New Yorker" Looks at the Culture of Consumption,* when *Advertising Age* runs a monthly section dedicated to luxury, when a hip magazine like *Nylon* gives itself over to an entire issue under the title "So Much Luxe: Dress for Excess," it is only a matter of time before the professoriate climbs aboard. And indeed a few of us have, as shown by such books as Marilyn Halter's *Shopping for Identity,* Gary Cross's *An All-Consuming Century,* Daniel Miller's *A Theory of Shopping,* and Rachel Bowlby's *Carried Away,* as well as collections like those edited by Pasi Falk and Colin Campbell (*The Shopping Experience*) and Daniel Miller (*Shopping, Place, and Identity*).

Academics especially have spent entirely too much time concentrating on the dismal side of shopping: the postdecision letdown that often follows the act, the whoops! put-it-in-the-attic side. As one wag has said, the reason that American homes average more than two thousand square feet, double the size of the average 1950 home, is that we need the extra space to store the unnecessary stuff we don't use. Plus, settling on the gloomy side of the equation makes some sense because the down side lends credibility to the usual interpretation of the shopping act, namely, that we should have better things to do, better things to want, better ways to use aspiration.

But clearly, most people don't. Although works of high culture are self-evidently richer and deeper and more full of meaning (as my colleagues never tire of reminding each other en route to the mall) the evidence has somehow not made its way out of the academy. The joys of shopping now exist, as Diesel knows, for both sexes. And shopping for the new luxury is extra special, as Diesel also knows. After all, what Diesel is selling is, at one level, just blue jeans, machine-made denim. The scene in the ad is dreamy for a reason. They're not just blue jeans. In a sense Diesel is selling you back what art also sells you—your dream life. Hard to believe, but blue jeans and dream fantasy are joined at the hip.

If you want to appreciate the function of opuluxe in modern dream life, observe its function in Hollywood, the dream factory. In fact, have a look at Richard Gere and Julia Roberts in *Pretty Woman* (1990). This self-conscious Hollywood confection of materialism plays out the high-cult Pygmalion myth through the redemptive powers not of art but of consumption. You make yourself over not by reshaping the interior form (the classical myth), or by tweaking the exterior form (*My Fair Lady*), but by buying and displaying branded stuff. You change yourself by switching accessories.

Essentially, you change the self by changing the drapery. And the drapery in this case is quite specific. It is the opuluxe fashion of designer *names* merchandised around the world in franchised boutiques. This is not haute couture but something more commercial, more mass-produced, and far more interesting because it is not so coherent and much more customer creative. It is the usually incomplete creation of the personal self as extension of other selves. And it has a name, *second-stream luxury*, for it flows below the upper crust to the common consumer, our modern Carrie.

The Diderot Effect

The entire process of creating a commercialized self has a name as well. It is called the Diderot effect. The insight into how commercial stuff fits together was not noted first by a modern Marxist, an academic sociologist, or a window shopper but by a late seventeenth-century essayist—Denis Diderot. In his *Regrets on Parting with My Old Dressing Gown*, the French philosopher explored what was to become a modern condition.

As he looked up from his desk and glanced around at his study, Diderot noticed that it had been transformed by mysterious forces. It was once crowded, humble, chaotic, and happy. Now it was elegant, organized, and a little grim. What happened?

Diderot suspected that the cause of the transformation was right before his eyes. It was his new dressing gown. A week after he began to wear the gown, it occurred to him that his shabby desk was not quite up to standard. So he got a shiny new one. Then the tapestry on the wall seemed a little threadbare, and he had to find new curtains. Gradually, he replaced the entire contents of the study. Why? Not because he wanted a new study but because he needed a sense of coherence, a sense that nothing was out of place, a sense of a center.

In modern marketing this is not known as the Diderot effect. That's too fancy. Instead it's called creating a consumption constellation, entering a brandscape, conforming to a fashion, making an ensemble. No matter what it is called, the pleasure and the pain remain the same. Achieving that sense of completeness is, in that linguistic barbarism unique to our times, to create a *lifestyle*. A lifestyle is an emblematic display of coherent brands.

When this consumption of brands inside constellations is elaborated, it becomes a "look," a fashion. And creating fashion is what defines the modern self. Diderot could not have known how dressing the self—the microcosm created by the individual and the macrocosm created by vast groups consuming similar objects—was to become the basis of modern commercial culture. But it certainly has. For instance, look at the difficult passages of life, like adolescence, courtship, first job, marriage, raising children, demonstrating success, or even retirement, and you will see that they require entire ensembles of matching goods. "Am I ready for the Chevy Suburban?" asks the modern Prufrock, not, "Do I want kids?"

Pretty Woman *as Exemplum*

Here's how *Pretty Woman* tells Diderot's fable of commercial transformation. Richard Gere is a successful buyout artist, the modern version of Veblen's buccaneer class. So he's in Los Angeles to gobble up a shipping concern owned by the sweet-natured Ralph Bellamy. Bellamy likes to do a little socializing so Richard needs a woman, not for sex but for business. He needs a dinner partner to make small talk between big deals. He needs eye candy, an arm trophy, something to go with his Armani suit.

He finds what he needs in a young hooker played by Julia Roberts. The problem is that she is a little rough around the edges. What to do? Well, since he is staying in the penthouse of the Regent Beverly Wilshire, and since this hotel abuts Rodeo Drive, and since we are continually informed that this is the street of consumerist dreams, the answer is obvious. He gives Julia a handful of bills and tells her to get "presentable."

As the camera works its way up and down Rodeo Drive, we see what is essentially an MTV music video of the Diderot effect via second-stream fashion. We are treated to our own window shopping, see the names of the stores—Louis Vuitton, Gucci, Chanel, Diamonds on Rodeo—and overhear snippets of casual conversation from shoppers. This place sparkles with answered prayers, whispers of dreams come true. It is indeed the Enchanted City where the yellow brick road of American consumerism ends. This is the Shining City, if not on the hill, then at least in near the shore.

But, alas, when Julia tries to remake herself, she only meets with hauteur and disdain. She is still too much the country bumpkin, what with her being dressed in tank top, red short-shorts, and black buccaneer boots that come up almost to her groin. When she goes into a particularly snotty store and asks how much things cost, the wicked stepsisters/sales clerks cackle, "I don't think this will fit you" and "It's too expensive," and, finally in unison, "Please leave."

Unable to resolve her changeover problems, Julia returns to the hotel, where she comes under the wise tutelage of Barney, the Jiminy Cricket of this consumerist fable. Barney is the concierge of the Regent Beverly Wilshire and under his gruff exterior beats the heart of you-know-what. Not only does he instruct Julia in fork etiquette (count the tines) and posture (always stand straight) but he provides the secret passageway to the Enchanted City. He calls his pal Bridget—played by Betty (Elinor Donahue) of *Father Knows Best,* so you know things are on the up and up—who is a salesperson in one of the ritzy shops. Betty understands Julia's problem. She'll help.

So Julia gets the first opuluxe object in her trousseau, takes the first step in her journey upward from the street to the penthouse: *the* little black cocktail dress. This is to be Diderot's new dressing gown. Cue the studio orchestra. Stop the dialog. Let the camera lovingly pan the scene. In her form-fitting elegant dress Julia has become . . . a knockout accessory, eye candy, a trophy, an indulgence, for herself, yes, of course, but especially for her man. No Marxist need apply. She is clearly happier for the experience.

One dress is not enough. This is just the core, the dressing gown that needs to be expanded, made coherent, part of an ensemble, accessorized. So the next day Julia returns, this time with the Man or, rather, with his credit card. "Wake up! Time to shop!" he tells her as he rouses her from dreamland. Richard in his Armani suit and Zegna tie is ready for battle. Together they revisit the evil and snooty stepsisters who have tried to keep Julia in her place: away from the transformative powers of luxury. As they stride into a typical boutique, he pulls aside the smarmy manager and lays it out in capital letters. "Look," says Richard, "we want the salespeople around here to suck up to us." "And how much money will you be spending?" asks the unctuous manager. Will you be spending "profane or really offensive amounts?" Richard assures him that offensive barely describes what he has in mind. "She has *my* card." The eye-rolling manager retorts, "And we'll help her use it."

Major sucking up occurs as we segue back into MTV land. Leaving the pupa, Julia is entering chrysalis. We see her butterfly wings slowly unfold as she exits the store in white suit and hat, a vision of perfection. This time the music is Roy Orbison's "Pretty Woman."

And what is her first act, now that she has crossed the divide? She goes back to the first store, the store where she was humiliated by the nasty saleswomen, and of course they do not recognize her. No more Eliza Doolittle; she is now Richard's Fair Lady. So she tells them who she was. She asks if they work on commission. Yes, yes, we do, they chirp. Ah, ha, she says, then take this! and she turns on her heel and walks out saying, "I have to go shopping now." We see them downcasting their eyes and grinding their fingernails into their palms in distress. Touché, Julia.

After a series of scenes lifted from countless bodice rippers and slick magazine ads, Richard lavishes on Julia the fruits of sucking corporations dry. The joyful twosome take a trip via limo and private jet to San Francisco to see the opera. The seats are high up. Not to worry that he's scared of heights, says Richard, they are "the best." Little by little we start to see the moral of this fable taking shape. The best is often confusing, but *having* it is not confusing at all. How can you be the best without consuming the best? That's the job of luxury. Luxury is the tribute paid to the best for being the best. As the Cadillac ad said, "The *Penalty* of Leadership."

Now the other side of the myth kicks in. As Julia is learning that you are what you consume, Richard is thrashing around. He is learning that display is not enough. Like the pony in the barnyard joke, emotions must be in here somewhere. While she has been changed by consuming opuluxe, he's going to be changed by consuming her. Revenge of the eye candy.

This takes a while. Richard still thinks that pushing money at Julia will solve his problems, but she knows better. Although she has given him everything—remember, she's a hooker—she has saved "kissing on the mouth." He gets kissed and in so getting also gets her heart. And one of his own. Richard goes back to Ralph Bellamy and changes his business tactics. No longer Dracula, he is now Robin Hood. Together they'll cooperate and save workers' jobs! Next, he pops his greedy lawyer in the kisser for upsetting Julia, and finally—cue the string section—he goes after Julia herself.

He no longer wants her on his arm or in his bed. He wants her in his life. But she is still wary of being an accessory, so Richard has to do a little work.

He has to hop into the limo and cross the tracks into the bad side of town. Then he has to climb up (he hates heights, remember) the fire escape and there, meeting her on the fire escape landing, ask for her hand. Fully savoring the fabular nature of his endeavor, he queries, "So what happens after he [the fairy tale prince] climbs up the tower and rescues her [the maiden in distress]?" And Julia, without batting an eye, responds, "She rescues him right back." The triumphal horns sound, Roy Orbison returns to the microphone to sing the coda, the camera pulls pack, and we are reminded by a jiving street wanderer that this is indeed the land of dreams.

Shut up and Shop: First to Rodeo Drive

But when we consider what this movie really says, we realize that the land of dreams starts at a cash register. The land of dreams is not on the wrong side of the tracks where Julia lives; it's where she did her shopping. And so, in the winter of 1999, I decided to find out just what these streets are like. As *Time* magazine noted nearly forty years ago, "If luxury had a lap, Beverly Hills sits square upon it" (February 21, 1964). So I tiptoed out of the ivory tower, slid past the groves of the academe, and went out to shop.

My overarching plan was to visit the best-known streets of opuluxe in the United States: Rodeo Drive, Worth Avenue in Palm Beach, and then the top of Fifth Avenue and upper Madison Avenue in Manhattan. Here we have the causeways of capitalism gone ritzy, what Americans have for the Rue St. Germain in Paris, the Via Condotti in Rome, or Bond Street in London.

I was going to start in Beverly Hills not only because of *Pretty Woman* but also because that's where Americans found our thoroughly modern Sister Carrie, the material girl Monica Lewinsky, desperately seeking something for Bill. The fable works both ways. You can transform Eliza Doolittle into my fair lady, but you can also win Professor Higgins with a little gift. We know Monica from her Gap dress, rather like Julia's little black cocktail dress. What she buys Bill on Rodeo Drive is a Zegna tie. In *Monica's Story* the author Andrew Morton blames Beverly Hills and Rodeo Drive for Lewinsky's concern with such frippery. Is that true? I wondered. So I would go there and find out.

I knew I couldn't do this alone. I hate to shop, and look what happened to Julia the first time she tried it, so I asked my daughter Liz, who was twenty-two, to join me. It wasn't hard to convince her to come down from San Francisco to give it the old college try. She had just graduated from Stanford and was a little at loose ends. I promised her that doing field research with her dad would be fun and educational. I even promised to pay her.

It was a dreary day when we left the Radisson Beverly Pavilion Hotel, which is sort of like a high-rise Howard Johnson's with a fancy name, to begin our studies. I had cased out the street the night before and, frankly, was a bit disappointed. Rodeo Drive is just as the movie promised, but the surrounding territory looks like downtown Boise, Idaho. Lots of low whitish office buildings don't give you the sensation of easy-living Beverly Hills. Even Wolfgang Puck's famous restaurant Spago looked a little dreary, sort of like a dive.

In fact, all of Beverly Hills was a disappointment. I remembered seeing an ad for L'Ermitage, "The city's newest luxury hotel now open for your amazement," which coyly invoked: "Like most things in Beverly Hills, we invite you to judge us on our looks." Not a good idea. The city has even come up with a slick new slogan: "The Province of Beverly Hills, America's only truly European city," possessing "the exuberance of Baden-Baden, the conviviality of Florence along with the daring of America." I'm not convinced.

Our plan was to start at the top of Rodeo Drive and work our way southward, back down to the Regent Beverly Wilshire hotel. I hoped that by the time we entered its hallowed halls, we would know what Julia learned: Clothes may not make the woman, but fancy accessories certainly help.

So we started at Tommy Hilfiger's Miami-esque mansion, which, as we soon learned, was not what we were after. This store looks like Bloomingdale's with fresh-faced youngsters wandering around looking for waves to ride. Nor was Ralph Lauren's ersatz hunting lodge our idea of Rodeo Drive opuluxe. It looked as if everything had been sprayed with a micron-thin patina. The distressed floors, the cracked leather chairs, the make-believe family portraits, the endless horse-and-dog stuff; even the sales staff seemed to be a little pasty and wan. No, we wanted to be intimidated, not jollied. We wanted to be dissed by the sales staff, just as Julia had been. (What we really wanted, perhaps, was the Rodeo Drive of the 1970s and 1980s, when Fred Hayman ran the show, when people went shopping in double limousines [one for the family, one for its purchases], when Gucci had a private second-floor salon for special customers who had to have a key to get in, when Arab harems would appear and strip a store to its cur-

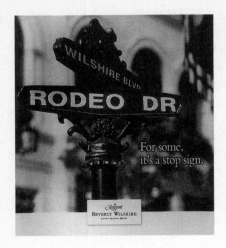

For some, it's a stop sign.

For some it's a stop sign. For others it's a green light.

tain rods. Clearly, this new version of Rodeo Drive had been Gap'd, Niked, and Polo'd.)

Yet we persevered. We finally hit pay dirt at Giorgio Armani. Here we met a new kind of store with a new kind of salesperson, called "an ethnic" in the trade. I don't know how to say this without sounding like a Neanderthal, but the people who help you in stores like Prada, Gucci, Versace, Fendi, and what I call the Italianate branch of opuluxe are not at all like the old-time salespeople I remember from my youth. At places like De Pinna and Peck and Peck you would be "assisted" by some rather tweedy and refined older white person. Often these people would be wearing a tape measure around the neck and have scuffed shoes. They sat down a lot. The more modern salesperson is edgy, a little nervous, and seems asexual, on purpose. Dressed in black, and thin, almost haughty, these salespeople were not solicitous but just there, around the store. They are always moving. At the door, also dressed all in black, was the guard. He was huge and wore a radio earpiece, but I don't think it was connected to anything. He didn't move at all.

Was there a reason for this? A kind of imperialism gone bonkers? A subversion of order in which the hauteur bubbled up from below? Was this the famous World Turned Upside Down of the Marxists? Or was it just trendiness carried to an extreme? Or was it a carefully calculated attempt to associate these objects with a street culture eternally sensitive to what's happening now? It's like the merchandisers of luxe have exchanged one kind of snobbism for another. I saw the same phenomenon in Manhattan and, to a much lesser extent, in Palm Beach. No matter, it did have the effect of generating panic, at least in this twilight yuppie.

The Armani store is filled with light, higher-than-high ceilings, pulsing music, stuff neatly but almost neglectfully arranged, and, as far as I could see, a staff totally lacking in sales interest. I saw something I hadn't seen before. I saw customers patting the clothes, fondling the fabrics, touching the buttons. The Gap has its merchandise piled high on tables, expressly so that people can get stuck, like guests at a feast. If so, they were gorging themselves here at Armani. E-commerce, I thought, will learn that opuluxe is not so simple as "price it right, move it off the shelves." It was like being in a petting zoo.

I was finally approached by a nice young man named David and, flustered, I asked him what I should be looking at. I was new in town. He didn't express much interest, so I just wandered around the store touching things, trying to figure out why all this stuff seemed so ugly to me but meaningful to my daughter. Meanwhile, I watched David wait on a young woman from the Middle East as she was trying on a beaded dress. I glanced at the price. It was more than $20,000 and she seemed pleased to have David's attention. The Euro-pop music and the greenish hue were driving me nuts, so Liz and I left.

I had no idea how to proceed. A number of art galleries are located along Rodeo Drive, and I have always felt comfortable in museums, so we took refuge in Art Brilliant. The gallery name was not kidding. Here was gaudiness on steroids, but at least I could function. I may not know the lingo of clothing, but I can speak artbabble. A vast painting of Michaelangelo's *David* was front and center, right in our path as we entered the gallery. It had been painted à la Francis Bacon except that gold replaced Bacon's gray skin. David looked like he had swallowed a stick of phosphor because he was lit up like a Christmas tree. In fact, everything in this gallery was covered in gilt. I was fascinated. The entire gallery was filled with barely disguised knockoffs of Old Masters done in lamé. I asked the proprietor if he didn't think this was a little reckless. He looked quizzical.

Art was no palliative for my shopping problem, however. We would have to buck up and get back out on the street. At Hugo Boss, an Italian men's store, I started to get a sense of what was happening. This store looked like an industrial warehouse where stacks of just ordinary clothing were piled up. But what struck me was the profusion of T-shirts. It wasn't that there were different varieties but that they all had wildly different prices. All they had in common was *Boss* written on them in various sizes.

Price Points

When I asked about this, the perpetually distracted saleswoman told me that it had to do with "price points." And what were these price points? They were, she explained, plateaus that customers had in mind, not of objects but of purchase prices. When someone bought a Hugo Boss object, she said, the consumer already had made a "choice of classics," so now all that remained was how much the shopper was willing to pay. Did I want the $20 T-shirt or the $40 T-shirt? All that separated them was the logo. So, essentially, the question was, as I rephrased it to her: How Boss-y did I wanna be? She was not amused.

This price-point information was to be the breakthrough that I needed because it allowed me to speak to the very people with whom Julia Roberts had had such trouble. Recall that when she asked them, "How much is this?" they cackled in glee. What she needed to ask was "How much Gucci/Vuitton/Boss/Chanel/Ferragamo . . . is *in* this?" In other words, if what you are buying at these stores is affiliation—in a sense the advertising—the question is, how much of it do you want?

But here's the counterintuitive key: The more you pay, the smaller the logo. In other words, if you are consuming the second tier of the product line, the name will be writ large. When you move into the first line, the name condenses, but the power increases, like the historical conflict between discreet old money and flashy new money.

Logocentricity

And the reward that you harvest by moving to the first tier of second-stream fashion is that you are now superior to those with the big name/logo, now superior to the way you were when you first started to buy opuluxe, now demanding of others that they carefully decode you and your elevated position. The phenomenon is rather like Bentley and Rolls-Royce. The cars are the same, but the Rolls has the ostentatious grill. To the cognoscenti the Bentley is classier. But you have to know the Rolls to know the Bentley. (And please forget that they are both now owned by Volkswagen.)

Over the course of the past few decades, trademarks like Ralph Lauren's polo player, Chanel's back-to-back *C*'s, Gucci's *G*'s, and Louis Vuitton's initials have become status symbols that come at price points. Once that price has been paid too often, the value is diluted, and the designer has to invoke the Veblen effect by upping the price and lowering the logo noise. Now that even the most inexpensive products are strewn with designer graffiti and a plain version of practically anything is impossible to find, the time may come when the logo-free garment will be the rarest and most precious of all. And, in an ironic reversal, we will be obliged to pay more for it. When every product is conceived as an advertisement of the "design," consumers who refuse to serve as human billboards will have to compensate the company for the attendant loss of publicity.

This absence of all the usual indications—with the logos hidden, with no design element so distinctive and consistent that it could serve as a signature for the brand (as quilted leather has for Chanel, for instance, or Prada's single red line or Gucci's red and green)—means connoisseurship becomes knowing how to read a secret code. Only someone who was really in the know could trace this handbag to Louis Vuitton or that scarf to Hermès. Like Russian dolls, as you get deeper into the land of opuluxe, the price rises, the size of the logo diminishes, and the confines of the club become more and more circumscribed.

So here's how I proceeded. I would say to the clerk that I wanted to buy a present for Liz that was, say, *very* Gucci, or *very, very* Gucci and could he show me such an object? I explained she was just starting to appreciate good things and could he help her along? This was the Open Sesame, because the clerks instantly knew what I was after. They would take me to various objects, not by category like handbag or shoe but by the size of the badge on the object.

Often this was done by showing me the actual designer's name in various sizes. So a purse with *Prada* on the side in large letters would be considered "Prada." *Very* Prada might have larger or smaller letters, but the items that were the *most* Prada would have almost no inscription. Only the cognoscenti would know. I was told over and over in various stores, not ever in these words but with various looks, that the large logo was arriviste and the teeny logo was arrival. This was the level I had heard of, the level described by the apt term *dog whistle* because there would be no "observable" marking, just some really sublimated marker like something written under the lapel, marked on a small button, or hidden in the stitching.

I kept marveling at how subtle this was, how clever, as if the real art of luxury was getting close to art. That's why Art Brilliant was filled with the imagery of the Old Masters made modern. This was connoisseurship applied to consumption. After a while one doesn't talk about the object but about how much interpretation the object can absorb. Intentionally or (more likely) inadvertently, this stuff was calling our motives for buying luxury goods into question by posing a challenge: Are you willing to embrace a product that makes recognizing the brand difficult, if not impossible? Are you willing to be such a devotee to art that you ask Michelangelo to please remove his name from the painting, or else you'll scratch it off for him? But you can't go too far. The image has to be recognizable to your cohorts.

The Concept of Heat

The other concept that I happened on to was the concept of "heat," or the absence thereof. Overhearing a conversation between two other savvy shoppers about what was in, and what was about to become in, I decided to broach my sales helpers with a plaint, "Can you show me what's about to be hot?" Or equally successful, "What's about to become cool?" I thought I'd be laughed out of the store. I mean, it's so shameless, so obvious and unsubtle—so just in from Bakersfield. Instead I was instantly accepted as though I was far from the first to ask such a question. Invariably, I was led to some scarf, shoe, parka, or bag, and we would stand in front of it as if experiencing an epiphany. "This," I was told, was "about to happen."

What was happening? How did they know? Did these people listen to a morning squawk box like brokers learning what stock to pimp for the day? Or was this a trait of the new luxury that needed study? Malcolm Gladwell, in *The Tipping Point: How Little Things Can Make a Big Difference*, has approached the general subject of social epidemics by using medical analogies like the flu to describe how human passions spread. And in *Butterfly Economics: A New General Theory of Social and Economic Behavior*, Paul Ormerod makes the case that economists have picked the wrong science as a model of markets. It's not the mechanics of physics that underlies consumption; it's the biology of living organisms.

Both observers seem to me to be on to something important, something at the center of luxury consumption. Math-based economic theory assumes that people know what they want and infers this from observing what they buy. But in reality people often do not know what they want until they learn what others are consuming. Desire is contagious, just like the flu. That's why there is always a sellout Christmas toy like Pokémon or Cabbage Patch, why some movies cost more to market than to make, why certain universities become superhot, why some restaurants have long lines, why Nobel Prize–winning economists at Long Term Capital Management stampeded to sell the Thai baht in July 1997, and why mutual fund managers all piled into the same dot-com stocks.

Here's the popular image of butterfly economics—the beating of butterfly wings in the Congo causes a tornado in Nebraska. Chaos theory! How exciting. But here's the more appropriate image—ants at the picnic. In the mid-1980s entomologists did a series of experiments with ants. They placed two food sources equidistant from and on opposite sides of an ant hill. The scientists kept the food piles equal in size, no matter how much the ants took from each. There was no reason for the ants to prefer one restaurant, so to speak, to the other. Logical economists would predict that ants would split the piles evenly, waiting in equidistant lines. But no. Instead, because the ants can signal each other as to where food lies, the distribution fluctuated wildly, even swinging from a 80:20 ratio to a 20:80 one (Lehmann-Haupt 2000:E9).

The clear conclusion is that while organisms may possess the skills to act rationally, they often don't. Individuals are not calculating machines with fixed tastes but rather social animals who interact with and are influenced by the flock, the tribe, the in crowd. As they say in advertising, you drink the advertising, not the beer; smoke the commercial, not the cigarette; drive the nameplate, not the car. So too in consuming the new luxury, you buy the trend, not the object. And how do you know the trend? You check what the other ants are doing. I never tried out the ant analogy with the sales staff, but the salespeople's willingness to show me where the forerunner ants were going made me think that they would have been sympathetic.

The Peaceable Kingdom

What struck me was that when I spoke this lingo, I encountered no tittering, no irony, no eye rolling. The salespeople did not smirk or turn on their heels and say that I was a rube. Even though, of course, this is exactly what I was. Years ago, if I had walked into the old Abercrombie & Fitch or the old Brooks Brothers or the old J. Press and said these exact words, I would have been laughed out of the store. Or sneered out.

But this new version of luxury is refreshingly candid, albeit subtle. You are being sold the signifier at various price points and no one balks at the process. This explains how the stores themselves are organized. It's rather like General Motors putting the Cadillac Esplanade over the Chevrolet Cavalier chassis or slapping the Cadillac logo on an Opel and calling it the Cimmeron. But as Cadillac can testify, such subterfuge is not without risk.

Designer opuluxe is a bit more complicated. At the macrolevel you have Armani and Armani Exchange, or Ralph Lauren and Polo Sport, or Donna Karan and DKNY. In each case the noise of the label is simply being turned up or down. Ditto the price. Ditto the heat. And this is not only a code for clothing—it works in all accessories. So Cartier has successfully developed a second tier of jewelry and watches under the label "Les Musts de Cartier" (as in "must have") and Van Cleef & Arpels has introduced what it calls "well-priced" engagement rings to attract a less-affluent clientele. Tiffany sells a host of trinkets on the cheap, my favorite being necklaces that have as one link a badge shouting "Please Return to Tiffany & Co.," and a four-inch-square porcelain jewelry box done in Tiffany blue. This is hardly dog whistle; it's more Ah-Ouga.

All this consumer decoding of the progressively ambiguous labels also explains how certain objects get into the opuluxe category. I had always wondered why these uptown stores all sell almost exactly the same things. The minute you see a handbag, you quickly see scarves, T-shirts, shoes, dark glasses, watches, perfume, and luggage. The inventory didn't make sense to me until I realized that all the objects have to be able to carry the freight of the label in such a way that viewers can unload it. No one much cares about labels on socks and pants. It also explains why, if you are going to put your logo on underwear, as Tommy Hilfiger, Calvin Klein, and Ralph Lauren do, you have to first feature droopy drawers so the name can be seen. Or maybe vice versa: the underwear comes first, *then* the drawers droop. As I write this, what is the new object making its way to the designer shelves? The umbrella. Looks normal until you unfurl it, and then it becomes a bumbershoot of logos protecting you from all kinds of inclemency. Cost? Vuitton, $225; Hermès, $355–$520; Prada, $156.

What the Suitcase Carries

And, of course, labeling also explains why luggage is so important. Not only do you carry your logo'd stuff in luggage, the luggage carries you. Look at any of these luxe stores and you will see a disproportionate amount of store space dedicated to carrying cases of various sizes and styles. And on these cases you will see the billboarding of the monograms from Gucci, Hermès, Vuitton, Fendi, and the like. Affiliation also explains such bizarre cross-pollination, called cross-branding, between opuluxe brands, such as the Lexus line of Coach luggage and the Coach edition of the Lexus.

Not by happenstance did these now-opuluxe retail stores often start out by producing the most mundane carrying cases, often pouches for medical materials and mail service during the Napoleonic Wars (as I was repeatedly told). What a nifty irony that the outside of the case itself now carries the most important information for producer and consumer alike. What I couldn't help but appreciate was that there are now such efficient ways of moving your stuff—duffel bags, for instance, or carrying cases with embedded wheels—but that these heavy *reliques de temps perdu* have not been replaced. Just the opposite. They are the same cumbersome models; their anachronistic dis-utility is part of their value. They have to be toted by someone else. I saw a 55" x 22" x 26" wardrobe case at Louis Vuitton priced to go at $18,200. It reminded me of the steamer trunk I took to summer camp. Veblen be praised.

The coach as Coach, the car as suitcase.

A Soupçon de Vuitton

I spent more than an hour in Louis Vuitton chatting up the affable staff about carrying cases. It was important to the salespeople that I know that M. Vuitton had made his living not just by making the cases but by packing trunks for wealthy women. The grand dames trusted him with their valuable things; he was a eunuch of luxury. In fact, he did this so well that he became a "packer" to Eugenie, empress of France.

One thing led to another and in 1854 Vuitton opened his own trunk shop. An early innovation: making the rounded top of a stagecoach trunk flat. Voilà! Trunks made for stacking! Should I be concerned that all this Vuitton luggage, all emblazoned with the signature checkerboard pattern, weighed a figurative ton? No, not at all, that weight would remind me of its provenance. Liz could barely heft a makeup case. Clearly, Vuitton was invoking J. P. Morgan's famous comment that if you had to ask the price of a yacht, you couldn't afford one. If you have to lift one of Vuitton's suitcases, you shouldn't have one.

And if I am too put off by having Vuitton's initials all over my luggage, I was assured by my long-suffering saleslady that I could order my own initials embossed for a slightly higher price. In fact, it turned out to be about twice as expensive. No matter, Louis's monogram was *not* there to show off but as a sign that I had bought the very best. It was a tribute to my good taste, not to his aggrandizement. After all, any company that had made trunks with special louvered trays to carry fresh fruit for a sultan of Egypt, tea cases for a maharajah, a secretary's trunk for Leopold Stokowski, a leather case to hold the America's Cup, my helper assured me, could go on quite well without my patronage. She was getting exasperated.

Was there any limit to these initials? I was shown the telltale monogrammed canvas wrapped around armoire trunks, wardrobe trunks, steamer trunks, shoe cases, attachés, soft-sided luggage, garment bags, cruiser bags, umbrellas, dog cages, sports bags, cosmetic cases, whiskey and cigar boxes, jewelry cases, cosmetic pouches, shoe bags, shopping bags, backpacks, ice buckets, soft-sided portfolio bags, courier pouches, all manner of clutches, belts, briefcases, ring-binder organizers, wallets and change purses, checkbook covers, credit card holders, passport holders, key- pen-, eyeglass-, golf ball-, cuff link-, cigarette- and photo-holders, shoulder bags, clutch bags, airline pilot map-case bags.

Liz and I left Louis Vuitton exhausted. We had had it with his initials and wanted to see something else for a change. I soon became interested in how far I could extend my "how much of the brand can I buy" conversation before one of the salespeople would rebel. I encountered no trouble saying something like this: "My young lady friend here [pointing to Liz] likes fine things. Can you show us something very very Fendi?" Nor did I have trouble with this variation: "My daughter [pointing to Liz] is having trouble at school, and I thought if I bought her something very, very Fendi, it would help her with her studies." In fact, even when I said I don't care about anything other than the logo—the bigger the better or, ironically in some dog-whistle cases, the smaller the better—I was never met with disdain.

How Much Brand Can You Buy?

Did these people have no shame? Or no sense of irony? I thought I was being so gauche, so déclassé, so bourgeois, so parvenu. In fact, the more outrageous the place—Prada, Gucci, or Versace, for instance—where the salespeople were the most weirded-out and convoluted in their all-black uniforms and freeze-dried hauteur—no one ever treated me as though I was out of line with this line of questioning. If I mentioned money, they might recoil, but if I talked brand display, they seemed to understand and accept. I often thought they found it refreshing to cut to the chase and indulge in only brand bombast.

This was puzzling to me. And still is. I now think this is because this "how much of the brand can I buy" is the conversation they are having with their paying customers. Not in such a bald form, but it must be close. As I looked around at the people who were actually buying this stuff, they seemed a decidedly lower class than what the store was claiming for itself. About a third of the shoppers I saw were tourists, mostly from Asia; another third were women of varying ages (not trophy brides as much as clusters of teenage girls fresh from the Gap), and then the occasional husband-and-wife team, which I thought was touching.

I wondered about these men-in-tow. While I saw a few men actually shopping, I saw many who were along for the ride. They didn't look unhappy, however. They were clearly enjoying the process. Was opuluxe part of courtship? Or part of consolidation? I remembered that the famous impresario of Rodeo Drive, Fred Hayman (who sold his eponymic store—

Fred Hayman Beverly Hills—to Vuitton), had a massive pool table to give men something to do while their wives or girlfriends tried on designer clothes. Those days are clearly over. There were a few single males, perhaps rogues or hubbies in search of presents. No gray-haired dowagers with chauffeurs in tow. And no Julia Roberts.

Demographic Pitch

I also know this customer-below/product-above configuration is a danger in advertising when the split is too wide. Products can move down-market from trend spotter to trend adopter to trend destroyer in a nanosecond. Hot doesn't become cool if it gets into the wrong hands. It gets trashed.

Nothing can do more damage to an opuluxe object than to have it held in the wrong hands. Gucci found this out the hard way in the 1970s. Instead of "aim high, sell low," Gucci aimed low and sold trash. Cadillac won't publicly admit it, but its executives cringe every time Hollywood shows pimps driving Cadillacs. Teenyboppers can quickly degrade a brand. So can the "wrong kind" of foreigners. As Calvin Klein has learned, you don't want to find your shmatte in J. C. Penney's.

This truism really hit home by the time I got to Giorgio's. On the first floor was all the merchandise I had seen elsewhere—the shoes, dresses, scarves, and pocketbooks. What was overpowering was the scent of the famous perfume, Giorgio. I know now why it is called an elevator emptier. But when I told the saleswoman, Dorothy, that I wanted to buy "a lot of Giorgio" and didn't care what the object was, she escorted me upstairs. There, spread out like an aisle at Kmart, was a cornucopia of Giorgio stuff—sweatshirts, bathrobes, towels, T-shirts, you name it—all the souvenir stuff of Disney World. On each object was the huge ersatz crest of Giorgio for all to see: the two rearing stallions furiously pawing the air. And here the price points were in line not with opuluxe but with the usual trinkets of "my trip to Los Angeles." It was almost as if the store had capitulated, given up the fashion charade and just admitted the truth of the sweatshirt: "My parents went to Beverly Hills and all they got me was this lousy sweatshirt."

"Was this 'sell the logo, forget the object?'" I asked Dorothy. She smiled. She kept repeating, "But it's okay, it's okay." With the exception of Dorothy, I had been unable to crack the facade of sobriety. No one would admit any humor whatsoever in this process. Of course, no one else had this great secret garden upstairs. But having seen it, I suspect Giorgio's will not be in business much longer.

The Environs of Rodeo Drive

Although I had certainly seen how young the customers for opuluxe really were, two other developments alerted me to just who was buying this high-priced, highly inscribed virtu. First, if you want to know who wants to get in on this audience, just look at what surrounds the southern arc of Rodeo Drive. True, Barneys New York is a block from Rodeo on Wilshire, and, true, Saks is expanding its fashion presence with a new men's store in the old I. Magnin building, and, true, Bloomingdale's is opening a store on Beverly Drive, a block east. All these wannabe stores are a cut below the boutique mystique. In fact, they often participate in this kind of retailing by having interior sections of their selling space partitioned off to featured designers.

But the real insight is that Planet Hollywood, a prole endeavor if ever there was one, with $8 hamburgers and $17 T-shirts, is cheek by jowl with this retail royalty. When the investors (a consortium of movie stars, including Sylvester Stallone, Arnold Schwarzenegger, Bruce Willis, and Demi Moore) announced plans in 1995 to open a theme restaurant down the block from the stately Regent Beverly Wilshire hotel, the backlash was epic and revelatory. Planet Hollywood did open, albeit with unheard-of neighborhood requirements, such as free parking for patrons at night, last call for alcohol at 11 P.M., early closing hours, and heavy restrictions on noise. As I write this, the company is filing for Chapter 11 protection, but the damage to Rodeo hauteur had been done. Maybe the WWF Smackdown diner will be next.

Across the street from Planet Hollywood is NikeTown, drawing a never-ending throng of sneaker buyers who gawk at shoes floating through transparent pneumatic tubes and wonder who is behind the one-way glass in the VIP shopping room. As opposed to Planet Hollywood, Planet Nike will stay in orbit, endlessly dumping more of the "wrong" consumers out onto Rodeo Drive. But, as I realized, these were the "right" consumers for this kind of Rodeo Drive stuff.

My Shopping Ends

My shopping day ended, alas, in tears, not because of the mallification of Rodeo Drive but because of what was happening between Liz and me. At

Tiffany the little research team fell apart. My fault and I apologize. Here's what I said to the saleswoman. I was just in town from Florida to see my daughter. Cue Liz. I said that she was attending junior college here in Beverly Hills. She is thinking about leaving school. She loves Tiffany's stuff. She especially loves the blue boxes. I don't want to spend a lot of money, but I want something "really Tiffany" and "really cool" that will keep her in school.

I look over to Liz and she seems to be holding up well, so I return to the sales clerk, who looks rather like my daughter. In fact, all the salespeople in chi-chi jewelry stores were unlike all the salespeople in the Franco-Italian places in that they were terminally WASPy. The saleswoman suggests a little ring, but I say that's too much. In fact, I confess I really want the cheapest thing I can get that will (1) keep my daughter at the books and (2) get her the blue box. The saleswoman suggests "Diamonds by the Foot," which consists of a chain attached to a stone attached to a chain—just what it says. And she pulls it out like it was a string of licorice.

I look over to my beloved Liz, and there are tears welling up in her eyes. We're out of there like someone just rang the dinner bell. What did I say wrong? Was it the school part, the blue box comment, the comments on how many yards would I have to buy to keep her in school? Liz wouldn't tell me. She told me later that what was upsetting was that the saleslady was looking at her in mild disgust, like she was some kind of spoiled daddy's girl. And when the saleslady said, "Yes, school can be tough," that did it. Liz had had enough of this charade.

LIZ COMMENTS:

What I thought was by far the most interesting part of the experience was the incredibly seductive nature of the objects themselves. Here I was on Rodeo Drive, conducting research; it was meant to be a purely academic, role-playing expedition. This was an experiment in how the other half—the decadent, materialistic half who threw money away—lived. I believe myself to be everything the woman in Tiffany thought I wasn't: intelligent, self-sufficient, not given over to the whimsical spending of large amounts of money.

Still and yet, when the saleslady pulled out the Gucci bag of the moment, and when my dad pretended he was thinking of buying it for me, there was part of me that was thinking, quite simply, "I want that." Everywhere we went, I spent longer than was necessary inspecting the evidence. I was a sucker. Watching the woman in Armani try on the $20,000 beaded dress, I was

*momentarily entranced—and more than slightly jealous. The stuff was just so
BEAUTIFUL, and when I looked down at my Old Navy sweater, I couldn't
help but feel a bit wanting. And that part of me just kept thinking, "Maybe
some day . . ." And so luxury sucked me in, even as I knew I was there solely
to be critical of it.*

*And, in the end, I wanted to leave Rodeo Drive for the same reason I often
avoid fashion magazines: not because I don't care about such trivial stuff, but
because I DO care, and when I look at these beautiful things, I'm left with an
aching feeling of desire and a slight dissatisfaction with my current life. Luxury is incredibly powerful, and it gets to almost all of us, even when we're told
it's meaningless. Luxury 1, Liz 0.*

Destination: Worth Avenue, Palm Beach, Florida

My next opuluxe shopping experience was with Liz's mother, my wife,
Mary. In late spring we drove down from Gainesville, where we live, to
Palm Beach. There we would meet a colleague of mine, a sociologist, Rod
Webb. En route I assured her that this was *my* trip and she was along as a
team member and that we most definitely were not going to buy stuff but
to do research. No crying, no buying. She seemed to agree.

I should have known better. Mary is a second-wave feminist. By that I
mean she wants to be paid the same as a man for doing the same work, and
she doesn't want to be told how to spend what she earns. She is not at all
upset when the sisterhood rails against the male hegemony and claims that
women are being infantilized and reified. She just goes shopping. When I
would quote her such passages as Tolstoy's "The whole trade in the luxuries of life is brought into existence and supported by the requirements of
women" (from "The Kreutzer Sonata"), she wouldn't bat an eye. How silly
to think otherwise, was her response.

To make matters worse, she had just read an article by Malcolm Gladwell in the *New Yorker* on the selling of men's pants that proved her point.
Two Canadian psychologists had men and women sit in a crowded waiting
room preparing to see a supposed Godot for an important appointment.
Then they were taken from the office and told the truth. There was no
Godot. But what could they recall from the room? This was not a memory
test but a test of awareness. Of course, the guys drew a blank. They were
lucky to remember what kind of chair they had just sat in. Mary quoted
Gladwell's insightful conclusion:

If you think about it, it was really a test of fashion sense, because, at its root, this is what fashion sense really is—the ability to register and appreciate and *remember* the details of the way those around you look and dress, and then reinterpret those details and memories yourself.

When the results of the experiment were tabulated, it was found that the women were able to recall the name and the placement of seventy percent more objects than the men, which makes perfect sense. Women's fashion, after all, consists of an endless number of subtle combinations and variations—of skirt, dress, pants, blouse, T-shirt, hose, pumps, flats, heels, necklace, bracelet, cleavage, collar, curl, and on and on—all driven by the fact that when a woman walks down the street she knows that other women, consciously or otherwise, will notice the name and the placement of what she is wearing. Fashion works for women because women can appreciate its complexity. But when it comes to men what's the point? How on earth do you sell fashion to someone who has no appreciation for detail whatsoever? (1999:53)

I pretended not to pay attention because I knew she was laying pipe. No matter what she promised, she'd be shopping before long.

Not Rodeo Drive

Worth Avenue looks a bit like Rodeo Drive in that it is about four blocks of two hundred clustered shops, complete with little alcoves and alleyways leading into little quaint courtyards, where yet more shops are situated. Many of these alleys open onto courtyards brimming with potted plants, marble statues, and tiled fountains straight out of a Moorish palace. If Rodeo is industrial modern, Worth is pastoral quaint. The Italianate buildings fronted with arched colonnades, the brilliant pink and purple bougainvillea cascading over sparkling white walls, the graceful palms lining the street, and the balmy Florida air embracing it all—how uncommercial.

I was startled, however, to find exactly the same stores, almost the same sales staff, same inventory, same awful Euro-pop music—same golden arches, as it were. I was getting the distinct impression that whoever designed these franchises had spent too much time inside museums: the focused lighting, the use of heroic display space, the mock labeling below the object for sale as if it was precious and needed a gloss to be understood, and especially the same overly prominent theft-detection systems blinking on and off.

But two things immediately were different. This street fit its environment. Palm Beach is an island, and the only thing industrial about it is that it is industrially rich. To the east side is the ocean, to the west is the famous Everglades Club and then a marina on Lake Worth, to the north are the massive marble trust offices of Chicago and New York banks, and to the south is the dinky Everglades Golf Links. And, second, the shoppers I had seen on Rodeo Drive were weekend rookies. Perhaps they had all seen *Pretty Woman*. They were mostly kids, really. These people here in Florida didn't need the movie, they lived the life. Here were the geezers from Greenwich. Of course, I was visiting in February, in season. Doubtless things are different in August.

Where Rodeo Drive looks to be just a jazzed-up regular shopping street, on Worth Avenue everything seems to fit. It wasn't always so. When the sewing machine heir Paris Singer and his amateur architect friend Addison Mizner first arrived in 1918, Worth Avenue was just a dirt road in the middle of a swamp. Singer and Mizner tried to open a World War I veterans' rehabilitation center here but couldn't get anyone to come. No matter. It was a ruse, historians believe, to obtain building materials that otherwise were unavailable during the war. In mock desperation the pair turned the veterans' building into a private social club called the Everglades. To keep the Everglades Club from being isolated after it opened, Mizner and Singer built some shops nearby, creating the avenue's two original courtyards, Via Mizner and Via Parigi (named by Mizner for Paris Singer).

So if Rodeo Drive seems to funnel out from the lobby of the Regent Beverly Wilshire hotel, Worth Avenue sort of slides around the corner from the Everglades Club and then flows toward the ocean. In the years after the war, between 1918 and 1931, nearly fifty homes, shops, and public buildings were constructed; you can see the coherence, at least until you end up at the rather dreadful Esplanade, which anchors the avenue on the east. This monstrosity of a mall, opened in the late 1970s, does have a Wilshire Boulevard air to it and maybe presages what is to come. The company that built it used a chauffeur-driven Rolls-Royce equipped with a bulldozer blade to break ground for the project.°

°Rodeo Drive has diluted its brew with NikeTown, the Rainforest Cafe, and Planet Hollywood, but Worth Avenue has struggled to maintain the magic. Palm Beach has a clever code that demands that each store be "town-serving," that is, have mostly island customers. So if your store has a branch in the local West Palm Beach malls, you'll never get onto the island. Adios, Kmart.

If Rodeo says new money, Worth says old. In fact, the clientele is old. I saw many more dowagers with dogs, old duffers in green pants without socks, and not many teenage girls with Discover cards. It is also old New England with a vengeance, old Canada, and old Western Europe. If I saw a good bit of the new Pacific Rim in California, here you had just a taste of South America.

True to the spirit of our times, Worth Avenue shares one characteristic with other glitter gulches: no bookstores. Doubleday used to be here. No more. Worth Avenue, like Rodeo Drive, is a glossy magazine world, as I gleaned while poring over *Palm Beach* magazine.

Affiliation in Atomistic Societies

If I had learned about price points in L.A., here I learned about controlled status anxiety. Rod was a big help in pointing out what is a given to sociologists, namely, that in nonmarket societies an affiliation with group endeavors like church, job, and ancestry is crucial, but in atomistic societies like our own, everyone is cut loose. You are what you can get, and you get what you can get by shopping for it. What you are is not what you make but what you consume. In bowling-alone societies shopping is often a central self-creative act.

People will do anything to get affiliation, and that is exactly what these designer shops facilitate. You essentially buy a link into a chain of associations, a chain that also holds other people who are in a consumption community. In a sense they allow you access to your own Everglades Club. Except now it's called Versace, Chanel, Prada, Gucci, and the rest. You can even get a charge card with the designer name on it—like the Armani MasterCard. These charge cards have proved very popular because they do not just force salespeople to acknowledge your superior status—they announce it to your companions.

While it is easy to see how this induction process worked in the past, it is almost impossible to see how current consumption carries on this role with people who seem to have it all. Yes, people in social distress—middle-class adolescents in L.A. and Manhattan are the most obvious example—consume their way into meaning. But was I really seeing a playing-out of this anxiety on the well-fed and -made-up faces of my fellow Worth Avenue shoppers? I would keep an eye on my fellow shoppers for the tell-tale symptoms of dreaded status anxiety.

Meanwhile, working the street, as I now came to call it, was a delight. I knew how to behave in the stores. I had my trusty wife with me and she knew the drill. I could even embellish the story so that it had a provocative variation. After we entered the shop, my wife would wander away. I would whisper to the salesperson: "My wife and I are having a little marital trouble. She likes good things, luxury. I am hoping to buy her something a little Versace that will make her realize how much I love her. Can you help?"

This worked best in jewelry stores, a kind of emporium that has always terrified me. Remember, I got hung up in Tiffany's Los Angeles store. People who sell rocks are either young women, if you look like you are a gawker, or like Gale Gordon (the actor who played all those awful businessman/banker roles in *Beverly Hillbillies* and on *The Lucille Ball Show*), if you are a serious buyer. But now enlisting their aid in resolving matrimonial distress proved the icebreaker.

I found that the admission of base desire endears you to salespeople of opuluxe, whether it is making sure you have the maximum number of little *G*'s on your Gucci purse, *F*'s on your Fendi luggage, or diamonds on your Cartier bracelet. In fact, the jewelry stores make it easy to resolve affairs d'amour because they all have their signature built into the bauble. I remember hearing once that the jewelry business was an industry built on the male erection and here, if needed, was proof.

To students of advertising, selling precious stones is the archetypical success story of opuluxe. Diamonds, for instance, were not in demand until in the late 1940s when the De Beers Corporation approached the N. W. Ayer and Son advertising agency in Philadelphia. Diamonds had been a commodity to be bought and sold, not a keepsake to be held. The market fluctuated as stones were dumped on the market by individual holders. Couldn't Ayer do something about this? De Beers asked. And indeed the agency did. Ayer created the most successful opuluxe slogan in the world, "A Diamond Is Forever," thereby transforming the mineral—pure, hard, and of almost no commercial value—into a metaphor of undying love.

Walk into any of these fancy jewelry stores like Tiffany, Van Cleef & Arpels, Bulgari, Cartier, and you can see how successful De Beers has been in managing the glut of diamonds produced from the vast new fields in Zaire, Ghana, Namibia, and especially in Botswana. Without panic the cartel has even absorbed the bigger fields found in the Argyle mines of Australia and bigger ones still in Siberian Russia. Diamonds are anything but rare. But they can be sold that way. And with a little help from the application of a designer name, their value can be supercharged.

While most expensive jewelry looks to me like boulders dumped into cement, I learned at Cartier that I could buy necklaces that were held together by the easy-to-decode panther link and at Tiffany that the Jean Schlumberger–designed jewel-encrusted birds were easy to spot; at Van Cleef & Arpels I got an education on the "invisible setting," which is easily recognized by its profusion of four-leaf clusters. In other words, what was happening at these jewelry stores was a replay of what first happened fifty years ago with Rene Lacoste. The little alligator was out there for all to see; here it was how these stones were set. These stores were branding a brand.

This explained why Worth Avenue marketers would allow a store like the Mariko Boutique, which was filled with parodic costume jewelry, to be in the same neighborhood as the real stuff. Clearly, the send-up only made the real stuff more valuable. And it paved the way to understanding what really perplexed me later in New York: Why did these prestigious stores allow counterfeit goods to be hawked on the street, not just in street fairs but right outside their own doors? Clearly, imitation *is* the sincerest form of flattery, and almost as clearly the knockoff makes value for the real thing just as the donkey makes the thoroughbred. Parody may momentarily subvert the subject, but at the same time it makes it worthy of subversion.

Find a Space and Brand It

Sometimes you can observe the almost Darwinian mutations not just of parody but of mimicry. You can see the erstwhile luggage stores like Gucci, Vuitton, Hermès, and the designer-name stores like Chanel, Versace, and Ralph Lauren move onto the turf of the jewelry stores and poach their objects. The moment you have an object that can carry a name—like a watch—you start seeing the watch companies like Rolex or Omega being elbowed aside by the fashion names like Gucci or Chanel. Occasionally, a brand like Tourneau seems to be shriveling up before your eyes, while savvy ones like Lucian Picard are quickly moving in the other direction. The watch must be brand nirvana in the designer galaxy; there for all to see is the name in the center of time, affiliation for all time.

Watch faces have already been colonized. Sunglasses are going fast. As far as I could see, every one of the major designers had a pair of sunglass-

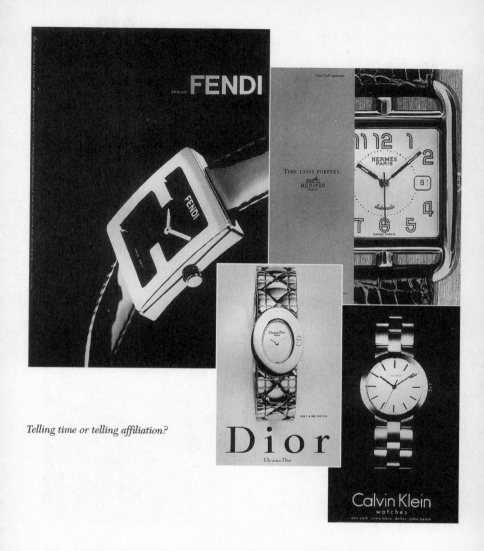

Telling time or telling affiliation?

es with her or his name or icon heavily embossed on the temples. Again, what a propitious venue for designer opuluxe for, as the eyes of a stranger meets your eyes, he or she sees first "your" designer, then who you are.

In a store dedicated to opuluxe eyewear, Palm Beach Eyes, right across the street from Friedrich's Optik, Rod and I were chatting up the salesperson about the different frames and why anyone would ever pay more than $150 just for some bent plastic. Totally unbidden, an attractive woman of about fifty came over and gave us a complete description of how she can tell what brand someone is wearing and how far away she has to be to make the

Seeing or being seen?

conclusion. She liked this kind of recognition, for it could be done without even looking down. You maintain eye contact. You make your judgment.

Her observation became a central insight. She said that there is a direct correlation between distance of knowledge, price of object, and status of wearer. If I can tell at forty feet that you are wearing Versace spectacles but can only tell at twenty that you are wearing Gucci, Gucci wins. It's more valuable. Again, the inverse ratio of opuluxe label and brand value, at least to cognoscenti. And what was the most valuable optical accessory? According to her, Cartier sunglasses. And how do you know who's wearing them? She pointed to an itty-bitty *C* at the temple.

Little did Foster Grant know when it penned the line, "Who's that behind those Foster Grants?" in the mid-1960s that the company was unfolding one of the central truths of modern opuluxe. Eyeglass frames are not just luggage for the face; they are billboards for the self.

Worth Avenue also had its share of art galleries. To my eye at least, the stuff was a cut above the explosion-in-a-lamé-factory of Rodeo Drive's Art Brilliant. My favorite was Johnnie Brown's (the inside joke is that this was the name of Mr. Mizner's pet monkey) Select Fine Art. In the Johnnie Brown Select Collection of Fine Art, I saw a collection of throw pillows with needlepointed inscriptions. They said: "If you want breakfast in bed, sleep in the kitchen." "Mirror, mirror on the wall, I am my mother after all." "The best antiques are old friends." The infamous Keane paintings of wide-eyed naifs would fit in here. Since everything is these stores is part of a "collection," perhaps associating these pillows with the collection of a pet monkey makes sense. But, yet again, it showed that part of the community that is consuming opuluxe is really the people who take Thomas Kinkade to be a great painter, Rod McKuen a bard, and John Tesh a classical composer.

It was here, mulling through this gallery, contemplating the size of modern signatures, that I realized that my wife was no longer with us. She had slipped off into one of the little alleyways and disappeared. But which alleyway? The Via Parigi, the Via Mizner, Via Roma, Via Bice? Without her I was unable to function in the designer boutiques. I needed her to magnetize the conversation.

I learned this the hard way by going into Chanel with just Rod. Charlotte tried to help me, but it was hopeless. What was my wife's size? What did she like to wear? Colors? All I could do was fall back on my old patter that I didn't care what I bought so long as it was a "hot signature item" and that I wanted the women "at the club" to know that I had spent a bundle. It didn't work. Charlotte pegged me for a bounder.

When I saw Mary later, she was loaded down with stuff. It was all from different stores. She didn't look at all sheepish. I told her that I needed her by my side, that we were a team, anthropologists doing fieldwork, just like Mary and Louis Leakey on the savannah. But I knew what

I was seeing. She wasn't listening. She was afflicted. Was it luxury fever or simple affluenza?

No, the affliction is called the Gruen transfer, named after the architect of early shopping centers, and it describes what happens when a shopper goes off looking for a particular object and then just drifts into becoming a shopper, a person with the diffuse impulse to buy . . . to spend. Early on, sociologists noted this phenomenon about mall shoppers, and it is one of the raisons d'être of your neighborhood mall.

Mary didn't seem bothered by the affliction. In fact, her response was unambiguous. She said that she didn't want to be on the team. She was embarrassed to be in the stores and have me talking about buying her something but never really doing it. Shopping as tease was no fun. Besides, she was spending her own money. And she enjoyed it. She now said Liz had called her after the Rodeo Drive fieldwork to report that being the pawn in Dad's game was no fun. I was chastened to realize that neither of them enjoyed doing research with me.

MARY COMMENTS:

I didn't think it would bother me to play Jim's sidekick. These stores make me very uncomfortable. I feel like a fish out of water, suddenly ashamed of my shoes and my clothes. I find myself flipping my handbag over so the Nine West tag won't show. As if. For me, the only reason to own the stuff they sell on Worth Avenue would be so that I could walk into those stores without feeling like the sales clerks are all judging me. I imagine a lot of sensible women who don't give a damn about the labels they're wearing may feel this way.

So, theoretically, I should have enjoyed going along with the act. But the idiot role he assigned to me made it even worse than going in as a regular shopper—here I was, someone without a badge on her body indicating that she knows how to dress according to high fashion, being described as a FAN who wanted to impress her friends by having something from the store. Clearly no taste, and no idea of taste, and such a ditz that I couldn't communicate to my husband what was special about it or what was in the store that I liked—he had to find a clerk to work it all out, man to man.

If that's not awkward enough, as I wandered around, I started finding things I actually liked. I started treating it like a regular store where I might take something home. After all, wasn't my husband looking at a $25,000 Tiffany diamond spider? Well, then, what about those nice $200 Paloma Picasso ear-

*rings? I mean I could really WEAR them, and while I wasn't used to spending
that kind of money on earrings, suddenly it seemed like a bargain.*

*When my older daughter was a toddler, she knew she could get stuff from
the supermarket and was a devil to take grocery shopping. But she didn't realize that the things in toy stores were also accessible, because we never
bought anything while she was along. Until she figured it out, she was an
angel in toy stores—like an enchanted visitor to a museum. I've thought of her
a lot since we went on that trip, and how close I was to the moment when it
suddenly dawned on her: maybe I can HAVE this stuff.*

Planet Manhattan: The Mother Ships

A few months later it was time to visit the mother ships of opuluxe in New
York City. Although Mary was with me, I was essentially on my own. She
made that clear on the way down from Vermont. The stores are all there
on Fifth Avenue and upper Madison. Huge hulking stores, no longer boutiques. These were holding up skyscrapers or in gentrified mansions. Some
of those on side streets are of manageable size, but most are monsters.
Some people attribute this change in size and uptown address to the opening of Barneys New York in September 1993. Although uptown Barneys
got badly bitten by its own snarling persona, its executives did show that
the new luxury could lure a new crop of young well-to-do customers to a
street that had been a prime shopping area for an older, if no less affluent,
audience. They also defined a new attitude of disdain.

What I thought was eerie about midtown Manhattan luxe is that these
stores were all elbowing aside the great churches of mercantile Christian
culture. From St. Patrick's to St. Thomas to the Fifth Avenue Church to
Christ Church, all the way up to St. James Church, these stores were gobbling up what was once prime liturgical space. Were they becoming the
new pulpits from which the word goes forth?

It was very hot in the city the day I took to the field. Many of the luxe
stores had their front doors open so you could bask in the cool air-conditioned air as it streamed out onto the street. What conspicuous waste!
However, the doors of the august churches were all closed, and often no-
tices were posted to keep off the steps, especially if you were eating. I wondered: Did the stores leave their doors open on purpose to show that at the
heart of luxury is waste? And, conversely, were the churches closed up for
the same reason in reverse?

As in Beverly Hills the other emporia that surround these shops are the commodified fun houses of low-life American commercialism. Side by side with luxe shopping is NikeTown, the Original Levi's Store, the Warner Bros. Studio Store, the Disney Store, the temples to Coke and Sony, and, of course, the Harley-Davidson Cafe. Although the designer stores won't give out traffic information about who comes into their emporia, the Warner Bros. Studio Store at Fifth and 57th claims it is visited by more than twenty thousand people a day. Clearly, the audience wearing the Looney Tunes T-shirt is also at least looking at a Cartier watch. Indeed, customers at the Warner Bros. store on Fifth Avenue held shopping bags from Tiffany. Somehow these audiences are cross-pollinating.

The Shopping Bag

The shopping bag was like powder on the heinies of migrating bees as they moved from hive to hive. The bags were emblematic on purpose, and they told me much about what's happening. Have a look.

Years ago, before the rise of opuluxe, the shopping bag was simply a place to carry stuff. Who didn't know the Lord & Taylor bag with the elegant script, the simple blue of Tiffany, the pink of Thomas Pink, or the decidedly unflashy Bonwit Teller or B. Altman? It was the ubiquitous museum store bag, however, from the Met or the MoMA, often announcing a particular show, that transformed the container into the announcement of self. Your bag showed you were hip. Just as museum di-

The shopping bag is a postcard that says where you've been and what you did there.

First came the museum, a place to hold stuff; then came the bag to hold stuff you bought at the museum.

rectors learned that all exhibits end in the souvenir store, so too did they realize that the bag, like the exhibit poster, was an important part of the experience.

This was not lost on their cousins in retail. Sometimes the bags do indeed capture the essence of the store. The Victoria's Secret bag is sexy, the GAP bag is commonly chic, Moschino's is humorous, Calvin Klein's is spare, Givenchy's is elegant, Vuitton's is sophisticated, Harry Winston's is subtle, and so on.

I was beginning to realize the depth of penetration of faux luxe into the American middle class by just watching the bags move in and out of various stores. One could learn much by counting the number of Disney bags that came into Armani and how many Dolce & Gabbana bags made their way into Harley-Davidson. Perhaps a future doctoral dissertation might discuss the number of these bags moving through McDonald's, as well as how many McDonald's bags make their way in the opposite direction.

But to understand the allure of the new luxury it was more important to take my eyes off the bags and watch Mary. As she had demonstrated, she

*The frigid vampire women of Versace
wait for dinner.*

could no longer be trusted. I had learned from the ensuing credit card bills that she had spent almost $400 (all right, all right, of her own money) in Palm Beach. and now I had to watch her like a hawk. We were okay at the Versace mansion, five all-marble floors of really decadent and, to the eyes of us both, very unattractive stuff. Where was Edward Gibbon when I needed him? The Versaces, those Italoluxe barbarians, had so self-consciously exploited the motif of Manhattan as the modern Rome about to be taken by the barbarians that it was as if the designers were saying, "Come on, Puritan America, just try debauchery, you'll enjoy it."

On the first floor of the Versace mansion Carlos gave us the once-over with the standard handbag spiel. It went something like this: The salesperson would assure me that what I was looking at was the new classic. I would say something like, "Oh, you mean like the Fendi baguette, the Prada bowling sack, the Vuitton graffiti?" And he would say, "Yes, just like those, a classic, an instant classic." There was never a hint of irony. In this case the classic was a new fabric that he called "pony." "Pony," I said, "like in small horse?" Yes, he smiled. It was clear that now in the late 1990s fur of all sorts had made its comeback, and so merchandisers needed to find a new social code that could be broken. Thus pony, yes, as in diminutive horse. (I found out later that it was really cow.)

And it was also clear that here in Manhattan, another Puritan code—namely, that opulence not be lavished on children—had been smashed. If Palm Beach habitués had made a fetish of pampering your pet in public, their grandchildren bore the brunt of unwanted indulgence back home in New York. Not only was there an FAO Schwarz line of children's wear but almost every designer store had a signature item just for tots. Still, somehow, moving opuluxe to the level of infantoluxe seemed a little much. It was the death of childhood, not the nurturing of it. A silver spoon literally in your mouth. Gag.

In Versace, for instance, you could buy sneakers and warm-up suits for small fry encrusted with the golden Medusa. And the prices for such stuff were not impish. A Moschino Junior pinstripe suit for a four-year-old carried a price tag of $368, while a Christian Dior jacket to fit an eight-year-old came in at $92, and even a teeny weeny T-shirt can cost as much as $72. At Saks you can buy a cashmere sweater for your "little luxury" for $252. Clearly, here Veblen peeked and saw what was happening. This is surrogate

Never too young for little luxuries, like a cashmere sweater for $252.

conspicuous consumption, excess galore, and it is certainly repulsive when inflicted on the innocent. For what kid would want to be stuck in tiny jeans and denim jackets topped off by a mini baseball cap? Or better yet, what baby would want a Baby Guess? denim and leather-sleeved jacket for a hundred bucks?

I was having trouble with this kid stuff and so was Mary. She wanted to go shopping without me. So we separated. She off to Liz Claiborne and me to Fendi, Prada, all the way up to Ralph Lauren's mansion on upper Madison. Wandering alone around these stores in Manhattan, it was not hard to get a sense of who the shoppers really were. Whereas I saw Asians and middle-class Americans buying stuff on Rodeo Drive and WASPs at play on Worth Avenue, here in the city, the hurly-burly was all over. Young proles on the prowl. Inside the stores I was as likely to be brushed by someone in a slingshot T-shirt as someone in full iconic battle dress.

As I hiked up to Ralph Lauren's mansion next to St. James Church, and a block away from the Frick Museum, I passed signs of note in store windows. Clearly, this whole area was a battleground of retail forces. Opuluxe was in ascendance; highcult was in remission. The Madison Avenue Book Shop was almost empty, displaying a window full of books on how to be your own best friend and how to find help for life's problems. Over in the corner was Louis Auchincloss's latest novel. I passed a young man with this proudly emblazoned on the front of his T-shirt:

BEEN
there
DONE
that
SEEN
it
BOUGHT
everything

On the backside was "Bloomingdale's."

I was still profoundly confused about how shoppers knew what stores they were in. For instance, even after all my research, if you dropped me into Gucci or Prada, removed all the insignia, and asked me to tell you which was which, I'd be unable to do it. The dog whistle was still pitched too high for my ear. I'm clearly not alone because when I asked people to tell me the difference, they too were confounded. In fact, Teri Agins, writing in the *Wall Street Journal*, tried to help out by providing a side-by-side comparison. Here's what she found, expressed in simple dichotomies:

Gucci	**Prada**
Los Angeles	*New York*
Goldie Hawn	Uma Thurman
Brad Pitt	Willem Dafoe
Bamboo/calf bag	Black nylon backpack
Swingers	Intellectuals
Hip-huggers	Flat-front pants
Skin-tight	Boxy
Frivolous	Utilitarian
High tart	High concept
Boisterous	Ethereal
Stiletto	Clunky square toe
Strapless	Patchwork
Edgy	Minimal
Caviar	Truffles
Single-malt scotch	Vodka on the rocks
Bikini wax	Eyebrow wax (1999:B1)

While I realize that this good-to-eat/bad-to-eat may be helpful to many, it only reminded me of Byron's response to Coleridge's metaphysics: "Will someone please explain this explanation?" No matter, I knew enough about what was important to me. I'd never buy anything at Prada, no matter what. This is because the store is now squatting in the residence of my favorite old Doubleday bookstore (724 Fifth Avenue). Forget never, forgive hell!

I did feel at home, however, in the mother ship of Ralph Lauren, Inc. It takes every inch of the twenty-two thousand square feet of the old Rhinelander mansion at 72d and Madison, and somehow seeing his stuff in this setting was far less troubling than seeing it in the modern Rodeo Drive building. The floors, the windows, the walls, everything fit. This is the world I still recognized, the world hijacked by Ralph Lauren and sold back to me, complete with horsey logos. This was English faux luxe, a hunt club, dark walls, oriental rugs, Stubbs horses and dogs on walls, cracked leather chairs, claustrophobic closeness, the Social Register cracked open on the table, make-believe ancestors in the stairwells, pastels and cotton, smiling faces, patina squeezed from the tube. This was not the Euroluxe of Prada, Gucci, Fendi, Chanel, Versace, Armani, and the like. This was Bond Street of the 1960s. Lauren was easy to understand, and here both the salespeople and the customers seemed relieved. After all, he was just Ralph Lifshitz from the Bronx.

On the way back to my hotel I·stopped in to view the antithesis of Laurenesque clutter, the melancholy emptiness of Calvin Klein. If the French and Europeans have colonized the middle levels of outrageous expense, the Americans now own the edges. In Calvin Klein's home store everything is dedicated to angles, abruptness, ennui, contrived and aggressive simplicity. Sit on hard wooden benches, if you must. Be a monk. Hunt for merchandise on your own because the one place you won't find it is where you think it'll be. Stock seems to be kept at a minimum and is displayed with a kind of just-gone-out-of-business frugality. No hip-hop music here. But a kind of thick angst. Well-practiced weltschmerz. No rugs, no wall hangings, no soft light, all sales staff in black. Calvin seems to be saying, no wimps allowed. If you want comfy, go Ralph; if you want sparseness, Calvinism is for you. Once again, trust the bag to make the pitch.

The Importance of Counterfeit

Coming out of Calvin Klein, I was struck once again with the importance of what is happening *outside* these stores. On Worth Avenue, and to a less-

The understated elegance of the bag reflects the store.

er extent on Rodeo Drive, the store environs are tightly controlled. But in Manhattan the streets belong to the people, Mayor Giuliani notwithstanding. And there were people on almost every corner selling counterfeit versions of the stuff inside the stores. Rather like the Mardi Gras carnival that occurs on the sacred grounds of the medieval church, these street fairs were just yards from the cathedrals.

One of the most perplexing (and ultimately revealing) aspects of Euroluxe is its seeming irrationality. Why would any one in his right mind pay for Chanel perfume, a Hermès scarf, Armani sunglasses, a Rolex watch, or a Prada backpack if he knew a perfect "replica" brand existed just steps away? But if you go to any large city—New York, Rome, London, Tokyo— you will see street merchants peddling illegal copies of branded luxury items, from the "snide" bejeweled watch to the ringer designer perfume, with seeming impunity.

While counterfeit goods do indeed undermine the retail value of such goods as CDs, software, books, artworks, and movies, and while they pose a threat to such industries as pharmaceuticals, detergents, liquor, and automobile parts, with opuluxe they seem to have an opposite effect. In fact, the Veblen effect—the inverse movement of the price of a luxury good and its perceived value—goes hand in hand with the counterfeit effect—the replication of the object *means* that the original has aspirational value.

I had seen this on Worth Avenue with the inclusion of costume jewelry, but what you see on the streets of New York is the outrageous hawking of designer objects, not just in scattered market fairs but right in front of the retail stores of the same name. It is startling. While American designer objects, such as Donna Karan purses and Hilfiger shirts, are also included, the counterfeit inventory is decidedly French and Italian, via Mexico and Korea. We may giggle at the obvious rip-offs of designer names (often badly misspelled) that are being hawked by vendors, but one would think that the manufacturers of the Euroluxe would be outraged. And, of course, this is magnified tenfold by the profusion of Internet sites selling counterfeit. So why don't they stop it?

They do . . . to a point. Per usual, the Americans are the most concerned about copyright protection. While the entire replica market is estimated to be about 5 percent of retail sales worldwide—about $80 billion a year—the consumer of the counterfeit opuluxe is most likely *not* going to be the purchaser of the real McCoy. In fact, the genuine buyer of the genuine article has the sensation not of being gulled but of having achieved a kind of perfect transaction. She knows she has The Real Thing, and in a special way she now has the added luxury of integrity.

Once again, such paradox should alert us to the complexities of the new luxury, for if conspicuous consumption were the dominant goal, displaying the badge would be enough. Many people who drink Evian water simply refill the bottle from the tap. But others insist on purchasing the brand and then tossing the container when finished. And it's those consumers who tell us something about the shift in luxury, the shift from moving outward to moving inward, from conspicuous consumption to consumption as reward, from display to epiphany.

My Shopping Days Are Over

So at the end of the twentieth century I had seen the most expensive real estate in the United States. The most expensive retail turf in this country is Fifth Avenue between 49th and 58th Streets, then East 57th Street between Fifth and Lexington Avenues, Madison Avenue between 61st and 72d Streets, then Rodeo Drive, Michigan Avenue in Chicago, and finally Worth Avenue. Assuming the people who pay these rents know what they are doing, somebody must be buying this stuff and the myths behind it. And indeed they are.

They are often not buying from these stores on these magical streets, however. For what I saw was essentially the display case for the real market. The real transactions are made inside department stores like Macy's, Nordstrom, Neiman Marcus, Saks, Bloomingdale's, and the like, where the seeds planted in public are harvested in private. Go into almost any large department store, and you will see what are essentially stores within stores—pocket boutiques—selling this branded opuluxe. How those brands get their value is the job of another institution, the communication of meaning not through commercial display but through commercial speech, not through the store but through the advertisement, not on the street but in the pages of glossy magazines and big-city newspapers. So let's have a look inside the myth factory and see how the stories are told.

4.

Where Opuluxe Is Made and Who Makes It

LVMH AND CONDÉ NAST

> In the factory we make cosmetics; in the drugstore we sell hope.
>
> —Charles Revson, chairman, Revlon Cosmetics

Charles Revson didn't quite get the trifecta. What you make in the factory and what you sell in the store depends, to a considerable extent, on what you can first create in the mind of your consumer. Making meaning for otherwise interchangeable products has been one of the most important developments of the modern world. Without it the industrial revolution would have sputtered out of control.

In a sense there is no such thing as a luxury automobile, a luxury purse, or a luxury lipstick. Rather, there is the *concept* of the luxury car, purse, or lipstick. Luxury is a social construction, and most often it is given meaning through a system of speech acts that, for lack of a better word, is still called *advertising*. Before you consume the product, you consume the advertising. Think of it this way: Luxury is the last thing you hear before you hear ka-ching.

One of the more delicious ironies of the new luxury is that while Europeans, especially the French, continually bemoan the Americanizing of their mass culture, they—especially the French—still construct our sense of opuluxe. They excoriate our attempt to Disney-fy their entertainment and McDonaldsize their diet, but they attempt to Frenchify our sense of elegance. The French love to publish books like *No Thanks, Uncle Sam*; *The World Is Not Merchandise*; *American Totalitarianism*; and *Who Is Killing France?* *The American Strategy*, to name just a few, conveniently forgetting not only their imperialistic past but also their carefully expansionistic present (Flahive 2000:A31). Around the world, opuluxe is owned by the French and to a lesser extent, the Italians, and to a much, much lesser extent by the Americans, the Japanese, and the Germans. To be sure, this tilt toward Western Europe is the predictable result of associating old luxury with tradition, elegance, pedigree, patina. But it is also because Europeans, especially the French, have learned much from their New World cousins—and nothing more important than how to sell the sizzle, not the steak.

What Katharine Hepburn said of Fred Astaire and Ginger Rogers could be said as well of European luxury and American salesmanship. If Fred gave Ginger respectability, she gave him sex appeal. If Europeans gave us the concept of high culture, we showed them how to give it pizzazz.

The business of modern luxury goods, like most successful enterprises these days, is all about adding value to machine-made products of the same inherent value. This oxymoron is at the heart of high-end consumption. Whereas the big American-based fashion houses like Calvin Klein, Donna Karan, or Ralph Lauren focus on design and marketing ("le luxe à l'americaine," the French call it), the Europeans, especially the French, have exploited the critical link between the brand name and the mystique of handcrafted quality. And that link, more often than not, is forged in the language, in a story, in a myth, in a brand. And that brand is often constructed on the glossy pages of a handful of magazines.

Luxe and quality used to be connected in real life. The famously unprofitable couture fashion shows put on by Chanel, Dior, and a few other houses were meant to imbue perfumes and ready-to-wear clothes—which are mass-produced—with precisely that aura of luxury that a unique purse stitched meticulously by hand implies. No more. That Chanel purse that your aunt Lucille treasures from last Christmas was made from leather cut from computer-aided designs, sliced by ultra-high-speed water jets, and stitched by superfast sewing machines programmed by kids in Silicon Valley. The aura that surrounds it now comes not from the workshop but from a different kind of machinery—marketing.

Opuluxe, the French Connection

While the creation of luxury is based on maintaining the illusion of separation, of distinction, of uniqueness, of being custom made, of being *on* Rodeo Drive, *on* Worth Avenue, and *on* Fifth Avenue, the mass-merchandising of opuluxe is quite another matter. In truth, those nifty little boutiques selling shoes or purses or suitcases are really parts of vast and sophisticated retailing empires that most often have their headquarters in Paris, their stocks trading on the Bourse, and automated machinery doing the production, often in a third-world country. But where Chanel, Prada, Fendi, Gucci, Oscar de la Renta et al. *really* exist is in the minds of consumers. The companies that hold these names are every bit as rapacious as Philip Morris and every bit as sophisticated as the Church of Rome.

Whereas no culture has been more central in maintaining the mystique of luxury than the French, no company has been more central than the acronymic conglomerate LVMH. While the French account for about half of the world market for luxury goods, the bundled companies of Louis Vuitton Moët Hennessy control about half that. And with each day this company slowly increases its share of the worldwide market.

Whether they deserve it or not, the French essentially franchise the concept of deluxe to the rest of the world. Not by happenstance have they mastered *taste*, whether on the palate, whiffed by the nose, or seen by the eye. It's what they have for the silicon chip. And they have protected their near monopoly zealously. The English, ever eager to pay tribute to what they wish to subvert, have a clothing store chain called FCUK, which stands for French Connection United Kingdom, as well their general feelings about the matter.

If French cuisine revels in taking some particularly unappetizing part of some bedraggled animal and dressing it up for the royal palate, then the French luxury trade has followed suit. Until very recently, there was no aspect of fashion, no accessory, no innovation that did not take Paris as its pushing-off point. No matter that modern "French" designers often come from England (like Alexander McQueen), Germany (like Karl Lagerfeld), Spain (Balenciaga), or the United States (Claude Montana), the concept of Parisian is at the heart of what is tasteful to the hoity-toity, if not to the hoi polloi.

The men who dominate France's multibillion-dollar luxury goods business know this and have wisely nurtured the illusion. Rather like the mendicant orders of the Vatican during the Renaissance, they are obsessed with controlling the concept of luxury, the concept of handmade workmanship, opulence, and attention to detail. They see themselves as patrons of the arts, sponsoring foundations and exhibitions around the world. But they're also shrewd, ruthless, and prescient merchants with egos as vast as their empires.

Just as the Holy Roman Church had its headquarters in the Vatican, the luxe industry is run by a trade association of about eighty companies called the Comité Colbert. Unlike other sectors of French life, the government has wisely left it alone. The state neither underwrites its successes nor salvages its failures. And the captains of the Comité are glad of it because the illusion of spontaneous and unfettered French taste is central to the myth. The Comité guards the myth of French luxury carefully. It even has a business school, the École Supérieur des Sciences Économiques et Commerciales (ESSEC), dedicated to marketing French-based luxury.

The Comité Colbert

The Comité Colbert was set up by France's leading luxury goods companies after World War II to promote an industry that has been among the country's top exporters since well before the Napoleonic Wars. From Singapore to the Sinai to Seoul to San Diego no one questions the French connection with elegance and style. If you are going to flaunt something other than a car, chances are you will be doing it with something French or something Italian that the French now own or soon will.

Ironically, perhaps, the Comité is even responsible for the democratization of luxury goods. Until the 1970s many of its firms were not really firms at all but rather artisans working for an elite clientele. These roots ran deep and the individual companies, like families, often fought each other. Such operations were small, family owned and run, and often had no market outside their home city. Hermès started making harnesses, then saddles, for horsey aristocrats in 1837. Vuitton was in the carrying-case business during the Napoleonic Wars. Louis-François Cartier came to Paris in 1847. They were, in the patois of historians, *artisanal*. But the French mastered not just the manufacture of handmade elegancies but the stories behind them.

The fabricators stayed in guarded isolation until the 1970s, when a new generation of executives swept into several of the industry's top companies and set them on an ambitious new course. Some of these men (few women) were family members; others were not. But all were modern managers who thought about distribution strategies, emerging markets, and "brand creation." These were foreign concepts in the luxury goods business. Most of them came from the United States. But together with a healthy dose of applied Veblen, the Comité set in motion trends that revolutionized the industry, making extravagant meaning for ordinary objects.

Here's what it did. The members of the Comité diversified what they made, adopting a kind of "brand-umbrella strategy" under which they launched second-stream products for the newly affluent upper-middle class. So, for instance, under "Les Musts de Cartier" you find middle-market trinkets: scarves, wallets, lighters, fountain pens, and even an "American" Tank watch. Then, by licensing their names and logos to manufacturers that actually make the products, the luxury firms profited mightily from what is now called brand extension in Marketing 101.

Next they down-marketed the objects, making them available to the newly enfranchised middle class around the world. By targeting yuppies, as well as the acquisitive newly rich, the Comité Colbert expanded the concept of leisure class into something bigger—the concept of leisure and luxury for the "mass upper class." All it takes to join is money, and money, thanks to the credit card, is always available. To appeal to the upwardly mobile meant, first, satisfying the need for "pecuniary emulation," but it also meant making top-of-the-line items for ordinary object classes.

Many consumers of the new luxury could not afford Chanel haute couture or even an average-priced Cartier watch. What they could afford, however, were items that were expensive by comparative standards but not in absolute terms and that, because they were identifiably made by an upper-crust company, carried affiliation status. Thus came democratization, the twin of diversification, and it was the real *work* of the craft of luxury in modern times.

As French luxe was moving down-market *and* out into different lines, the Comité nurtured the development of worldwide distribution. In 1977 Henry Racamier, then boss of Louis Vuitton, started building a string of Vuitton boutiques round the world. Scores of luxury goods firms like Italy's Giorgio Armani followed Racamier's lead, though often on a smaller scale. In fact, the Italians formed a rival group called the Classico Italia, a consortium of twenty-three of the top clothing and accessory companies, to compete, but they have been a day late and a dollar short. Most of the Italian names like Gucci, Fendi, and Armani have been at least partially swallowed up by the French.

The French succeeded because the new upwardly mobile and socially anxious classes were remarkably similar around the world. American yuppies, French bon chic bon genre, English Sloane Rangers, Japanese Roppongi, and Russian neocapitalists all needed similar signature goods. They all traveled, so they all needed luggage. They all drank, so they all needed wine and branded alcohol. They all wore perfume, suits, watches, shoes, sunglasses, and the like. In fact, if you ever want to see the best inventory of what is opuluxe, just take a slow meander through any duty-free shop at any airport. And who owns most of those duty-free shops? The French.

LVMH

What the Comité did in macrocosm, LVMH did in microcosm. The company diversified, lowered price points, and aggressively advertised worldwide products, often with the same campaign. If there was going to be a global village, the consumers of French opuluxe would get there first.

Although the brand names that LVMH holds seem at first to be either in competition or in seemingly different categories, a deep-down coherence exists. Not only do these brands attempt to dominate the top of each category but each category dovetails with the others. So if you are a male who drinks expensive wine, you wear an expensive watch, sport fancy sunglasses, have custom-made shoes, wear shirts with French cuffs . . . all from LVMH. And if a woman, here are your perfume, handbag, shoes, umbrella, and scarf.

And what are these objects known around the globe? LVMH's prestige brands include Dom Perignon, Moët & Chandon, Veuve Clicquot, and Pommery champagnes; Hennessy and Hine cognacs; and Louis Vuitton, Loewe, and Celine luggage, leather goods, and accessories. LVMH owns the "house" establishments of Christian Dior, Givenchy, Kenzo, and Guerlain perfumes and cosmetics; Sephora in perfumes and retail beauty products; Fred in jewelry; and Givenchy, Christian Lacroix, and Kenzo in couture and fashion. The company owns a huge chunk of Fendi and a sizable stake in Gucci (the result of a failed bid for control with a rival French firm, Pinault Printemps Redoute). It even owns the American designer name Donna Karan.

Many of those stores that I saw on those quaint little streets were owned by this corporate octopus. As well, LVMH holds a controlling interest in the retail space through which other consumers of exactly these products pass—the airport-based duty-free shops. Ditto the shops aboard most cruise ships. And to make sure it doesn't miss the other end of the market, it owns the ancient British auction house of Phillips and is contemplating a move on Sotheby's. And in the future? LVMH is planning a worldwide chain of De Beers diamond stores in which diamonds will be marketed for the first time under the De Beers brand name.

Nameless, Faceless, Wizards of Oz

The man who understood how to assemble opuluxe into a coherent pattern came from the cold, flat, industrial north of France. Although Bernard Arnault showed early promise as a star student at France's prestigious École Polytechnique, one of the so-called grande écoles that funnel their alumni to the upper reaches of business and government, his real education occurred in the United States. After trying to establish a branch of the family real estate business in North America, he returned home in the early '80s. He was in his midthirties and he had learned one valuable lesson from consuming American commercial culture: Value does not reside in objects but in the perception of objects. Value is added after manufacturing is done. Or in the advertising slogan of *Rolling Stone* magazine that captures the constituent parts of LVMH, perception *is* reality.

With help from family and merchant bankers, in 1984 Arnault bought a dreary holding company called Boussac in order to get its unappreciated prize: the once-vaunted couture house of Christian Dior. Dior had been the name of French luxury for Americans growing up in the 1950s and this first postwar generation—the baby boomers—now had the disposable income and competitive desire to buy designer goods. Dior was to become the cornerstone of a luxury goods supermarket where a rising global bourgeoisie would one day shop.

Dior had previously sold its most valuable asset—its name on perfume bottles—to the uneasy merger of two great houses, Louis Vuitton and Moët Hennessy. To reclaim Dior's name Arnault started what was to be his trademark behavior: talk French, act American. The hostile takeover of LVMH was not the Gallic way of doing business and certainly not the way old-time luxury producers did business. Many members of the Comité Colbert were aghast, but of course Arnault was doing single-handedly what they were struggling for as a group: increasing the perceived value of his products, decreasing the predatory behavior of other producers, and expanding worldwide.

Arnault's specific insight was to see that all the objects of opuluxe, all the positional goods from all categories, were marketed as part of a coherent pattern yet could be purchased individually. Divide and conquer. Leverage the brand. More important than the concept of ensemble was the concept of the accessory, called the trimmings in the trade. The Diderot effect, long neglected by marketers, was finally being not just recognized but exploited with a passion. Sell the starter object, let the customer create the ensemble.

Arnault's grand insight was to control every part of the process from factory to store. Under his new plan you mass-produce the luxury objects, add different meaning to them through advertising in glossy magazines, and then sell them under different names. Just as gasoline, refined at one plant, goes out to become Exxon, Texaco, and fuel at Joe's Quick Stop, so LVMH makes handbags using technology developed by its sibling Loewe—a Madrid-based leather goods company—and sells them under various brand names like Vuitton and Dior.

And just as big oil is able to use its combined clout to negotiate favorable leases along the interstate highways, so LVMH is able to negotiate with big retailers for floor space. LVMH coordinates the selling function for its perfumes, for instance, which represent a combined market share of 25 percent. Alone, the brands would have had little bargaining power; combined, they are formidable. Ever wonder how Proctor & Gamble gets so much shelf space for soap, or how Coca-Cola takes up half the soft drink aisle? LVMH knows how.

Although the products cached inside LVMH seem different, they all share certain concepts, the most important of which is the notion that having competitive products does not mean that you cannibalize customers. Remember, in opuluxe you don't buy the product, you buy the advertising, the story. By holding what looks to be a multitude of discrete brands, you squeeze your competition. So the fashion houses of Christian Lacroix, Givenchy, Donna Karan, and Kenzo; the leather goods companies Vuitton, Loewe, Celine, and Berluti; or all the designer perfumes as well as Sephora, a French chain of perfume stores, share not just production and distribution facilities but clog the consumers' sense of choice. If a customer can keep only about six names of luggage producers in his head at once, why not own three of the names?

Thus the centrality of the designer persona and especially the designer's actual name. Arnault's strategy has been to hire designers capable of attracting attention and forge a brand identity around them. In so doing, Arnault can establish a consistent image by gaining control of licensed products and their distribution. Then he exports the brand (*leveraging* is the Marketing 101 term) to other products such as watches, sunglasses, towels, or whatever.

What I saw *in* the stores and *on* objects like those watches or sunglasses is at the heart of this kind of synergy. "Product pyramiding," as it used to be known, is the backbone of the leading luxury groups. Find a designer. Make it a brand name, stamp it on different things. Advertise it. After all, this is exactly what Martha Stewart is doing down at Kmart, Michael Graves at Target, and Lynette Jennings at Home Depot.

Arnault's lesson was not lost on his colleagues. It is certainly a lesson not lost on his bête noir, François Pinault. These titans of tip-top taste have had remarkably similar careers. Both took over moribund industrial companies and turned them into luxe leaders by following the game plan of consolidate, extend, down-market, and colonize. Pinault started with a sawmill, moved into media and wineries (he owns Château Latour-Martillac), and controls Europe's largest nonfood retail group, of which Le Printemps department store is the name most familiar to Americans. A few years ago he bought Sanofi's beauty products division, which owns Yves Saint Laurent couture and perfumes, to which he added other names: Oscar de la Renta, Van Cleef & Arpels, and a controlling interest in Gucci. His Artemis holding company owns Christie's as well as positions in a slew of other companies, including Vail skiing, Converse sneakers, Samsonite luggage, and U.S. Filter. Pinault Printemps Redoute has the same mass-marketing ideas as LVMH for exactly the same reasons: Consolidate opuluxe brands and then sell them globally.

The Battle for Gucci

It was inevitable that these two men would clash. After all, they shared the same idée fixe: Control opuluxe. In 1999 it happened. These two headstrong and deep-pocketed men went after Gucci, a company that just a few years earlier had been the barely solvent producer of leather bags and snaffle-bit loafers. Although Gucci was a parvenu among the artisanal work-shops, having been in business only since the 1920s, it had, by the 1980s, while still under family management, lost its cachet and its direction. For a while little G's were appearing on everything from cigarette lighters to thong bikinis. The Gucci family, riven by feuds, sold out to a London-based Bahraini holding company. Domenico De Sole, an Italian-American lawyer, became chairman and, more important, Tom Ford, an American designer, became major domo. Together they transformed the company into one of the key "stories" of the '90s and, in so doing, whetted the ap-petite of the French conglomerates.

De Sole and Ford's genius was in tailoring Gucci products to suit indi-vidual national markets. The company built up its Asian portfolio of stores while the region's property market was deeply depressed. Then, to protect the quality of its franchise, Gucci started buying back its stores and re-stricting its famous interlocked G's. In other words, it started behaving like the Comité Colbert. More savvy still was that De Sole and Ford in-stalled professional managers and computerized stock-control systems, closing Gucci's Milan office and fifteen of the firm's directly operated shops. Most savvy, however, they more than doubled their advertising budget, thereby harvesting acres of gushing editorial coverage in glossy women's magazines. They thereby restored the cachet of what had be-come a parody of opuluxe.

In what the press called "the handbag war" Messrs. Arnault and Pinault went after Gucci hammer and tong, tote bag and checkbook. The battle for this Italian company run by Americans and owned by London-based bankers, was waged in Dutch courts. Ironically, Investcorp, a Bahraini in-vestment bank that also owns Chaumet, Breguet, Ebel, Riva Yachts . . . began acquiring Gucci in stages in 1991 but then backed off. Gucci was in play. Arnault wanted to fold Gucci into his conglomerate, while Pinault wanted Gucci to take control of his luxe brands, especially Yves Saint Lau-rent, and extend them.

Before long the irascible French masters of the universe were suing each other for defamation of character, for libel, and for whatever they could find. They were indeed acting just like American leveraged buyout artists of the 1980s, barbarians at the gates of luxury. De Sole and Ford clearly wanted the power and prestige of independence under the um-brella of Pinault Printemps Redoute, as well as about $3 billion in new as-sets to manage. So when they sided with Pinault, the war was over. Except for one anomaly: Thanks to the bidding war, LVMH now owns a massive stake in its erstwhile rival.

Looking on with interest as the handbag war was waged was the other lux-omerate, Vendôme, the holding company behind such names as Chloé, Cartier, Piaget, Alfred Dunhill, Montblanc, Baume & Mercier, and Vacheron Constantin. Although the names are French, the holding company is Swiss. Vendôme is almost 70 percent owned by Compagnie Financière Richemont AG of Switzerland.

While Vendôme is often compared to LVMH, the Swiss group has kept a much lower profile. But once again, the capitalist desire to control the entire process, from design to advertising to retail shelf space, is the same. In an effort to leverage its luxury brands, Vendôme has opened what looks to be independent boutiques but are really all just sibling stores. Just stroll up Madison Avenue. There they are: Alfred Dunhill, Chloé, Sulka, and Montblanc, all side by side. This clustering is rather like what LVMH did by buying duty-free shops: It gives the company the illusion of different brands while harvesting the economies of scale. Most customers are oblivious that the intimate little shop is really part of a huge conglomerate that owns the quaint little shop next door.

While we know the names of the major automobile makers or oil companies or media outlets, few of the end users along Rodeo Drive, Worth Avenue, or Fifth Avenue have any idea about the clustering of these seemingly separate entities. So too, when you are shopping inside Bloomingdale's and you see perfume next to handbags next to ties, all marked with different names, little do you realize the entire quadrant of floor space belongs to LVMH or Vendôme. Admittedly, not all opuluxe is pumped through the channels of desire by crafty financiers using the magical illusions of craftsmen laboring over their tables, lovingly crafting unique objects. But most of it most assuredly is.

The exceptions almost prove the rule. For instance, the only global couture brand that looks set to stay in private hands is Chanel, owned by the secretive Wertheimers. Patek Philippe, the watchmaker, has a good chance of staying independent. Versace was in the process of going public when Gianni was killed. Now controlled by brother Santo and sister Donatella it will probably, if Morgan Stanley, Merrill Lynch, and Goldman Sachs have anything to do with it, make its way into some conglomerate. Armani, Ferragamo, and Blahnik will probably have been swallowed up by the time you read this. Small purveyors just can't compete, even though the myth of luxe is that they are doing exactly that. Who among its customers would know that Amsterdam-based Prada is not just the conduit for the designs of Miuccia Prada but a huge conglomerate holding sizable chunks of Fendi, Jil Sander, Church and Company, and, until a few years ago, a sizable portion of Gucci? Tiffany has long been public, Rome's Bulgari jewelers is publicly traded, ditto Hermès, as are the New York–based empires of Polo-Ralph Lauren, Inc., Bill Blass, and Tommy Hilfiger. In fact, the Americans, as Calvin Klein has shown, may not be able to make it on their own. Calvin's stuff has spent entirely too much time on the exit ramps of the interstates in cut-rate discount malls. The brands are too loose with the label, too recognizably . . . American.

The combination of the centrifugal forces of consolidation and centripetal forces of going global promises that in another generation probably only a handful of massive opuluxe companies will be left standing. As young consumers see midcult brands such as Nike, Benetton, and Diesel as hipper than couture labels, as competition increases for finite shelf space within mall boutiques, and as department stores like Saks and Neiman Marcus flood the market with store brands, opuluxe empires may topple.

But will Julia Roberts be next seen going into a big-box store for her Diderot makeover? Will she be shopping on the Web? Doubtful. If history is any guide, the allure of "dream shopping" will protect these special patches of glitzy retail. And as long as "elegance is power," as Oscar Wilde once said; as long as "going shopping" is an adventure in self-creation; and as long as Richard Gere is there picking up the tab, these stores on these streets owned by these companies will set the standards for a certain kind of taste.

The Media Really Is the Message

As we have seen, most of the value of the new luxury is in the story. Advertising tells that story. Advertising travels in a medium, either in print or electrons. The history of these media is simple. If they can't carry commercial speech, they won't survive. As they have evolved, various media have established themselves as part of how we understand the value of certain goods.

In 1999 BBDO New York, a major advertising agency, conducted a study of *current* consumer perception of media (Levere 1999:C12). Now admittedly, most research conducted by ad agencies is like a lamppost to a drunk—they use it when they need it—but the report did reaffirm the obvious. If the medium is the message, then we use different media when we want different messages. We go to the Internet for escape and for specific data on subjects like travel and health. We watch television for entertainment and breaking news. We listen to the radio for background. But we read newspapers and magazines when we are eager for information. That's why, as the study suggested, luxury objects are best explained in the most cerebral and slow-moving media: newspapers and, especially, glossy magazines.

This has not always been the case. If you were interested in observing the luxe life from the 1930s to the 1950s, you went to the movies, from the 1950s to the 1980s perhaps you watched television, but from the 1980s on you looked at mass-market magazines and metropolitan newspapers, usually those published in New York.

Opuluxe and Electronic Media

That the movies showed the post-Depression world how the other half lived in luxury is indisputable. In fact, the connection between economic destitution in real life and glamour in reel life has been made so often it was a cliché by the 1950s. This insight was certainly not lost on the producers of luxe. Harry Winston and Christian Dior scurried out to Hollywood to wrap starlets in their jewels and drape them in their couture for a reason. Who could forget the synergy between Audrey Hepburn and Givenchy? While viewers liked to see such glamour, only a very few of them ever bought it.

By the 1960s television continued the cinematic tradition of product education in which objects built character and vice versa. Of course, it happened on a slightly smaller scale. Not by happenstance did the concluding credits of shows like *Dallas* and *Dynasty* inform us what car companies were lending the Ewings or the Carringtons their snazzy wheels. Those of us who grew up on these shows learned a lot about frontier luxury by checking out what JR and Sue Ellen Ewing wore, how Krystle and Blake Carrington entertained, and especially how Alexis Carrington decked herself out.

Although product placement is now usually in the service of verisimilitude (viz Seinfeld and his never-ending references to everyday products), the introduction of luxe is still possible via the tiny screen. MTV has had a profound effect by showing how expensive goods fit together, as have such shows as *Beverly Hills 90210* and *Dawson's Creek*. Many people credit HBO's *Sex and the City* for selling thousands of Fendi "baguette" hand-bags. Every time the lead character, played by Sarah Jessica Parker, stuffed her underwear inside her baguette, sales at the Madison Avenue store sky-rocketed. Average price: $1,100.

Watch the Academy Award presentations for ten minutes and you will see the achievement of perfect unity by opuluxe marketers, name design-ers, movie makers, and television viewers. If the Nielsen numbers are to be believed, this is the Super Bowl for women, a seamless web of advertising, infotainment, and fashion display. Look, see, dream, buy.

Glossy Print Is Best

Since the 1980s new luxury has been introduced into households not, iron-ically, through pixels but through old print. No longer is this "I see it; I dream of it" but rather "I can have it; now how do I use it?" Thanks to down-marketing, credit cards, installment buying, and especially leasing programs, almost anyone can have almost anything . . . but perhaps only a knockoff product and perhaps only for a limited period of time. So *how* to consume has joined *what* to consume.

The ability to inform a newly affluent and fashion-conscious clientele is what has caused the explosion of "second-stream lines." This is the stuff I saw not in the windows but on the floors of those stores in Los Angeles, Palm Beach, and Manhattan. So the question for opuluxe producers be-comes how to draw attention to the stuff that generates the value for the really profitable mass-market stuff. How does it fit into a coherent con-sumption pattern? In Diderot's terms the job is to isolate the "starter" items and then show how they unfold into an ensemble. To do this, the worldwide conglomerated producers have revived two old venues, the boxy newspaper ad and the glossy magazine ad.

By far the most influential nonindustry papers are *The New York Times* and the *Wall Street Journal*. Although the *Times* is usually dismissive of the concerns of style and consumption on its editorial pages, it is positively fawning in its fashion columns. In the "Styles" section of the Sunday *Times*, and especially in the Sunday magazine and the *Fashions of the Times* sup-plement, the gray lady is nothing but a debutramp. In fact, she is often scandalous. As well, the *Journal* usually pays opuluxe no heed, but every Friday it gives over an entire section to "Weekend Journal." Again, during the week both papers pretend a patriarchal standoffishness in favor of Really Important Things, but when the weekend comes around a little Saturnalia can't hurt. Recall that the church did not just tolerate Mardi Gras; it supported it.

And, while the *Times* and the *Journal* usually approach the subject of new luxury with a wry loftiness, you can see that lurking just below the surface is a real interest in what money will buy in the modern world. You don't need this, the newspapers seem to say, but here it is anyway. The advertisers, never much for the vaunted concept of the wall separating editorial and commercial, show what's what.

As with almost all innovations in newspapering, taking consumption seriously has been forced on the papers by advertisers eager to address this urban and affluent audience with their wares. Look at *The New York Times* during the 1990s and you can see this operating in slow motion. The increase of infotainment throughout all sections, the inclusion of Tuesday's "Science Times" section to showcase computer ads; "Dining In, Dining Out" on Wednesday for food and wine ads; "House and Home" on Thursday for furniture and real estate ads; the two-section entertainment sections on Friday for endless movie ads; the jazzy "Styles" section of Sunday for designers' ads. Look at how the *Times* uses color. Advertisers demand color; things show up better and it leads to better product recall. Notice as well the appearance on the front page of stories that used to be deemed tabloidish and were therefore relegated to the back sections, stories on marketing, advertising, e-tailing, and e-commerce, on the getting and spending of . . . ugh, money. The Gucci story, the handbag war, for instance, was well covered by the *Times*.

The *Times* has been running a jazzy national TV and print campaign under the tag line "Expect the World," which clearly is meant to appeal to younger readers. All these changes are attempts to find the "proper" readership for advertisers, not to find "All the News That's Fit to Print." If newspapers want to survive, they have to think of themselves not as delivering news or entertainment to readers but as delivering readers to advertisers. And the advertisers are clearly coveting the high-end market for opuluxe.

Luxury Alley

Of all the places in the *Times* where you can see the effects of opuluxe, none is more continually interesting than what I call luxury alley. This is the daily

Luxury alley, the first pages of the daily New York Times, *grows a column wider on Sunday, as it did on March 7, 1999, pp. 2–3.*

single column of display ads (double on Sunday) surrounding pages two and three and, when demand merits, pages four, five, and, once in a while, six.

The reason you will not see any low-life cut-rate interlopers in this space is that the paper presells all this space. And it sells it on the promise that no discounter will elbow its way into one of the ad positions. For around $1.2 million each, about twenty-five selected companies can lock up the space. And lock others out. The only time that riffraff advertisers are let in is during an especially slow month, like July, and only then if they don't misbehave with cost-cutting and knockoff vulgarities.

The corners have been presold to Tiffany (top outside right) since before World War II and to Cartier (top outside left). Calvin Klein and Ferragamo usually alternate in the "gutter" at the bottom, Saks has middle right, Tourneau has middle left. Other than that, it's the usual suspects: Mikimoto, Coach, Lord & Taylor, Bloomingdale's, Barneys, Chanel. Paul Stuart and Harry Winston are usually on page three. The only change during the week is that extra display ads of two columns by seven inches are sometimes added to page two and, when Christmas, Mother's Day, and Valentine's Day roll around, to pages three and four.

These ads do have a certain hypnotic allure. They are never flashy, always just an image, a little description, and usually the price. They show a signature item. Tiffany will show its settings, Cartier its bracelets, Hermès its scarf, Tourneau a watch or two. Even the department stores will remain true to character. Barneys will be edgy. No fooling around from Neiman Marcus.

And, more interesting, occasionally Saks will pose models in the same pose for what seems almost a year. In the late 1990s Saks showcased a woman with her head slightly tilted and a shadow across her downcast eyes. The point? To efface her personality and emphasize the clothing. Women's groups said nothing. Maybe in penance, the current tag line is "Live It Up."

These ads in luxury alley are metonyms of opuluxe. To be sure, they remind an affluent audience of the kind of product available, and they keep the name of the store in the public eye, but beyond that they maintain the company that they keep. You know they will be there every day, twice as deep on Sunday. In so doing they seem to say that before all else, before the news, before all the other sections, before breakfast and the commute, remember who we are and what we sell. They seem to say that the reward of a productive life is consumption. Up front, look here first. Have a look at what the advertising looks like when the luxe supplier (Saks) escapes the box format.

Give the "Gift of Style," say, a chinchilla jacket or a diamond necklace.

What these ads do not tell you is how precisely to use the product, how exactly to fit the product into a pattern of other objects, how to accessorize yourself with what it is that they are offering. They are flash cards of opuluxe. If you want to see them put together, you need to be conversant with another kind of print, the full-page and full-bleed magazine ad that the *Times* celebrates with its own bound version—*Fashions of the Times*—the personal style magazine.

Vanity Fair

What the *Times* runs as an occasional supplement is a standard magazine genre—the lifestyle magazine. The modern ones are different from their predecessors in important ways. If you look at the old *Vanity Fair,* from the 1940s to the 1960s, you will see that it is about pretty horses, formal gardens, high fashion, long dresses, dogs, fingernails, more horses, still more dogs, comfy chairs, and who's getting married or is off to Europe. In a word, it's about what the duchess of Windsor is about. If you can judge a magazine by its ads, the old *Vanity Fair* was about tip-top elegance for a precious few.

Now look at the new *Vanity Fair.* I hold a copy in my hand. *Vanity Fair* comes monthly from a company that has probably done more to democratize and domesticate the posh than any other institution except Master-Card and Visa. If you buy the hardware on Rodeo Drive, Worth Avenue, and upper Madison Avenue, you get the software instructions from its glossy pages. Far more than television and the movies, magazines like *Vanity Fair* show how goods *work.* It's *Popular Mechanics* for the new luxury.

Many of these style magazines come from the presses and imagination of Condé Nast, the print fiefdom of the Newhouse empire called Advance Publications. You know these magazines because they are the staples of middle-class yearning. Of the seventeen or so magazines, from *The New Yorker* to *Wired,* the most profitable are the "how to consume" ones: *Vogue, Glamour, GQ, Vanity Fair, Architectural Digest, House & Garden,* and, most recently, *Lucky.*

In 1999 Condé Nast consolidated its sweep of the genre by buying Fairchild Publications (*Women's Wear Daily, W, Jane, Los Angeles Magazine*) from Disney. Although Condé Nast did this for advertising reasons (so it could sell space across a spectrum of opuluxe producers), it also tightened its grip on the introduction and use of new variations. The only competitors left on the female side are *Harper's Bazaar,* owned by Hearst Mag-

azines, and *Elle,* part of Hâchette Filipacchi Magazines. Opuluxe men's magazines are growing like Topsy, starting with the amazingly puerile *Maxim* for kids and ending up with the amazingly puerile *Robb Report* for adults. In between are magazines like *Details* and *GQ,* which are more temperate but no less materialistic.

Condé Nast magazines are about how things are supposed to look (including yourself), and that look has profoundly changed since Ronald Rea-

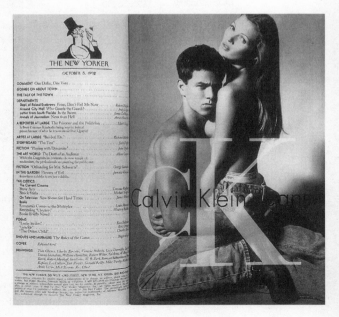

*Tina Brown takes over
The New Yorker, and
Calvin Klein elbows out
Eustice Tilley on
October 5, 1992.*

*Condé Nast touts its
magazines to advertisers.*

gan was president. When the magazines were overseen by Alexander Liber-
man, the Russian artist and graphic designer, the luxury movement was upward, pretentious, and quiet. Look at these magazines today, under the
watchful eye of a very savvy James Truman, and you will see that matters
have become downtown, raunchy, and almost defiantly middle class.

Old fogeys were not out of line when they predicted that Tina Brown's
transfer from *Vanity Fair* to *The New Yorker* announced this transition.
And Brown did not disappoint. In her first issue she slotted a Calvin Klein
ad featuring Marky Mark in his skivvies right next to the newly tarted-up
table of contents. I don't mean to imply that this was as much a conscious
editorial decision as it was part of a transformation wrought by publishers
interested in moving a different kind of product to a younger and newly affluent audience. Editors went along.

I also don't mean to imply that there is anything nefarious in this transformation. Just look at the made-over *New York Times Magazine,* which
now has only one article of more than 750 words and then prose snippets
and squibs sandwiched between ads so the entire magazine will not seem
to be entirely given over to selling luxury. But of course it is. Sometimes the
proximity is downright distracting, as in several recent foldout covers.

The occasional collision on the cover of the New York Times Magazine *as luxury gets too close to content (September 6, 1992 and March 19, 2000).*

Or look at *In Style* magazine, which is *only* the snippets and squibs, and you will see that the demand for images of opuluxe has far exceeded the supply of prose ligatures. Certainly, one sign of this transformation has been the replacement of high-fashion models as cover material with the featuring of nonmodel celebrities *and* their things. If you observe both the advertising and the text of such magazines, you will soon see that their real subject matter, the undifferentiated text, if you will, is the consumption and display of luxury lite.

An Issue of Vanity Fair

To see this conflation of small text and large ad, of pictures of things and paragraphs of how to use them, to observe the now long-broken Chinese wall between a magazine's editorial side and its advertising staff, let's have a look at a typical issue of *Vanity Fair*, this one from August 8, 1999.

Here's how the magazine shakes out before any formal text appears: Four pages, accordion style, of Guess? "raw denim"; two pages of Calvin Klein eyeglasses, two pages of a Bonnard-esque girl on swing for Estée Lauder perfume; two pages of Saks Fifth Avenue "defining style"; two pages of Prada with one page all blue sky; DKNY jeans; one page of David Yurman (watch); three pages of St. John (women's clothing); three pages of Victoria's Secret; and two pages of Lexus. Almost every ad is free of copy and in four-color bleed. These ads are mostly just luscious color pictures of solitary young people looking rich, indifferent, and bored.

After about twenty advertising pages, we find a contents page. On the facing page is the start of three pages of Ralph Lauren followed by two pages of Prada (again). Then the second page of the table of contents, this time featuring the columns to come. A page of Clinique, a page of Lucky Brand Jeans (the first ad with text and lots of it) and then a page of "Advertising and Promotion" for *Vanity Fair*. Here we learn that *VF* is cross-marketing with various film festivals, with BMW, and with Tourneau watches. Now two more full pages of Ralph Lauren, the *VF* masthead, then another page for DKNY, two more pages for Calvin Klein (kids' wear), and then the editorial/ownership page. Now, in succession, a page for Clerc (watch), two pages for Audi, Editor's Letter, Armani Classico page, contributors' bios, Waterford crystal, letters to editor, Evian, Cline (women's clothing), and, *finally,* the magazine text and columns start.

Editorial content doesn't catch hold for a while. Instead we have four pages for Cartier, full pages for Rena Lang (women's clothing), Dolce & Gabbana, Absolut Vodka on consecutive pages, Abercrombie & Fitch for two pages, Chrysler, two more Calvin Klein pages, Skyy Vodka, Sprint cell phone, Hugo Boss, Toyota, Kodak CD pictures, Finlandia Vodka, and then a six-page tie-in for BMW. Then Paul & Shark (men's clothing) and *The Thomas Crown Affair,* a soon-to-be-released movie about a rich, well-dressed man pursuing and being pursued by a well-dressed woman. Now halfway through the magazine come full-page ads for Claritin, the Sierra Club, Minolta camera, Bebe clothing, Complete contact lens care, Country Inn Specialties (premium breakfast cereal), Lincoln "America's Luxury Car," *The Muse* (a movie), Fuji digital film, and then twelve (12!) pages of Gucci interleafed with text.

From pages 128 to 196 *Vanity Fair* is all articles, no ads whatsoever. Stories on movie stars, movie directors, a woman who married a movie director, a restaurant, and a Las Vegas circus act are unfettered by commercial interruption. What an irony of our times that the *jump,* or the separation of text by ads, which was developed by advertisers to force readers through advertising, is a thing of the past. Whoever is reading this magazine is not having to be led through the ads. Know why? They are reading the ads and skipping the text.

From page 196 to the end we find full pages for Planned Parenthood, De Beers diamonds, and Acura, interspersed with text, until we come to a Gap ad on the inside back cover and a Tanqueray Gin ad on the outside. So here we have it: eighty-six pages of dedicated opuluxe with a big chunk going to Gucci (12), Calvin Klein (6), Ralph Lauren (5), Prada (4), Guess? (4), Cartier (4), and DKNY (3). The rest is lots of cars, camera film, vodkas, and watches. Some do-gooding, to be sure. A tip of the liberal hat to the street beggar but mostly a single-minded dedication to the new luxury.

Vanity Fair is a new kind of magazine. Consider this: In early magazines all the ads were bundled in the back of the book. In *VF* they are off-loaded in the front. The magazine is thoroughly materialistic. In fact, *VF* is far more materialistic than its cousins, the fashionistas. Compare it to *Vogue, Elle, W,* or *Harper's Bazaar* and you will see that *VF*'s focus is almost entirely on how to recognize branded things from the Land of Elegance, how to use these things, how to value things and privilege the people who own them. But mark this: These things are not out of reach. You can buy them.

VF most assuredly is not a fashion magazine, or even a style magazine, as much as it is a manual for new-moneyed consumers of designer objects. This is a lifestyle magazine with attitude, an advertisement with a chip on its shoulder. It is passive aggressive, in your face on one page and then meek and repentant on the next.

To be less mechanical, what *Vanity Fair* is, is *House & Garden* applied to the soma. Not the old *House & Garden,* which was about just what it said, but the new—since 1996—version, which is about how your house and garden are really an expression of you. The old *H&G* almost went under in the mid-1990s because the editors couldn't quite understand what was happening to their market. They thought it really was about houses and gardens. They took literally the generic term *shelter magazine.* The new editors realized that a house was more than a shelter—it was a husk, a second skin, something to surround and extend the self. The house is a closet.

If you want to see this really played out with an edge, look at its upscale cousin, *Architectural Digest,* which is a kind of sadistic version of *H&G.*

Don't even think of living like this, the magazine seems to say. Notice how its tables usually are set for twelve guests, although no one is around. And never children! Does Barbra Streisand really *use* that bathroom? But what *AD* flaunts, *H&G* accepts: Houses are brands, before all else they are an advertisement for/of you. Once the editors found out that they should treat the house as an accessory, their subscription base soared from 400,000 subscribers to 650,000, their delivery rate (the number of actual readers) rocketed to 796,000, and advertisers clamored to get on board (Brady 1999:33).

In fact, some of the *H&G* ads even say as much. A store that sells furniture shows its product over the headline "Expressing Your Inner World," while a fabric and wallpaper company claims, "Your Home Is the Canvas—Your Experience Is the Design," and a watch company says, "Design Is a Statement as Personal as a Signature." Almost all the ads in *H&G* implicitly or explicitly claim that their product is really an aspect of *your* style, of you.

The now-annual September luxury issue of House & Garden.

An Issue of House & Garden

Here, have a quick look at a special issue of *House & Garden* from September 1998. The special issue is titled "A Time for Luxury" and it essentially fills in the lifestyle gaps of *Vanity Fair*. This issue proved so successful that Condé Nast has made luxury a yearly offering, and its 168 pages of ads increased to almost 200. If the ads are reflective/predictive of audience concerns—and they most certainly are or else millions of dollars and lots of marketing savvy are being wasted—then we are being given a good look at the consumption community for this new class of consumable—opuluxe accessories for the house.

That these sister magazines share the same advertisers is logical and predictable. In a sense one is a "pullout" of the other. But what is striking is that the objects, the things themselves, are different. The names, however, remain the same. So if Calvin Klein is over in *VF* selling jeans, here he is selling sheets. And if Tiffany is selling rings in *VF*, in *H&G* it is showing flatware. Gucci goes from twelve pages of clothes to two pages of watches and luggage.

As might be expected, we find a slew of furniture companies, plumbing supplies, towels, top-of-the-line refrigerators and stoves, sealed window casements, window treatments, paints, and lots and lots of closet designs. After all, this magazine is about things for the house, things to make the house "homey," things to make your house you.

If celebrities, or at least models known to fashionistas, do the heavy lifting in showing the appropriate use of designer objects in *VF*, here at *H&G* the editors lend a hand. They have a defined and affable personality, almost as if they are meeting you at the door of your house. Admittedly, this particular issue I am looking at is self-consciously dedicated to valorizing luxe, but it is really only an extension of the magazine's usual take on the material world. Namely, how to consume and what to consume. You are what you buy. You are essentially a closet. This is the home of consumerist synergy as text and ad, story and sale; copy and picture finally meet in seamless celebration of self and things.

If the ads were segregated from text in *VF*, they are perfectly dovetailed in *H&G*. The articles *are* ads. There is no Chinese wall. Just the opposite. More important than the delineated stories are the educational columns. For instance, in "Domestic Bliss," a monthly column, we have a series of aphorisms on specific objects of consumption. From breathless sentences we learn how to choose stationery, how to place plants, arrange faux columns, organize rag rugs, use the proper fork at dinner, and even how to apply store design (in this case the literal design of a specific department of Saks) to your own house. "Domestic Bliss" concludes with this handy guide to luxury:

Luxury Hot *Contemporary Luxury*	**Luxury Not** *Past Luxury*
Line-dried clothes	Clothes dryers
Revival movie theaters	Satellite dishes
House charge	ATM cards
Fur rugs	Wall-to-wall carpeting
Ashtrays	Humidors
Dressmakers	Designer sheets
Candlelit chandeliers	Gas fireplaces
Coke in glass bottles	Frozen vegetables
Sex without fear	Psychotherapy
Legible liner notes	Cappuccino at bookstores
Bacon-and-egg breakfasts	Croissants
Farmers' markets	Roses
Outdoor kitchens	Dishwashers
Hand-knit afghans	Cashmere sweaters
Letters from friends	Federal Express

Having tried this in/out list on friends who claim to know better, what's luxury and what's not is more the result of the whimsical editorial need to separate and list than of any deep principle. But that in itself tells much about the nature of luxury in the way we live now. Whereas old-style luxe depended on the illusion of timelessness and the patina of old age, new-style is nothing more than what's marketable and new. The principle is that whatever is currently in is exactly what is out.

The other column that weaves its way through page after page is one called "Hunting & Gathering." This time the white gloves are pulled off and we get down to business. The column really should be called "How to Pass . . . " for it tells not just what brand of object to buy but how to use (i.e., display) it so others will read it (and you) properly. So, if you are concerned about what *brand* of watch, studio chair, perfume, paint, pen, sheets, wine glasses, napkins, piano, picture frame, luggage, milk choco-late, terra-cotta pot, wallpaper, or slippers to buy so that you can feel "washed over" with luxury, here's the place to learn.

Lest the point be missed, if you go to the back of the magazine, the index of the book as it were, you will find pages called "Sources: Where to Buy It." Here all the "Domestic Bliss" objects and all the "Hunting & Gathering" objects are listed by store name. In other words, some of those focused shoppers I had seen as I wandered on Rodeo Drive, Worth Av-enue, Madison, and Fifth, the ones who clearly knew what to do, had doubtless perused the pages of such a how-to magazine as *House & Gar-den*. They had done the Hunting. Now they were doing the Gathering.

The rest of this issue of *H&G* was predictable. A six-page insert from TAG Heuer showing that you need many watches because watches don't keep time, they keep variations of your self. A well-crafted essay on Voltaire and luxury under the headline "The Revolutionary Writer Didn't Condemn Luxury, He Praised It—And His Argument Is Still Sound" ar-gues that luxury is more a goal than an actuality. "Luxury has been railed at for two thousand years, in verse and prose, and it has always been loved," says the sage of Ferney (Klepp 1998:140).

There are several pages of cross-marketing between *H&G* and various hotels around the country where you can go and see objects showcased in the magazine. And there are many—ten, to be exact—short articles com-plete with lush photos of what are essentially ensembles of things. So we see someone's garden and stuff, someone's den and accessories, someone's table settings in which posh is contextualized—*Architectural Digest* on the cheap.

Lest you think that I have unfairly targeted women's magazines for ads rich in the allure of opuluxe, just take a look at any mature man's fashion magazine like *GQ* or any young man's magazine like *Details,* both from Condé Nast. Better yet, look at magazines analogous to *H&G* where fash-ion is not foregrounded but gender-specific tasks are. Look at any of the slew of money magazines like *Worth,* for instance. Clearly, the prime audi-ence is middle-aged males, husbands, perhaps, of the *H&G* readers.

The most interesting new magazines are anti-opuluxe magazines. As I write this, two such new magazines are being brought to market. Time Warner is releasing *Real Simple,* and *Simplicity* has been launched with backing from the investment bank Goldman Sachs. They join the *Art of*

Simple Living, a magazine begun in 1999 by Brown & Williamson (yes, that Brown & Williamson, the tobacco company). Let me get you through the first twenty pages of *Real Simple.* Here's what you see before you get to the table of contents: ads for Ralph Lauren, Estée Lauder, Baby Gap, Clinique, Ann Taylor, Lancôme, Jones New York, Lucy.com, Gymboree, and Revlon. The first real feature not pitching a product comes on page fifty-eight, right after the "to-do" list, a nifty little collection of tips that is no more than a guide to major advertisers. If you want to see the oxymoron expressed visually, take a look at the front and back covers.

With 110 pages of ads and 400,000 copies heading into circulation, *Real Simple* is Time Warner's biggest magazine launch ever. Aimed at women in their thirties and forties who earn more than $60,000, it has features on everything from how to streamline bill paying to the fastest way to clean your bathroom.

Real Simple arrived just as the company was shelving *Life,* an interesting exchange. In its own words, the magazine is "dedicated to simplifying

The back and front covers of the inaugural issue of Real Simple *from AOL–Time Warner, April 2000.*

every aspect of a woman's life." For many practicing Voluntary Simplicity, this last sentence sounds simply ludicrous. But more important is that it shows how consumption has even become the method of nonconsumption, rather like eating to lose weight, a modern variation of bombing a village to save it. Buy more to spend less; get more stuff in order to simplify your life.

5.

How Luxury Becomes Necessity

THE WORK OF ADVERTISING

*Advertising did not invent the products or services
which called forth jobs, nor inspire the pioneering
courage that built factories and machinery to produce
them. What advertising did was to stimulate ambition
and desire—the craving to process, which is the
strongest incentive to produce. Mass production made
possible mass economies, reflected in declining prices,
until the product that began as the luxury of the rich
became the possession of every family that was willing
to work.*

—Bruce Barton, chairman, BBDO

I know what you're thinking. You are thinking that this may be an interesting subject but that it really doesn't pertain to you. You are certainly not
buying this stuff. You don't like luxury, let alone *love* it. You are not duped
by advertising. You can be perfectly happy without most things. In fact, all
you need is a few good books, a few interesting ideas, a few friends, a few
good conversations, a few sunsets, and you are content. You have those
core values that politicians love to invoke. Well, me too. It's all the other
people that I'm talking about. Not us. So when I talk about *us* and *we*, you
know I really mean *them*.

That said, let's be honest about materialism. While it's fun to sound superior, and to *be* superior (and this kind of new luxury we've been dis-

cussing is especially easy to feel superior to), human beings like *things*. We buy things. We exchange things. We steal things. We donate things. We live through things. We call these things "goods" as in "goods and services." We do not call them "bads." This sounds simplistic, but it is crucial to understanding the power of luxury. The still-going-strong industrial revolution produces more and more things—not because production is what machines do, and not because nasty capitalists twist their handlebar mustaches and mutter "More slop for the pigs," but because under it all we are powerfully attracted to the world of stuff.

The balderdash of cloistered academics aside, human beings did not suddenly become materialistic. We have always been desirous of things. We have just not had many of them until quite recently, and, in a few generations—who knows?—we may return to having fewer and fewer. Still, while they last, we enjoy shopping for things, and see both the humor and truth reflected in the aphoristic "born to shop," "shop 'til you drop," and "when the going gets tough, the tough go shopping."

Department store windows, be they on the city street or inside a mall, did not appear magically. We enjoy looking through them to another world. It is what capitalists have for voyeurism. Our love of things is the *cause* of the industrial revolution, not the consequence. Man (and woman) is not only *homo sapiens,* or *homo ludens,* or *homo faber* but also *homo emptor*.

Once we know how to mass-produce things, we need to learn how to mass-consume them. Marketing begins before things are shipped to market. At the center of marketing is always advertising. Before all else, modern advertising is tied to mass-produced things and only secondarily to services. Manufacturing both things *and* their meanings is what modern industrial culture is all about. In a sense Condé Nast and LVMH are really just different sides of the same culture. I call it adcult, and it is so much the culture that surrounds us that, like fish in water, we hardly know it's there.

Why Luxury Is at the Center of Adcult

Once production is tied to machines, then advertising is not just possible, it's necessary. If your machine is just like mine, then what they produce will be identical, fungible, interchangeable, parity items. To separate them I have to say that my soap, cigarette, baking powder, patent medicine, or shoe is different from yours. I have to tell a story. This is especially true with top-end products, from bottled water to pashmina scarves. So as a producer, I have to be able to make a claim of distinction, although common sense should tell the consumer it will be feckless. And the higher I go, the more irrational my claim will become. After all, I am no longer selling the product, I am selling the concocted distinction, the story.

As we have seen with new luxury, common sense is always held in abeyance. If we were using common sense, we would all be reading *Consumer Reports* and buying the same brands. But we most assuredly don't. In fact, the heart of luxury is the irrational acceptance of magical thinking. If we could own this one item, *then* things would somehow change. No one ever marketed luxury as necessity, but we have seen the truth of Motley's witty quip: "Give us the luxuries of life, and we will dispense with the necessaries." Or the equally insightful comment by the nineteenth-century critic Theophile Gautier, "I would sell my bread for marmalade." Or the concocted nonsense for Sub-Zero refrigerators, seemingly endorsed by the minimalist Frank Lloyd Wright.

A Frank Lloyd Wright quotation of dubious provenance for Sub-Zero refrigerators.

So if France and, to a lesser extent, Italy have provided most of the machine-made low-level fashion luxuries, the United States adds the users' code, the gloss as it were. "We bring good things to life" is no offhand claim, but the contribution of the last century. Advertising is how we talk about these things, how we imagine them, how we know their value.

In fact, in dealing with the aesthetic category of new luxury, advertising *is* their value. When you buy a Prada purse, a Hermès scarf, a Hugo Boss T-shirt, a Fendi belt, an Armani coat, Ferragamo shoes, you are really buying the "story," the advertising. The same is true when you are buying a Lincoln Town Car, a BMW, Mercedes, Cadillac, Lexus, or . . . Volvo S80. Clearly, these things in and of themselves simply do not *mean* enough. In fact, what we crave may not be objects at all but their meaning. New luxury in this sense describes objects whose value is almost pure magical story and, in so being, satisfies a very particular desire, the yearning for fixity. Nothing is *beyond* luxury. Once we have it, we can quit aspiring and relax. We hold the gold, the end of the road, *nada más*.

Branding Luxury

In advertising jargon these distinctions of perceived value are often achieved by *branding*. Branding is the central activity of creating differing values between fungible objects like flour, bottled water, cigarettes, denim jeans, razor blades, domestic beers, batteries, cola drinks, air travel, overnight couriers, computer chips, and telephone carriers. Giving such objects their identity, and thus a perceived value, is advertising's unique power. What really separates a Calvin Klein swath of denim from one from Donna Karan from Levi Strauss is the brand. In this sense new luxury is the ultimate branding of branding. The object as object almost evaporates. The luxury brand remains.

For whatever else advertising "does," one thing is certain: By adding value to material, by adding meaning to objects, by branding things, by telling a story, advertising performs a role historically associated with religion. The Great Chain of Being, which for centuries located value above the horizon in the world beyond, has been reforged to settle value into the objects of the here and now. Commercialized luxury has colonized much of the space once held as sacred. In this sense luxury is holy and its consumption is special, which is why reactions to it are often explosive.

The real work of advertising is not to manipulate the doltish public but to find out how people already live, not to force consumers to accept material against their better judgment but to get in the path of their judgment; not to make new myth but to make your product part of an already existing mythology. Advertisers are not interested in what we claim to want, or in what scientists or moralists claim we should want, but in determining what indeed we do want as tracked by what, and how, we purchase. A simple product like bread, for instance, is laden with emotion and information. We squeeze it, we smell it, and we look at it. Then we buy it. We even do the same with products like wine, drugs, and cosmetics where our senses can't possibly help us out because of the packaging. Luxury is the turbocharging of this process and, if successful, the end of our searching.

The wise advertiser will always attempt to find out first what we are after and then fashion a campaign in which to position her product. Only a fool, soon to be bankrupt, attempts to change our patterns of desire. Alas, in truth, it is the advertising, not the audience, that is manipulated. This is what Marshall McLuhan meant when he claimed that audience works in the consumption of the image. For advertising does not invent desire, nor does it satisfy desire; it expresses desire with the hope of exploiting it. Over and over and over. That is why opuluxe flourishes in a world inundated with advertising. Its meaning is almost all relative and attributed. It depends on other advertising. And this is why such myths can be so profoundly destabilizing to unprepared cultures.

An Example of How Opuluxe Advertising Works

Let me illustrate the process with an almost totally ridiculous product: bottled and *branded* water. We all know that if we were rational, this product would not be taking over millions of feet of shelf space. We also all know that if we had to taste, say, ten different kinds of noncarbonated water, including New York City tap water, we would not be able to tell the difference. In fact, in taste tests Manhattan water comes out in the top quartile for "good tasting water."

So if you want to separate your water, you do it not by taste but by telling a story. Differentiation resides in language and imagery, not in product. If you want to charge a premium for your product, and if your product is simply H_2O, then you have to make it into a luxury via language

How to make a fungible
product luxurious by
telling a fabulous story.

codes. You have to *say* it has value by *showing* it does. You have to tell a
story. And to make this story work, other people have to be talking about
their water.[*]

Here is how Evian is making water into a luxury product. It is making
tap water into a beverage and a beverage into a brew and a brew into an
elixir. Just ordinary water is becoming a magical lifestyle accessory. So we
have a bartender pouring Evian as if it were the makings of a martini; a
woman bathing in Evian as if it were part of pampering the self (and not,

---

[*]The two largest soft drink bottlers, Pepsi and Coke, both have lines of bottled water, Aquafina
and Dasani. All they do is take their water from municipal systems and add mineral additives at
the local bottler. That's all they do—other than advertise. Pepsi, which got into the business first,
tested Aquafina in Wichita, Kansas. PepsiCo officials were amazed to find that customers were
not at all upset to learn that the water did not come from springs but was tap water—their own
tap water!—just cleaned up in a bottling plant. Who cares about the source? What drinkers liked
was the name, the label, the bottle, *and* the advertising (Hays 2000:C10).

one hopes, associating it with leftover bathwater—perhaps that is why the bottles are still half full), or as if it were something special to feed a loved pet like the goldfish. In each example the association is made with the outlandish in the hope that the brand will be separated from the rest of the interchangeable products and move upward into the Land of Big Profit. Needless to say, the venues in which Evian places these ads are magazines like *Vanity Fair*.

The ad is the easy part. Now the tricky part is that the consumers have to be not just willing to accept this association but willing to display the acceptance. Clearly, our desire not just to keep up with the Joneses but to separate from the Joneses is at the heart of such positional goods. Holding Evian in your hand is like waving a wand. You are too special for tap water. And this is a desire that marketing can exploit—but not create—by advertising.

Sometimes we want to stay away from the Joneses.

Adluxe in the Past

How was this aesthetic category—deluxe—constructed a generation ago, when this kind of advertising was in its infancy? While we may think that we are the first generation to be bombarded with appeals to luxury, such is hardly the case. True, we have more of it, and what we have is very subtle, but what is different today is (1) who is receiving the appeal, (2) the objects associated with the appeal, (3) the reasons for making the appeal, and (4) the medium in which the appeal is made. But, most important, as I have

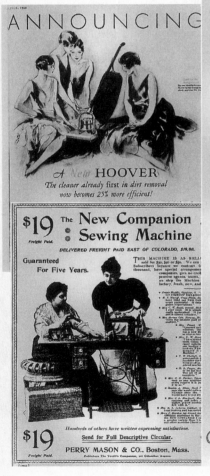

$6.25 is all you need pay down to secure a Hoover complete with household cleaning attachments. Now, anyone can afford a Hoover. Have yours delivered today!

It beats rugs gently; sweeps as no broom can; and thoroughly air-cleans — *electrically!* Its handy new air-cleaning tools dust, *dustlessly.* It keeps your home immaculate; saves time, strength, health; makes rugs wear years *longer.* Certainly, it's a Hoover! Delivered to any home upon payment of only $6.25 down! Your Authorized Hoover Dealer will explain our easy purchase plan.

THE HOOVER COMPANY, NORTH CANTON, OHIO
The oldest and largest maker of electric cleaners
The Hoover is also made in Canada, at Hamilton, Ontario

The introduction of technoluxe is almost always elegant.

said, is that you need lots of other advertising to make this kind of advertising work. Opuluxe advertising separates not just the product but the advertising from other products with other advertising.

In the early twentieth century luxury motifs were most commonly invoked as a way to introduce a new machine into the house. If you look at ads for sewing machines, washing machines, vacuum cleaners, and refrigerators, you invariably see the mistress of the house dressed in finery while wielding the unit. "Look," the ads says, "it's easy, clean, *and* elegant." Sometimes over to the side we see the domestic help—looking suspiciously French—patiently observing the mistress, almost as if the working girl knows she is about to be rendered redundant.

From phonograph to radio, the clientele for entertainment is decidedly a "cut above."

Of course, the appeal to luxury was already part of selling such disposable products as beauty soap or cosmetics, such treasures as jewelry and table settings, such social elixirs as liquor or cigarettes, or even plumbing fixtures (but only in the bathroom, please). And luxe is always just on the edge of selling cars and promoting air travel. But the good life is center stage, the focal point of things run by electricity whose primary use is family welfare, often family entertainment.

Here, for instance, is how the concept of recorded music in the home was introduced. The very idea that music could be consumed by small groups of listeners in private was the height of luxury. Families would gather to sing and play instruments, certainly. But only the wealthy could hire musicians expressly for the task of entertaining. After all, the provenance of classical music was exactly this—composers and musicians working at the direct behest of either the church or a wealthy patron.

So when Edison advertised his phonograph, he invariably chose ludicrous scenes, like the one aboard a yacht. And in a few years, as the cumbersome conical horn with the diaphragm connected to the round needle

Victor Exclusive Talent

The best friends you can have—who cheer you with their music and song, who unfold to you all the beauties of the compositions of the great masters, who through their superb art touch your very heart strings and become to you a well-spring of inspiration.

Painting adapted from the
Chicago Tribune cartoon of John T. McCutcheon.

Copyright 1913 by
Victor Talking Machine Co., Camden, N. J.

Victor-Victrola

[1912]

The opera comes to Main Street, thanks to the record player.

FREED·EISEMANN
THE RADIO OF AMERICA'S FINEST HOMES

RCA has made radio
not only greater — *but* simpler

Now — in Radio, too, *Social Prestige* has been established

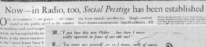

NO SQUAT
NO STOOP
NO SQUINT

Tune easily ... gracefully ...
speedily ... accurately ...
with Philco Automatic Tuning
on the Inclined Control Panel!

That's either an
Orchestra or a
LABYRINTH
RADIO"

Stromberg-Carlson

In the late 1920s and 1930s radio was
a sign of arrival.

was put into a polished cabinet, we can see exactly what this entertainment was becoming. For here we have the lord and lady of the bungalow formally dressed for a night at the opera, just like the rich. Check the foreground, for the miniature characters drawn from operatic repertoire have been domesticated and are now part of middle-class life.

These machines had a profound effect on music for, as the age of listeners dropped, the music of romance increased. Swing music, which for the Greatest Generation was what rock 'n' roll is for my generation, elbowed aside the delicacies of the classical canon. But the advertising pitch stayed the same. This was elegant, upper class, private, and rich. Note how, in ads for the home radio, listeners are behaving just like the Victrola listeners, sitting graciously while now the younger generation cuts the rug.

With time and acceptance the radio appears as an increasingly sophisticated piece of furniture. In the 1920s the cabinet becomes an image of prestige and doesn't just fit into the living room but transforms the room into a salon. With this machine the living room becomes the very kind of chamber in which classical music was once performed. With this receiver you become part of an aristocracy of taste that runs all the way back to the separation of classes in the late eighteenth century.

Thanks to transformations wrought by advertising, luxury becomes a staple of home entertainment, a story, if you will, of doing at home what the elite, in an interesting transformation, now do outside the home—namely, *consume* sound. If the highbrows now go out to have what used to come in, well, now with these machines, the middlebrows can have it

The introduction of television is a dressy affair.

both ways. Look at how radios were sold in the 1930s—as the elegant cabinet, every bit as polished as a piece of fine furniture—to transform parlor into palace.

When the hybrid radio-phonograph is introduced in the 1940s, elegance is assumed. And when the audio track is paired with the video receiver of the next generation of entertainment, the pieces are all in place. Early ads for television from the 1950s recapitulate the history of home consumption of entertainment. Instead of a family sitting around the fireplace of radio, now it's the television with more sophisticated programming. The electronic hearth becomes a centerpiece of sophistication. You invite friends over. The men wear ties. The women dress formally.

The New Yorker *as Midcult Memory*

Looking at radio ads, one can certainly see how luxury can be used to generate value for an expensive and suspicious technological innovation—the category I call technoluxe. Association with accepted standards of elegance makes it easier to cross the threshold and enter the house. This kind of story not only shows you how to present the object and how to use it; it also implies how the object will change your life. For the better. Get the object and you get the status. Plus a cleaner rug.

Until the 1960s this appeal was, if not subtle, then at least not shouted. In the way we live now, we cannot *not* hear this pitch. Luxury, which was once hushed, almost as if connected with shame, is now touted as a necessary part of ordinary life. The shame of consuming too much at too high a level has become the shame of consuming too little at too low a level. Ironically, in this sense new luxury has become necessity. As consumption increases, the luxury eventually becomes generic.

To find the tracks for this counterintuitive observation, I looked back in ten-year increments at the November ads of *The New Yorker*. As Jib Fowles showed some years ago in *Mass Advertising as Social Forecast,* ads are more than a trustworthy barometer of what a culture is currently consuming—they are one of the most accurate predictors of what a culture is aspiring to purchase. They show the dream life of a generation. And there is no better time of year in which to see this than the four issues of November. For in this month producers of luxury objects are furiously laying the pipe that they hope will carry the flood of Christmas buying into their cash registers. And the most trustworthy medium for seeing how American middle-class taste for opuluxe changes in the vade mecum of urban consumerism is another magazine from the Condé Nast empire, *The New Yorker*.

I sent my graduate students into the library to leaf through only those ads that were larger than a quarter of a page. I wanted different eyes to go over the same material, and I wanted them to locate only those objects that either advertised luxury or implied it. The appeal had to be blatant for, as Russell Belk has argued (1996), the perfect gift *must* be drawn from the luxe category. Their working definition therefore was stuff at the top of a category, elegant or premium objects pictured next to certified posh, stuff that separates you from others and shows you have made it, arrived, succeeded.

In other words, I wanted images of what ad agencies thought were the yearnings of a mostly urban middle-class America from the end of the Depression to almost the end of the twentieth century. I wanted these yearnings to be for objects "suitable for giving" connected to the holiday season, although I realized that many objects would be consumable the year long. I wanted to find out what gets an object *into* the category of luxury as well as what gets it *out* of the category of the necessary. Or in advertising lingo, what is ahead of the curve, what is passé? What resolves status anxiety, and what creates it?

The Exceptions

The one genre of luxe that I didn't want recorded was technoluxe, all those machines for the home that I discussed earlier. Machines that run on electricity are already introduced as luxuries. "First costs" are expensive, and mass production makes them cheaper. Soon they become domesticated by the middle class and finally move into the class of necessities—that nifty welfare system of capitalism. Witness the telephone, the radio, the television, and the computer. They start as premium brands. They end up as generics.

What I didn't realize was the importance of such everyday items once coded as luxurious like the coffee maker, the garbage disposal, and especially the Polaroid camera, all of which make cameo appearances as opuluxe and then evaporate.

What I also didn't realize was the absolute centrality of tobacco in the democratization of luxury. The snuff box becomes the cigarette package, a display container that instantly announces your virtu. That this cigarette pack was flashed twenty-three times a day by the average smoker made it a prime site of opuluxe. In almost every issue of *The New Yorker* from the 1930s to the 1960s, a cigarette ad—usually for du Maurier or Parliament—and regular cigar ads—Robert Burns, Webster, and the ubiquitous Dunhill—show the intimate connection between taste in tobacco, the package, and elevated status. These ads immediately dry up as the federal government removes them from print advertising. But until then they are a rich source of luxe, for what surrounds addiction to nicotine is rarely vulgar and often sublime.

Exceptions exist. For instance, Marlboro started in the 1940s as a women's tearoom smoke and was the height of elegance. The Leo Burnett Company regendered it in the 1950s as a real man's smoke, and it exited the glossy pages of *The New Yorker* for more rough-hewn venues. This is one of the few examples of wrong-way luxury, a product made attractive by being made common.

The devolution of luxury. Thanks to Leo Burnett,
Marlboro goes from tearoom sophistication to Wild West independence.

The Material World for the Middle Class in The New Yorker

Starting in the late 1930s, just as the radio is being introduced by those elegant couples in their spacious living rooms, what else is being coded as deluxe? First, a general observation: The advertising load of luxury since the 1950s is almost the same percentage of pages, regardless of the period. The month of November carries about sixty unambiguous pitches for elevation to higher status through consumption. Over the years this has shrunk a little, and of course the magazine has shrunk as well. *The New Yorker* has lost ad pages as its core readership has wandered elsewhere. Still, the pitch for status elevation has remained remarkably stable. What has happened, and what is obvious even from skimming the pages, is that this appeal has spread out to cover a greater number of products.

In the 1930s and '40s the objects coated with glitter were cigarettes, alcohol, furs, tableware, luggage, crystal, watches, and perfume. A favorite luxe item was something now long forgotten: the cigarette lighter posing as a piece of heirloom jewelry. And, of course, with changing limits of political correctness, animal fur has gone from sea otter to seal to raccoon to mink to leopard to oblivion and now, at the beginning of a new century, is reappearing in such strange configurations as pony aka Holstein cow.

Most obvious and startling, however, is this. For the adult population between the Depression and the end of the Vietnam War, there is no doubt which consumer good carried the greatest weight of luxury. Alcohol. Clearly, the repeal of the Eighteenth Amendment in 1933 unloosed a tsunami of liquor. And, just as clearly, liquor had the allure of the still forbidden to the self-consciously sophisticated reader of *The New Yorker* throughout the war years. But the uniform coating of alcohol with luxury throughout the years was for me, and my students, an unexpected aspect of midcult American taste.

The thirst for branded spirits is an American hankering for what is usually a European product. Starting with Dubonnet, Martell cognac, B&B, Harvey's Bristol Cream, Hennessy cognac, Bacardi, Dewar's White Label, Drambuie, Vat 69, and Martini & Rossi vermouth in the 1930s and ending with Peter Heering liqueur, Christian Bros. brandy, Haig & Haig Pinch scotch, Cutty Sark, Marquis de Goulaine, Tattinger champagne, Vaklova Vodka, and Glenfiddich and J&B scotch in the 1970s, the stream of liquor as luxe was deep, powerful, and unremitting. In some issues of the late

1950s (November 22, 1958, for instance) almost every sixth full-page ad was for a foreign liquor, usually an after-dinner liquor or scotch.

Americans lost their taste for heavy drinks in the 1960s as domestic bourbon and especially gin, wines, and vodka found a younger audience. And, admittedly, the giving of liquor as a Christmas gift protected some of these brands long after they had gone out of style. But it is indisputable that liquor abruptly lost its appeal as a signifier of aspirational taste in the 1960s. Alcohol is still there in the advertising pages of the magazine, but its promise has changed. Now alcohol will help you have friends (especially lovers), but it will not help improve your social standing. It is no longer a luxury item. Ironically, bottled water is.

Meanwhile, cars have moved in the opposite direction. True, a few cars were separated by proclamations deluxe: Cadillac, La Salle, Packard, Lincoln, Imperial, Jaguar, and Bentley. But most automobile advertising was promising what alcohol now promises: Get the car, get the woman. Pig iron and plastic on rubber wheels is intimately connected in advertising with the sociobiology of human reproduction. Often, we see the woman down at the end of the car, just touching it, as if to say that they are a pair, buy one, get one free. Occasionally, a car will be positioned as a deluxe model, only to fall flat. Witness the Nash, the American Motors Ambassador, the Frazer, the English Austin, the Vauxhall, and the Jeep Wagoneer. Since the 1980s almost every car ad in *The New Yorker* invokes some aspect of luxury.

When men were competing in the marketplace only with other men, women had to dress them for success. For men the appropriate shoe, tie, and overcoat became markers of prestige, and advertising reflected it. Clearly, having a Harris tweed or a Burberry overcoat, a tie from A Sulka or Countess Mara, or shoes by Johnson & Murphy was a mark of arrival. At least until the 1960s. Men's formal wear was a staple of class consciousness as After Six, Rogers Peet, and F. R. Tripler were quick to announce. As well, aftershave was a luxury: Lenthenic, Aqua Velva, and Yardley were expected weekly invokers of luxe.

Women's clothing was always showcased as part of luxurious life, often surrounded by the already established signifiers like jewelry, furs, and cars. The typical ad before the 1980s never mentions the designer by name but instead cites the store: Bergdorf Goodman, B. Altman, Saks, Best & Co., Lord & Taylor, among others. And certain luxe items now out of fashion, like gloves, girdles, and hats, were coded with rising social class. Aligned with this, however, is the curious introduction of chemical fabrics and ma-

terials. While one might expect silk and wool to be de rigueur, the manufactured rayon, nylon, Koylon, Corfam, and Qiana were invariably announced as refinements.

Other objects may remind us just how socially constructed a category
opuluxe really is. Everyday table food, oddly enough, was sometimes positioned as a luxury item, again, at least until the 1960s. And not just packaged steaks from Omaha but Campbell's Soup and Heinz cucumber pick-
les. Coffee too—Cafe Rico, Yuban, Medaglia d'Oro—was invariably
pictured as part of a cultivated life.

Also part of that elevated life was the ability to recognize highcult reading. Having good-looking books (from numerous monthly book clubs)
promises a room in the house now no longer fashionable—the library. So
too does having good-looking stationery (especially Crane writing paper)
and proper display instruments (the Parker pen soon loses out to Montblanc). In the world before e-mail, when a phone call before 5 P.M. was
special, how you presented yourself on paper was a sign of status.

Even the magazines on your coffee table were coded for class. *Fortune*
advertised itself in the pages of *The New Yorker* as a sign of social arrival,
as did the introduction of *Newsweek*. And while modes of travel (U.S.
Lines; the Santa Fe, Great Northern, Cunard, and French Lines; United
Airlines; Matson; American Export Lines; KLM; Air France) all claimed
deluxe accommodations, you knew the degree by how dressed-up you were
at boarding. The ads showed you. Sometimes the destinations themselves
shifted their claims. In the 1950s, before it was taken over by college kids
on spring break, Ft. Lauderdale was a "destination of distinction."

Leafing through the ads of *The New Yorker*, one can see a subtle
change in the 1960s that was to become fully assimilated by the 1980s. Advertised luxe migrated away from the presentation varieties of jewelry,
tableware, luggage, crystal, watches, and perfume and started clinging to
all manner of manufactured stuff of everyday use. Alcohol became valued
as a social mixer, not as a social indicator; cigarettes were banished, as were
furs; and women's clothing became associated with designer names and designer boutiques, while men's luxury clothing almost totally disappeared.

But during those twenty years from 1960 to 1980 simple things like
sheets (Martex Percale), new destinations of indulgence (Palm-Aire Spa),
stuffed animals (Gund), chocolates (Godiva), real estate brokers (M. J.
Raynes, Inc.), credit cards (Visa), advertorial inserts featuring "places to
go" (Virgin Islands, Aspen, Cayman Islands) and magazines that described

Mocking the initials that feed it, The New Yorker *sends up not just its readers but its advertisers with its cover of March 20, 2000.*

them (*Condé Nast Traveller*), color printers (Tektronix), cruises (Radisson Seven Seas), goosedown cover-ups (Warm Things), to name only the most common, had the word *luxury* literally emblazoned over them. If the *New Yorker* ads could be trusted, luxury was already democratized and down-marketed by the 1970s.

If one takes anything away from looking at the advertising pages of *The New Yorker*, it is the hesitancy that older generations may have felt about invoking luxury had been put aside. To a world that had weathered the Depression and World War II, the idea of luxury, having the stuff of your "betters," was one tinged with ambivalence, even shame. True, a good smoke, a good drink, a fancy table setting, or a display of jewelry could separate the aggressive consumer from the pack, but the repertoire of such objects was relatively small and hard to get at. Too, the concept of sating the self, of making common things too uncommon, of asking for two helpings of dessert, was still a taboo. Indulgence still carried the stigma of selfishness.

If you want to see the shift, simply look at *The New Yorker*'s cover for March 20, 2000. As with many covers, it's a joke that is serious. The woman (trophy bride?) is decked out in opuluxe names, literally. She is covered in designer initials, Fendi, Chanel, Louis Vuitton, Yves Saint Laurent . . . , while her hapless man (husband?) is decked out in his appropriate initials, IRS on his tie and IOU on his handkerchief. Wink-wink, the cover seems to say, this life is shallow, but it's precisely the life offered you by the advertisers. And bought by many of the readers. Yes, yes, we are above it, the cover says. No, no, you are not, say the ads.

If we can trust the *New Yorker* advertising, the concept of accessorizing the self by consuming bits and pieces of a luxe ensemble had fully unfolded by the 1980s. And the idea that almost any class of objects could be topped with a distinct brand of unsurpassed quality was not simply contemplated but actively being accomplished. Absolutely everything the woman on the cover wears is a billboard of affiliation. It is the triumph, albeit perverse, of commercial speech, of advertising, that such value could be loaded into the most mundane objects and that these inscribed objects then could be separated from the rest of the category. It also is a sign of human yearning that this seeming irrationality could spread so quickly through so many different object and social classes. This is no longer the world of meaning for New Yorkers—it defines us all, all over the world.

6.

From Shirts to Tulips

A MUSING ON LUXURY

> *He took out a pile of shirts and began throwing them,*
> *one by one before us, shirts of sheer linen and thick*
> *silk and fine flannel which lost their folds as they fell*
> *and covered the table in many-colored disarray. While*
> *we admired he brought more and the soft rich heap*
> *mounted higher—shirts with stripes and scrolls and*
> *plaids in coral and apple green and lavender and faint*
> *orange with monograms of Indian blue. Suddenly,*
> *with a strained sound, Daisy bent her head into the*
> *shirts and began to cry stormily.*
>
> *"They're such beautiful shirts," she sobbed,*
> *her voice muffled in the thick folds. "It makes me*
> *sad because I've never seen such—such beautiful*
> *shirts before."*
>
> —F. Scott Fitzgerald, *The Great Gatsby*

If I had to pick the defining moment of modern American commercial culture, this is it. The scene is over in a second, but it holds a century of modernity. It's the industrial revolution in an eyewink. Jay Gatsby, a mysterious man whose most important creation is himself, is showing what he's got, what he's made of, what he is. He is doing this in order to make the woman of his dreams, Daisy Buchanan, into the woman of his life. Daisy is his image of perfection, a southern belle, what World War I was fought for, what machines spin for, the green light at the end of the dock, a woman whose "voice [was] full of money" (old money) and whose attention is what he yearns for. She is respectability, the consumption of status, luxury.

So here is Daisy standing before Gatsby's temple of shirts with her cousin, Nick Carraway, a fresh-faced newcomer from the Midwest. Nick does not yet understand. Clearly, Daisy is falling apart because of what Gatsby has. But why?

There are many reasons. Most of us who read the novel in school understand it in what might be called the academic way, Marxism lite. This interpretation leans to the Left. Here's how it goes in classrooms from coast to coast: Before us in this scene, boys and girls, is the American tragedy of consumption turned rapacious, of dreams benightmared, of the imagination losing its way, of capitalism gone bonkers. Here is a man, Jay Gatsby, who has dedicated his life to self-aggrandizement, albeit in the name of misguided love, and who has enthralled himself to stuff—manufactured stuff—in hopes of buying respectability. That he should think he can win the heart of his love by stuffing his closets with expensive shirts is nothing short of tragic.

The Buchanan Moment

In this version Gatsby is a man whose misunderstanding of What Really Matters is so pathetic, so sad, so—dare we say?—American, that we can only hope Nick learns from his example. Alas, Daisy is already a goner; clearly, she is lapping up his feast of plenty. Shallow woman-child.

As English class continues, the standard interpretation unfolds into academic moralizing. Why doesn't Gatsby realize that there are things that *really* matter, things like community, like faith, like family, like literature and the arts that plight the troth of love with so much deeper passion, that can give life *real* meaning. How can he be so crass, so vulgar, so, okay, let's say it all together . . . so American!

And now, class, look at Daisy through the same *Utne Reader* lens. What is *her* problem? Has she spent entirely too much time down at Neiman Marcus, too much time flipping through catalogs, too much time watching the Home Shopping Network? Has she spent too much time clicking through indulge.com? Is she such a simple-minded luxury bimbo with such mixed-up values that she should go ga-ga over a pile of men's shirts?

Does she believe that you fill the shopping cart to fulfill the self? And what does she mean, "It makes me *sad* because I've never seen such beautiful shirts before"?

The professor gathers steam. What *should* make her sad is the plight of the rain forest, urban sprawl, the sea turtle, and the inequitable distribution of money. Or if that's too magnanimous, couldn't she at least think about the laundry costs of messing up all those carefully folded shirts, which will now have to be relaundered, re-ironed, and refolded by some vassal of imperialism?

Go onto any college campus in this country. Sit in any classroom when this novel is discussed. This is the standard interpretation. I know. For years I taught it this way.

But another plausible interpretation of this scene is one that we most definitely do not discuss in class. If we did, we would be called cynical at best and brainwashed at worst. We would be called this, however, not by our students but by our peers. Here it is: Daisy is seeing objects, manufactured objects, of such beauty that she is profoundly moved. She is not duped, not foolish, not ditzy. These are objects well made, beautiful to look at, and pleasurable to touch.

There used to be no greater academic heresy than to think that the material world carries deep meaning, albeit not as deep and long-lasting as the world of ideas. But meaning nonetheless. In fact, the masculine academic world has dedicated itself to the enthusiastic denigration of getting and spending as a meaning-making endeavor. Perhaps because we consider material indulgence as vaguely female, and therefore somehow less admirable than the stoic male approach, the invocation of dress shirts, specifically, Gatsby's elegant shirts, has become a kind of touchstone for true believers. Condemn them and you have depth. Find them alluring and you are shallow.

Take a look at the cover of Roger Rosenblatt's book of collected diatribes against the world of opuluxe. There they are: Gatsby's shirts piled sky high, an apt metonym of consumption out of control. The pile looks eerily like the inside of a modern Gap store, all the clean aseptic manufactured clothing piled almost to the shopper's eye, as if to announce not just abundance but neverendingness. Here, the pile seems to say, take a handful, what's a shirt, even a wildly overpriced one? There're plenty more.

When William Safire, wily commentator on the passing scene, wanted to criticize the shallowness of mallcondo culture in his *New York Times* col-

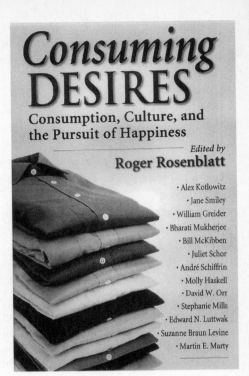

Consuming
DESIRES
Consumption, Culture, and
the Pursuit of Happiness

Edited by
Roger Rosenblatt

· Alex Kotlowitz
· Jane Smiley
· William Greider
· Bharati Mukherjee
· Bill McKibben
· Juliet Schor
· André Schiffrin
· Molly Haskell
· David W. Orr
· Stephanie Mills
· Edward N. Luttwak
· Suzanne Braun Levine
· Martin E. Marty

*The shirt as apt analogy for
overconsumption.*

umn, he started his piece on "I spend therefore I am" by invoking these shirts. He asks himself, why do I own thirty-eight dress shirts? (1999:A25). How can this be? He knows full well, for if anyone appreciates the rich history of men's shirts as representatives of needless glut, it is Safire. Maureen Dowd, his female counterpart, would not start her version of consumptive melancholia by counting the number of blouses in her closet. Maybe the female version of unnecessary consumption would be purses or shoes. But shirts, that's the manly trope.

Why Shirts Matter

I have a confession to make. While doing research for this book, I spent a lot of time looking at things like Gatsby's shirts. As you know, I spent hours skulking up and down Rodeo Drive, Worth Avenue, and Madison and Fifth Avenues. As you'll find out, I even went to Las Vegas and was amazed. I became a discount luxury mall rat. I've pulled off at every off-price outlet from one end of Interstate 95 to the other. I've looked at catalogs, hundreds of them, every magazine Condé Nast publishes, ads, thousands of ads, and lots of movies, Fox TV, HBO.

You name it, if it's sold at True Value Hardware store, I have no idea what it's about. But if you can find it in Gucci, Prada, Louis Vuitton, Hermès, Ferragamo, Neiman Marcus, and the rest, then I've fondled it. Most of the stuff is just ridiculous, eyewash really, sparkling motes. Some of it is obscene. Versace. And none of it is necessary. But to a student of material-

Other shirt piles in the spirit of Jay Gatsby.

ism, understanding Daisy as she buries her tear-stained face in these shirts is to understand the irresistible power of luxury, where it comes from and why it won't go away. Daisy Buchanan is many things, but what she is not is singular. She, not Jay Gatsby, is at the heart of commercial culture. He's the messenger. The shirts are the message.

Face it: Understanding luxury is to the student of material culture what figuring out the incest rituals of the Trobriand islanders was to anthropologists, proving Fermat's last theorem was to mathematicians, reading the Rosetta Stone was to linguists, and breaking the Germans' Enigma code was to the Allies. I'm not saying I can do it, but I am saying that much of the industrial revolution, and thus much of Western culture, is traveling in Daisy's tears.

The Dress Shirt Covers Much

So maybe we should start with the specific object and then try to understand the emotional effect. This focus on the material seems so mundane, so bourgeois, but an object is always at the heart of deluxe. Certainly, one aspect of this scene that we pass by is the role of men's dress shirts in the 1920s. The term *dress shirt* was a recent coinage to separate the formal shirt from the workaday shirt, and it betokened a garment whose primary use was the display of status.

Fitzgerald was one of the first American writers to use brand names instead of generics, so when Gatsby says to Daisy and Nick, "I've got a man in England who buys me clothes. He sends over a selection of things at the beginning of each season, spring and fall," he is telling us something specific. But what that is is often lost on the modern reader.

Gatsby is saying that *English* shirts matter. Until well after the Second World War, the English made the very best shirts in the world. And this was not just because they had the best power looms but because shirtmaking was still a craft of great hands-on sophistication. When the transplanted David Ogilvy wanted to sell Hathaway shirts in the 1950s, he knew what to invoke. Here is the body copy from one of his most famous ads:

> American men are beginning to realize that it is ridiculous to buy good suits and then spoil the effect by wearing an ordinary, mass-produced shirt. Hence the growing popularity of HATHAWAY shirts, which are in a class by themselves.

David Ogilvy's Hathaway shirt man from the 1950s.

The man in the Hathaway shirt

HATHAWAY shirts *wear* infinitely longer—a matter of years. They make you look younger and more distinguished, because of the subtle way HATHAWAY cut collars. The whole shirt is tailored more *generously,* and is therefore more *comfortable.* The tails are longer, and stay in your trousers. The buttons are mother-of-pearl. Even the stitching has an ante-bellum elegance about it.

Above all, HATHAWAY makes their shirts of remarkable *fabrics,* collected from the four corners of the earth—Viyella and Aertex from England, woolen taffeta from Scotland, Sea Island cotton from the West Indies, hand-woven madras from India, broadcloth from Manchester, linen batiste from Paris, hand-blocked silk from England, exclusive cottons from the best weavers in America. You get a great deal of quiet satisfaction out of wearing shirts which are in such impeccable taste.

At the end, just past this peroration, Ogilvy concluded with the comment that he must have known was not true but was true enough. (Anyway, after all the nonsense about "ante-bellum elegance" in the stitching, the reader is too exhausted to care.) In keeping with the Savile Row ethos, he claimed that the shirts are made by "dedicated craftsmen . . . [who] have been at it, man and boy, for one hundred and twenty years."

Now, I am sure that Hathaway's shirtmakers are craftsmen, and I am sure the shirts have been made since 1837, but in the twentieth century they have been made—as Ogilvy surely knew—not by "man and boy" but

In the pink, indeed.

PINK PERFECTION

*'I have the simplest tastes. I am always
satisfied with the best.'*

OSCAR WILDE

by rows of female stitchers. But the point Ogilvy was trying to make is that these are *English* shirts, implying they are made by English shirtmakers.

And well he should have invoked the Englishness of these shirts, for the English had developed all kinds of devices and measures, like the Shoulder Device, which meant that they could produce a custom-made shirt from barrel cuff to straight collar that fit perfectly. It was the envy of the sartorial world. And, of course, when the ad lists the various fabrics, it is clear that most come from the British Empire.

Such handmade dress shirts came in Gatsby's day from the same locale as today, Jermyn Street, where generations of shirtmakers have plied their arduous trade. For instance, the original Thomas Pink made his mark as a bespoke tailor in eighteenth-century London by knowing how to cut, cross-stitch, and especially hand fit his shirts to individual clients. Pink's shirts were not easy to come by. In fact, the phrase "in the pink" describes one's well-being and fiscal health. Back in Thomas Pink's day, if one could afford to have clothes made there, one had rosy prospects indeed. In fact, being in the pink is probably an apt definition of the affect of consuming luxury.[*]

The most demanding part of the shirt was the collar, and this, to those versed in the finer nuances of the craft, is where expertise really shows.

---

[*]One revealing turn of fate: Thomas Pink is now a minor subsidiary of LVMH.

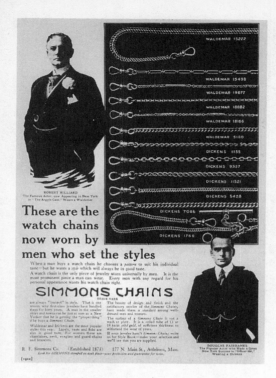

Forget the watch; these vest chains were deluxe emblems of male power in 1912.

Top-quality shirts have a soigné, flattering, quality to the cut of a collar that makes it stand up along the neck without pinching or bunching. To the well-trained eye this soigné-ness is to the shirt what patina is to furniture or what a silversmith's marks are on flatware.

For Gatsby this collar was probably made of two pieces with removable "bones" and sewn flat so the collar would stand up and make the human face look imposing and important. Thus the collar of a shirt was to a man like the neckline to a woman. It defined gender, and when it was aggressively masculine, it tapered out onto the shoulders with the hint of epaulettes. On the platform of the shirt the male wears the vest and on the vest the paradoxical signs of social dominance: chains.

We now scoff at the comment that clothes make the man, but my grandparents' generation didn't. They knew better. Before the appearance of the totally machine-made shirt, the handmade dress shirt was an almost fetishistic component of men's apparel. Men looked at shirts as we now look at cars. Needless to say, the buttons would be real mother-of-pearl.

In true luxe fashion what was once an elegance has become common-

The dress shirt was not always as common as it is today. These ads are from the 1920s.

place. Men's shirts are now in the category of "who cares?" But they were once a display garment, like women's pocketbooks or shoes are today. Collared shirts, dress shirts, white shirts meant that you were not doing day labor, that you were not working with your hands, that you were important, that you were somebody.

Look at ads with the Arrow Shirt man, many by J. C. Leyendecker, roughly contemporaneous to Gatsby, and you can see how the shirt was "positioned" before the appearance of artificial fabrics like polyester and the totally machine-made shirt. With the rise of computer-generated stitching programs, laser cutting "guns," and permanent-press fabrics, the dress shirt as distinctive badge has disappeared, becoming just a T-shirt with collar and long sleeves. Nowadays the only way to generate luxury with a shirt is to put little symbols on the chest, as Brooks Brothers, Ralph Lauren, Yves Saint Laurent, Tommy Hilfiger, et al. do today. Little wonder that the ever-nostalgic J. Peterman catalog carries a Hemingway cap, a D. H. Lawrence waistcoat, and an insignia-free Gatsby shirt.

Daisy's husband, Tom, a man of substance and bearing, certainly had expensive shirts, so these shirts of Gatsby's must be really special, literally marvelous. And they are—not just in number but in various colors—no small feat. That we are being told that they are in "*sheer* linen and *thick* silk and *fine* flannel" means that the skill usually lavished on formal dress is here lavished on Gatsby's everyday wear. This man knows no variations; all is sumptuous, deluxe.

I don't want Daisy's sobbing to carry too much weight. No doubt about it, she is a foil to Nick's gathering sophistication. But I don't want her sobs passed off as shallow materialism. Indeed, she is a kind of debutramp. No doubt. And she neither loves too wisely nor too well. True. But this scene is not the rapture of a luxury bimbo. Recall that our hero, Nick, is also taken in by the blandishments of the material world. He loves the parties, the cars, the liquor, the swimming pool, the good life. He may be able to finally transcend the pleasures of luxury, but we should never pretend that these pleasures are not there or that they are not a major part of his aspirational life. They are.

Mea Culpa: *The Author Experiences the Buchanan Syndrome*

My own little epiphany, my Daisy Buchanan Moment, as I call it, was not so emotive. But it was no less sudden. It happened to me at the men's tie counter at Ralph Lauren's mother ship in Manhattan. This store, the gentrified Rhinelander mansion at what is the top end of Luxury Lane (upper Madison Avenue), is five stories of unmediated Gatsby (née Gatz from Wisconsin) or in this case unadulterated Lauren (née Ralph Lifshitz from the Bronx). It reeks of confected, concocted, pasted-on patina, make-believe family coats of arms, signet rings on demand, and all that is phony about modern luxury. My dad would have gagged before he crossed the threshold.

Everything that is Ralph Lauren's "signature" is here in this store. The signature is writ in huge flowery cursive. And it's just too much. The disease is not Anglophilia, it's Anglomania. This Lauren Unlimited is so Disneyesque a version of Olde England that you half-expect a battery-operated animatronic version of the Great Cham, Dr. Johnson, to be puffing away on a stogie, sunk into one of the overstuffed machine-distressed leather chairs. This place gives *parvenu* a bad name. *Faux* doesn't come close. It is the affliction of affectation.

But, still, I like ties, no matter the setting. I like silk rep ties, not too heavy but heavy enough so you know they are there around your neck. I like the feel of silk when I'm tying one—you know, when you are making the knot and throwing the long end over the short one, how you can have a sense of sort of cracking a whip and being a big shot? I like doing that and I can tie a tie perfectly in about forty-five seconds. When Fitzgerald described Gatsby's shirts as being of *thick* silk, I could feel what he meant.

Well, doing field research for this book, I was moving my hands through the *thick* silk ties in a display box. I was just turning them over while looking at all the terrible bric-a-brac on the walls, all the fake ancestry, etchings of sporting animals, and bookshelves of husks of Victorian novels. Quite suddenly, I felt this terrible rush of pleasure. This stuff, this terrible overpriced stuff, this stuff with that little dreadful polo pony on the fat end of the tie, was making me feel . . . what? Fantastic and a little sad, and in a moment I realized—I *really* wanted one of them.

In a snap, rather like what I imagined Daisy must have felt, I realized the emperor has clothes. All right, I didn't break down and sob, but I gasped that I now knew their attraction. I felt a rush of guilty pleasure and then it was gone, the powers of repression setting me straight once again, protected by the ballast of cynicism. I remember looking up, hoping no one saw my little breakdown.

I have felt the Buchanan Moment before around things. Every September in the 1950s I would ask my dad to take me down to the car showrooms so I could gaze silently with a wild surmise at the new models from Detroit. I would literally hold my breath at the Cadillac dealership. My dad was embarrassed. I remember that, just as he was reading John Kenneth Galbraith's diatribe on Americans' love of luxury, and particularly the tail fin of the 1958 Cadillac, I was also hyperventilating over exactly the same object.

Sell Them Back Their Dreams

Marketers understand this. They even talk about specific luxury objects in terms of "dream values." Here, just listen to a few marketing men:

> Advertising doesn't always mirror how people are acting, but how they're dreaming. . . . In a sense, what we're doing is wrapping up your emotions and selling them back to you.
>
> —Jerry Goodis, *Have I Ever Lied to You Before?* p. 26

> It has often been said that Madison Avenue is in the business of selling dreams. Advertisers have discovered a powerful truth: Dreams sell. Advertisers have learned that they can make their sales pitch more effective if they wrap their products in our dreams and fantasies. There are people in and around advertising (like myself) who spend a good deal of their time trying to understand our dreams—not our individual idiosyncratic dreams, but our collective dreams, America's dreams, the world's dreams.
>
> —Sal Randazzo, *Mythmaking on Madison Avenue*, p. 1

> We are here to sell dreams. When you see a couture show on TV around the world, you dream. When you enter a Dior boutique and buy your lipstick, you buy something affordable, but it has the dream in it.
>
> —Bernard Arnault, CEO, LVMH

And in a recent book, *Selling Dreams: How to Make Any Product Irresistible,* Gian Luigi Longinotti-Buitoni even coins a term, *dreamketing,* meaning dream marketing. Well, he should know. He is the scion of the family that once owned Italy's Buitoni pasta and Perugina chocolate business. He's now head of Ferrari's North American sales. And if ever there was a product drenched in dream value, it's Ferrari. Just mention that name and most boys can hear the distinctive whine. Like Daisy Buchanan, they may even become tearful—well, choked-up.

As Longinotti-Buitoni makes clear, it is exactly the same kind of aura that surrounds all luxe, whether it be a cigarette, a watch, or a bonbon. It's not enough to use the best design or the best distribution system. You must be able to modify the customer's sense of perceived value. You do that, essentially, by telling a story, often something that resembles a fairy tale.

Some years ago the most comprehensive study of upper-level consumption was undertaken in the United States by the International Research Institute on Social Change (RISC). RISC is a consulting group funded by multinational companies based in Switzerland and active in seventeen of the world's major markets. RISC took a representative sample of the U.S. population (aged fifteen and older) and interviewed the group members each fall. The study is still going on, and its findings are occasionally made public (Dubois and Paternault 1995).

In all, three thousand people were interviewed in person, at home, using a combination of self-completed and face-to-face questions. RISC asked respondents about their acquisition habits and feelings relative to a set of thirty-four luxury brands. This "home" list was developed on the basis of answers obtained from an unaided awareness test. A wide variety of objects are represented—perfume, jewelry, fashion, leather goods, alcoholic beverages, stereo equipment, and the like. Here is the list in alphabetical order:

Armani	Lancôme
Bang & Olufsen	Lanvin
Bulgari	Laura Ashley
Cartier	Lenox
Chanel	Louis Vuitton
Chivas Regal	Montblanc
Christian Dior	Omega
Christofle	Oscar De La Renta
Daum	Pierre Cardin
Dunhill	Ralph Lauren
Estée Lauder	Remy Martin
Givenchy	Revlon
Gorham	Rolex
Gucci	Shiseido
Guerlain	Waterford
Hermès	Waterman
Lacoste	Yves Saint Laurent

The home list was generated by weighing three criteria: aided awareness (which brands do you know by name?); recent purchase (what have you bought in the last two years?); and, most interesting, "dream value" (imagine that you are given the possibility of choosing a beautiful present because you won a contest—which would you choose?). On the basis of these categories, the respondents were asked which five brands they liked best.

If Anglo-American culture showed the world *how* to expand and colonize using trade, then the most obvious thing that this list shows is that the French showed *what* to trade. The list contains about as many French as non-French brands, which is consistent with the estimated 50 percent market share enjoyed by French brand names in the worldwide luxury market.

While the awareness and purchase indicators used in generating this list are rather standard, the "dream value" measure deserves additional comment. It is the key to understanding the importance of luxury. When consumers are asked to describe their spontaneous associations with the concept of luxury, the theme of "dream" almost inevitably emerges. In the world of luxury brands here's how it goes: awareness feeds dream, purchase makes dream come true, purchase redirects dreams to the next object.

The essence of the paradoxical nature of the marketing of luxury goods is this: The spirit of Tantalus lives deep in the human breast. We are drawn not so much to inevitable disappointment (although that often happens) but away from melancholy angst.

RISC is too smart to evaluate the nature of human desire for luxury, but I'm not. Once we are fed and sheltered and sexually productive, our needs cease to be biological and culture begins. Luxury objects get value not from production as much as from consumption. Who is buying the object becomes more important than how it is made. The consumers who are most important are naturally those who seem to have resolved their problems. They "have it all"—wealth, power, youth, and, of course, most obvious in advertising, sexual attraction. Such people used to be those who wielded economic, political, military, or even ecclesiastical power. Now we have a new class of aspirational lifestyle, the pure confection of dream value—the consumer of opuluxe, the consumer of dreams. That's Gatsby—the new man of consumerist dreams.

Take a look at how Hermès sells the same unremarkable product, the cravat. Nothing sophisticated about it. The young man is clearly dreaming, and in his dream, coming down from the heavens, is his wish fulfilled. Hermès, Messenger of Dreams, is an entire campaign based on the same trope: the dreamer at the bottom, the object dreamed about coming down from the heavens. Opuluxe does indeed colonize the lands of religion. What makes it modern, of course, is that Hermes delivers his divine message within the walls of a ritzy boutique. Hermes was also the god of commerce.

Hermès, Messenger of Dreams, brings a . . . tie, while Madame Dean, another messenger of dreams, brings a . . . corset.

The placement of the product above the head of the dreamer is hardly happenstance. This is, after all, the world of the sublime (sub = below; limen = threshold). And that this world above the horizon should be intimately connected with the world below consciousness is to be expected. This is the nexus of yearning and redemption.

If you want to see this for yourself, just look at the ads in any fashion magazine, and you will see they are essentially snapshots from a recognizable portfolio of scenes of yearning. They are visual clichés we share of what constitutes the good life or, at least, a life better than the one we are currently living. Little wonder they are coated in the dim half-light of dreamy desire and sleepy wishes.

We All Grow up Through Buchanan Moments

Clearly, these ads for opuluxe are a kind of *Zerrspiegel,* or fun-house mirror, of our inner yearnings. In my own life what happened in the Ralph Lauren store was just one of hundreds of such moments, most of which I experienced during early adolescence. Whether we repress them as we grow older or whether their disappearance is a natural condition of consumption fatigue, I don't know. All I know is that while I was once bombarded by them, I am now entertaining other illusions decidedly less drenched in opulust. In fact, many of my illusions now are informed by the desire to be free of things. To rephrase William Blake's "Proverbs of Hell": The road of excess consumption may finally lead to the palace of Voluntary Simplicity.

As I grew up, I would imagine myself in a tailored suit looking like Gary Cooper. Sometimes just smelling cigar smoke would trigger the fantasy of material wealth. Feeling cashmere, silk, leather, or well-worn pure cotton sheets gave me momentary sensations of yearning. In the 1950s, for reasons best left to analysts, seeing women in Dior suits triggered fantasies of accumulation. I loved magazines like *Life* and *Look* that were full of pictures of stuff and technicolor movies starring Gregory Peck and Cary Grant wearing business suits, driving cars, buying and selling, commuting on the train, having big offices, toting attaché cases.°

I can't have many Buchanan Moments at my age on my salary, so most of them have to be memories. Still, I remember them vividly. I experienced a powerful one in Cripple Creek, Colorado, in the summer of 1952 when I was nine. For my birthday I got a pair of elegant cowboy boots. I had always loved boots. In fact, I had really wanted a Royal Canadian Mounted Police uniform, complete with high black boots, that I had seen in the FAO Schwarz catalog. Things are power. I know this desire is at the heart of jackbooted fascism, and I usually repress it. But I didn't know it then.

So when I was a tyke, I rhapsodized over those new cowboy boots. They took my breath away. I was so excited when I got them that I wore them to bed. And the next day I tucked my pants into the top of the boots, even though my dad had introduced me to a real cowboy who said that this was not the style. Although I loved them, their beauty made me strangely sad.

°In fact, I think the abiding allure to adolescents of such barely repressed sexual myths of conquest *and* consumption (as in the James Bond sagas, for instance) is that it allows us to put objects into a predictable pattern so that we know the car, the champagne, the cigarette, the watch, the hotel well before the entertainment begins, before the female lead appears, and we can dream the dream. Little wonder that the price of product placement for Bond movies is higher than for any other genre.

They were not perfect for long. I was distraught when they got dirty, rather the way owners of off-road SUVs must feel when the Lexus RX 300 cruiser gets muddy.

Another bittersweet blast of luxury fever blew over me in the parking lot in Stowe, Vermont, at the base of Mount Mansfield after a day of skiing. I was about fifteen. Someone from New York City had left his Aston Martin idling while he was in the warming hut. A cluster of teenage boys stopped in their tracks and just listened to that car. No one dared get near it. When I backed away, I had tears in my eyes. Were they from the exhaust? I was totally confused that I could feel so strongly about a car. Later, at Christmas, I remember thinking that I could understand how the wise men felt as they beheld the Christ child in Bethlehem. I knew it was sacrilegious to make such a comparison, but I also knew it was true. I also felt a little sad that such a beautiful thing should exist, that I could never have it, that it would go away.

The Buchanan Moment as Plot Device

Although we usually don't understand the new luxury in this manner, if you observe popular culture, you will see it being attested to in the most materialistic of the television genres, the sitcom. For here, in the intimacy of the sitcom, we find the dynamics of individual yearning for specific luxury objects played out over and over. Critics contend that it is exactly this repetitive plot device, from Lucy's wanting a fur coat in the 1950s to the deep material aspirations of the young couple starting out—be they traditional like Rob and Laura of *The Dick Van Dyke Show* or slightly off-center like *Will and Grace*—that fuels the materialism of young America. But I say just the opposite: What we are seeing here more nearly mirrors what we all move through, namely, the palliative dream powers of opuluxe.

Remember how George Costanza so rhapsodizes about velvet on *Seinfeld* that he gives up his apartment and moves in with a girlfriend in order to surround himself with the fabric? In true *Seinfeld* fashion the material obsession is indulged only to be then parodied. George finds out that all the velvet furniture is not owned by the girlfriend but by her boyfriend. When the boyfriend comes to gather his velvet, George is distraught. All ends happily as the parties work out a ménage à trois or, really, including the velvet, ménage à quatre. Still, it is George's exultation, his erotic pleasure—in what? a fabric!—that we all understand.°

Now I admit that putting forward an explanation of the dream value of the luxury impulse by invoking a southern belle from fiction, a loopy second banana from television, and a tenured college professor is something even Judge Wapner would throw out of court. If you want to be reminded of the dream's power, just turn back to chapter 2 and look again at that *Saturday Evening Post* cover of August 15, 1950.

Better yet, go back into nineteenth-century literature and observe the interest in deluxe of the first generation of artists who dealt in the fruits of the industrial revolution. For here in literary culture you will see an unselfconscious interest in the world of things just before the Victorians attached shame controls.

Opuluxe in High Culture

For instance, look at Fitzgerald's favorite poet, John Keats, describing another lover, Porphyro, who, like Gatsby and his shirts, piles up luxuries to tempt the object of his affection, Madeline. Here in the climax to *The Eve of St. Agnes* Porphyro rolls out his temptations.

> *While he from forth the closet brought a heap*
> *O candied apple, quince, and plum and gourd;*
> *With jellies smoother than the creamy curd,*
> *And Lucent syrops, tinct with cinnamon;*
> *Manna and dates, in argosy transferr'd*
> *From Fez, and spiced dainties, every one,*
> *From Silken Samarcand to cedar'd Lebanon.*
> *These delicacies he heap'd with glowing hand*
> *On golden dishes and in baskets bright*
> *Of wreathed silver: sumptuous they stand*
> *In the retired quiet of the night,*

°As Morris Holbrook explains in *Daytime Television Game Shows and the Celebration of Merchandise,* this feeling runs deep, especially for viewers of *The Price Is Right.* Look, see, desire, scream.

Filling the chilly room with perfume light. —
"And no, my love, my seraph fair, awake!
Thou art my heaven, and I thine eremite
                    (264–77)

Just as Gatsby has gone to his closet to find the shirts to wow his love, these comestibles that Porphyro wheels out seem to do the trick as well. Madeline moves into the dream world of luxury and then returns to the here and now:

Her eyes were open, but she still beheld,
Now wide awake, the vision of her sleep:
There was a painful change, that nigh expell'd
The blisses of her dream so pure and deep:
At which fair Madeline began to weep,
And moan forth witless words with many a sigh;
While still here gaze on Porphyro would keep;
Who knelt, with joined hands and piteous eye,
Fearing to move or speak, she look'd so dreamily
                    (298–306)

I am not trying to defend the invocation of the luxurious (at least not yet). I am only trying to establish that the reaction to the material world can often be profound and transformative because it draws so much from dreamland. Salvation that used to be promised in the world beyond is now sited in the world of the here and now. But the promise is the same: Consume this sacred potion and, like Alice, you will go deep into Wonderland.

Just look, for instance, at the Victorian novelists' concern with what is now the grubby world of commerce, and you will see that for them the land of luxury was the land of peace and contentment. Yes, they are suspicious and, yes, they criticize it, but the allure is undeniable. The literal stuff of a moneyed life is at the center of Thackery's *Vanity Fair,* the obsessive concerns of almost everything written by Dostoyevsky, the comic center of Gogol's fictional world, and the metronome of Trollope's masterful *The Way We Live Now*. Think only of the role of property, that necessary luxury of Edwardian times—the estate—and you will see how it forms the magnetic center of almost all the novels of Arnold Bennett and H. G. Wells. No wonder that the country mansion in Galsworthy's *Forsythe Saga* is almost a character to generations of materialists, be they consumers or spurners of the consumerist ideology.

And what of the American novels of the Gilded Age, novels by Henry James and Edith Wharton? What are James's late novels *about* if not about how luxury has settled into the social matrix, replacing abstract concepts like ancestry, club, and church. These people now have money. What are they going to do with it? What can they do with it? What does it mean? From a middle novel like *The Portrait of a Lady* to the late novels like *The Ambassadors, The Golden Bowl,* or *The Wings of the Dove,* the dilemma is the same. In a world untethered from received tradition, consumption of things takes on a metaphysical meaning. It becomes a way of creating the self and making it meaningful.

What was intricate and labored in James became more accessible in the novels of Wharton. Consumption is not defended in *The House of Mirth* and *The Age of Innocence* as much as it is simply acknowledged as the new way of organizing social position. Identity in Wharton's world is forged not so much with personality as with object display. Your social value comes not from within but from your external associations; you are classified almost from birth by your passage through things. Wharton's protagonists, from Lily Bart in the *House of Mirth* (1905) to Newland Archer in *The Age of Innocence* (1920), may rail against the mindless cant of a predatory system based on this new kind of "hieroglyphic display," but neither can overcome it. Her characters are every bit as trapped in a commodified system of tradition as those of Henry James. What finally separates them is the knowledge that they cannot escape. This new economic order based on conformity, envy, emulation, and display, the order so presciently explained by Veblen, has still not been subverted. It is, in fact, becoming accepted.

American culture of the twentieth century is still perplexed by this conundrum, however. Have we made a devil's bargain to exchange an old order based on abstract concepts of blood and faith for a new order based on concrete demonstration of goods and badges? On one hand, the material world has produced a cornucopia of plenty, the foamy top of which has been opuluxe. On the other hand, if such rarified objects carry meaning in the modern world, then those disenfranchised from such things are separated from meaning as well. That critical strain is apparent in Fitzgerald and Sinclair Lewis (recall Babbitt's yearnings for opulxue) and glaringly obvious in writers like Frank Norris, Theodore Dreiser, Jack London, Ring Lardner, and John Steinbeck.

When you look to see where this impulse is in the modern novel, you end up with the work of authors like Bret Easton Ellis and Tom Wolfe, for whom the material world is bloated, stultifying, and oppressive. But it is also highly charged with the systems of social value. Here, for example, is a modern version from Ellis's *American Psycho*:

> Price and I walk down Hanover Street in the darkest moments of twilight and as if guided by radar move silently toward Harry's. Price seems nervous and edgy and I have no desire to ask him what's wrong. He's wearing a linen suit by Canali Milano, a cotton shirt by Ike Behar, a silk tie by Bill Blass and cap-toed leather lace-ups from Brooks Brothers. I'm wearing a lightweight suit with pleated trousers. a cotton shirt, a dotted silk tie, all by Valentino Couture, and perforated cap-toe leather shoes by Allen-Edmonds. Once inside Harry's we spot David Van Patten and Craig McDermott at a table up front. Van Patten is wearing a double-breasted wool and silk sport coat, button-fly wool and silk trousers with inverted pleats by Mario Valentino, a cotton shirt by Gitman Brothers, a polka-dot silk tie by Bill Blass and leather shoes from Brooks Brothers. McDermott is wearing a woven-linen suit with pleated trousers, a button-down cotton and linen shirt by Basile, a silk tie by Joseph Abboud and ostrich loafers from Susan Bennis Warren Edwards.
>
> The two are hunched over the table, writing on the backs of paper napkins, a Scotch and martini placed respectively in front of them. They wave us over. Price throws his Tumi leather attache case on an empty chair and heads toward the bar. I call out to him for a J&B on the rocks, then sit down with Van Patten and McDermott.
>
> "Hey Bateman," Craig says in a voice that suggests this is not his first martini. "Is it proper to wear tasseled loafers with a business suit or not? Don't look at me like *I'm* insane."
>
> "Oh, shit, *don't* ask Bateman," Van Patten moans, waving a gold Cross pen in front of his face, absently sipping from the martini glass.
>
> "Van Patten?" Craig says.
>
> "Yeah?"
>
> McDermott hesitates, then says, "Shut up" in a flat voice.   (226–27)

What we are witnessing is the commodification of distinction: The trophies that once beckoned to us from the highest shelf have been brought down to eye level. They have been democratized, shared, drained, and now made ironic.

The Stendhal Syndrome

That art—painting, to be specific, not literature—should also be the conduit for the display of luxury is a paradox with a perplexing history. Return for a moment to the nineteenth century, before advertising and commercial culture captured the idea of luxury and made it both alluring and suspect. In 1817, at almost the same time that Keats was writing *The Eve of St. Agnes,* Stendhal was visiting Florence. In the Church of Santa Croce he was overwhelmed by the frescoes of Giotto. He noted the symptoms in his diary: rapid and irregular heart beat, a sensation of melancholy as if his life was draining away, feeling faint. In fact, he feared he would fall down. So he went outside to a bench, where he was revived by reading the poetry of Ugo Foscolo. Stendhal had seen something lavish, transcendentally opulent, and he was profoundly disoriented.

Now what separates the Stendhal Syndrome, as it is known in psychiatric literature, from the Buchanan Moment, as it is known in these pages, is both the trigger and our response to the stimulus. While we consider it fashionable to feel faint in front of a great work of art, or in front of a religious icon (Jerusalem is the third most common venue in which to be struck with this affliction, after Florence and Ravenna), it is certainly not something to contract down at Bloomingdale's or out in Las Vegas. Yet that is exactly where many of us go to achieve it.

It becomes the job of advertising, of what was then called attentioning, to site the sensation in manufactured objects. Ironically, romanticism, which seems forever at loggerheads with materialism, is a backhanded acknowledgment of the conjunction of mild euphoria and consumption. Wordsworth is forever criticizing the rise of urbanism, Blake is wary of the mass production of anything, let alone art, Shelley rails against mob taste, while Coleridge confesses his attraction to this new "hedonistic self-consciousness." Like it or not, social status, consumer behavior, and mild euphoria were starting to crisscross.

Here at the headwaters of the industrial revolution, luxury bubbles up in the strangest places. For instance, the early nineteenth century marked the first time a simple machine-made mutation, say, a color like Waterloo blue, became a subject of intense anticipation and meaning. Young women flocked to this color as they now cluster around some purse concocted by Gucci and displayed in *Vanity Fair.*

So here we have one Elizabeth Grant, daughter of an Edinburgh lawyer and landowner, describing a process never before seen in middle-class life and now, in the modern world, never not seen:

> We were inundated this whole winter [1815–16] with a deluge of a dull ugly colour called Waterloo blue, copied from the dye used in Flanders for the calico of which the peasantry make their smock frocks or blouses. Every thing new was Waterloo, not unreasonably, it had been such a victory, such an event, after so many years of exhausting suffering. And as a surname to hats, coats, trowsers, instruments, furniture it was very well—a fair way of trying to perpetuate the return of tranquillity; but to deluge us with that vile indigo, so unbecoming even to the fairest! It was really a punishment!
>
> (1911, 2:35)

Although Grant acknowledges the connection between consumption and meaning, between color and nationalism, the desire to express social belonging through affiliation with manufactured things was exactly what rattled the poets. Yet getting to this sensation was why the poets were so peripatetic, forever seeking the sublime in waterfalls of the Lake District, in the Simplon Pass, vistas on the Mediterranean coast. The poets even gave it a name. It was a "glory" experience, literally incandescent, awesome, *glorious*.

Before High Culture Was High It Was Often Lowly

In the modern world this sensation of experiencing awe in the material world can be found in two seemingly different places: in advertising and in art. Since I spend most of my time detailing its colonization and exploitation in commercial speech, let me quickly gloss it in "art appreciation." Read Holbein's painting, done well before the industrial revolution.

Assuming you know nothing about this image, what would you guess it says? Show this painting to a ten-year-old and you'll find out. Its point: "the things I have got" and, by extension, "the things you haven't got." For these are not whimsical things but sumptuous things, things that show who I am and that I am someone special. The men who stand in the painting—so obviously at ease with themselves—know what they are wearing, know what they are leaning on, know what they hold, know what we have to look at. They are certainly not wearing those clothes because they are comfortable. They have told the photographer/painter exactly when to snap the shutter.

Hans Holbein the Younger,
The French Ambassadors,
1533.
Courtesy of the Trustees of the
National Gallery, London

Don't even worry about any symbolism because, before all else, this image is about transcendental materialism, about the allure of luxury, of the sensations of display.

What is ironic is how our response to the picture has changed over time. When Holbein painted this image of the two French ambassadors in 1533, the objects with which the men self-consciously surround themselves were valuable *and* meaningful. The lute, the celestial globe, hymn book, telescope, Ottoman rug, merchant accounting log, surveyor's square, compasses, the arithmetic book are all signs of conquest and power, stuff to supply to conquistadors on their expeditions to gather yet more lucre. There is nothing haphazard here, this is the stuff of exploration, and exploration will demand the services of these ambassadors. They were venture capitalists—successful ones.

The curiously represented skull, which dominates the bottom of the painting, is a conventional *vanitas* symbol, not so much undercutting the luxury of objects as perhaps a memento mori, an acknowledgment that this too will pass. So in a sense these venture capitalists get it both ways: They get to show off their stuff *and* show how righteous they are. They get to appear at church in the chauffeured limo. He who dies with the most toys wins *and* gets to go to heaven.

Art history has a term for these so carefully arranged objects. They are called objets d'art not because they are objects *of* art—that is the modern configuration—but because they are objects worthy of being included *in* art. What they are really saying is what luxury always says, what Ozymandias shouted, "Look on my Works, ye Mighty, and despair!" Just a little envy, please, they seem to say. First, look at my stuff; then, judge me. If you dare.

The Tradition of Art as Vehicle of Luxury

And, in a way, we still give in. We don't look upon the objects *in* the work and feel the breath move out of us, we look *at* the work that depicts them, the framed work of oil paint on canvas, and gasp. Thanks to the followers of Stendhal, we have *learned* to fall faint before these works, but that is not to say that we don't faint away elsewhere. Because we do. Interestingly enough, the other places where the Stendhal effect occurs, after religious shrines and high culture museums, is at Disney World.

At the end of the nineteenth century, the most common place for women to faint was just inside the doors of the department store. To generate the sense of easy availability of luxury, department store managers would often pile shiny goods on shelves near the store entrance so passersby would think that a luscious cornucopia was just across the threshold. As Émile Zola wrote in his novel *Ladies' Paradise* (1883), a common street sight in Paris was so many shoppers milling at the store entrance that they spilled onto the street. "It should seem to people in the street as if a riot were taking place . . . that the shop was bursting with people, when often it was only half-full" (17).

Once inside, women were trapped in a glittering Aladdin's cave where everything was easy to touch and proximity to the ineffable was disconcerting. Before they became house police, the primary job of store walkers was to escort ladies safely through the emporium so they would not be excited by the goods. The early department stores were called lands of enchantment for a reason: They were magical.

It would be wrong, however, to see this as a woman's affliction. Oddly enough, it was Walter Benjamin, the dyspeptic and melancholy Marxist, who understood the transcendent joys of touch and feel in regard to manufactured objects. In *The Arcades Project,* an unstrung and often bleary paean to shopping the small streets and cubbyholes of Paris, Benjamin described the joys of the flâneur. The stroller in the dream world of objects, says Benjamin, is often taken into the world of slumber where the luxury of others becomes the indulgence of the self. The division between mine and yours is erased. Suffering what is rather like a contact high, the flâneur finds in the jumble of arcade opuluxe the momentary stays against confusion. He finds the eroticism of looking (scopophilia), the pleasures of touch, the celebration of finery, and the missing self, the sensual self.

Public Luxury Started by Those Who Battle Mammon

Benjamin urges us to realize that, from time to time, we need to acknowledge the power of luxury objects; these are the reciprocal demands of objects of desire. They own us; we own them. He is distraught at what private ownership does to this equation. And deeply nostalgic.

Certainly, in the art world we realize that the Renaissance was a time of exuberant and often bravura ownership of luxury by individuals. All manner of objects were gathered, decorated, and painted as personal display items, what today would be called positional goods. From the fifteenth century onward a handful of princes and super-rich clerics flaunted possessions to a degree not seen since the fall of Rome. Rather like the Gulfstream jets of our own dot-com billionaires, the great palaces of Mehmed II, the damask robes of the doge of Venice, the gemstones of Cardinal Francesco Gonzaga, and the tapestries of Charles V were part and parcel of a cult of aggressive individual display. When Antonio Cardinal Barberini died in Rome in 1671, his art collection, which he had hauled behind him from one palace to another, included 116 cartloads of paintings and 91 cartloads of sculptures, medals, busts, figurines, and pedestals, along with a large harp.

The German economist Werner Sombart argued in his *Luxury and Capitalism* (1938) that it was precisely such expenditures by the Vatican and the courts in the late Middle Ages that laid the groundwork for modern markets. True, private luxury was rather like our own, be it in the Renaissance, the Gilded Age, or the Age of Silicon. But at the same time public luxury was being amassed inside the very institution dedicated to often decrying its consumption, namely, the church.

Nothing so spread the lure of materialism as the Vatican, which knew one thing above all: Things that shine gather a crowd. Here was arguably the most material-oriented religion ever developed, not so much because the church fathers wanted it that way but because the parishioners clearly did—and could afford it. As with demons in general, Mammon became both a scapegoat of desire and an avatar of yearning.

The Relic as Community Luxury

Consider the relic. The late medieval church announces the absolute centrality of materialism by being constructed around a specific object. This magic totem, of sometimes outrageous and always dubious provenance, is housed in a reliquary, the more ornate the better. A box is then placed over this box, and over that another, until finally, voilà, the actual soaring cathedral, so massive it had to be supported by huge flying buttresses. When a new church was being constructed, often a shard of an already "certified" relic was transported into the new glittering box.

More likely, however, the rarity had to be "bought" on the open market in a most curious manner. The act of purchase was theft. Relics were often "stolen" by the very religious order that owned them, because only when an item had been stolen could the religious assert its luxury value. Because no market of buyers and sellers existed for relics—how could you ever be so sacrilegious as to sell a relic?—its theft meant that the object had worth. As we are learning, theft was a economic device of not just franchising wares but also of maintaining market value. We are aghast at the medieval commerce in what are so clearly bogus relics housed in such magnificent containers. But in many ways the traffic in relics is a mimic of the market for luxury—think precious stones, oil paintings, rare books—in which attributed value trumps any intrinsic value. Put it under glass, put it in a museum, put it near other objects of certified value, and you have just made it luxurious.

Ecclesiastical Objects Deluxe

The magic of luxury is the hallmark of the physical church as well as of the service. For instance, the mass itself is centered around the transubstantiation. Such magic almost demands an elaborate panoply of fancy objects, all of them capable of being fabricated to the highest standards. Furnishings such as altars, thrones, lecterns, scepters, croziers, umbrellas, fans, and, above all, the trappings and equipment needed for public processions and celebrations are all over the place. Liturgical apparatus of all kinds were used, then cast aside as newer models appeared—flashier models, bigger tail fins, more chrome, fancier countertops, ones more likely to arrest audience attention.

Convincing a populace that this is not bread and wine but the blood and flesh of the Redeemer would tax even the most experienced juggler of signifiers, so of course the objects of transubstantiation were continually overarticulated. In fact, this last-to-be-introduced sacrament had proved to be in continual need of reification and luxurification. Predictably, of all the liturgical objects the chalice is the most important to decorate. In fact, it is one of the most important containers in all Western culture, invariably deluxe. For this container is not just magical in itself but holds the central mystery of the entire religion. Transubstantiation happens beneath its brim. No other object in all Christendom is like this vessel and none the focus of more intense obsession. Entire crusades were dedicated to finding the actual chalice, the Holy Grail; little wonder the mimics were so ornate.

While the chalice is the most overwrought luxury object in the church, the Catholic mass is filled with a massive inventory of display items such as patens, caskets, chasubles, pyxes, tabernacles, plates, screens, candlesticks, bells, ewers, cruets, stoles, and ladles. Of course, this material bloat was exactly what so disturbed Martin Luther and caused him to call for a return to prosaic objects, thereby moving luxury from the public to the private sector.

Until the seventeenth century, however, those churches that prospered had one thing in common: intense luxurious decoration. Not only were they literally covered from top to bottom with ecclesiastical decoration like mosaics and murals but inside frescos were painted, often one on top of another, some lasting only a few years.

The internal spaces of the Renaissance church had the look of the glossy pages of modern magazines. While it may be heresy to compare flipping through the pages of the four pounds of *Vogue* with a trip through the Cornaro Chapel of the Church of Santa Maria della Vittoria in Rome, the journeys are not dissimilar. Altars were assembled, dismantled, and reconstructed with regularity. Panel paintings were moved around, taken out on parade, stored, traded, sold, repainted, cast aside. So too were illustrated manuscripts—holy books—made, showcased, and stored. It is almost as if the simple chalice had exploded as new technologies allowed public demonstration of communal riches.

The Book as Luxe Object

As is typical of the history of competitive consumption, one commodity jumped loose and became not just a signifier of wealth but also a carrier of information. First the chalice, then the book. The book, which had long been a decorative object and not a conduit of knowledge, became, as it moved from church icon to library display to scholarly apparatus to technical manual, a central repository of information. What was once valued primarily as an object to decorate became an object to transport valuable information.

We never refer to this ecclesiastical ornamentation as conspicuous consumption. Galbraithians never arch eyebrows over this. Please, shhhh, this is Art. Ecclesiastical luxury moves into art history as the baroque, then the rococo. It may seem ridiculous, but certainly no mention is ever made of the massive waste that might have been better spent on servicing the needs of the poor, building schools, repairing the infrastructure. We never mention its proximity to the ridiculousness of Cadillac fins; we never compare the high Renaissance with consumption fiascoes from the Dutch tulip bulbs to Internet IPOs; and we never see ourselves as acting out the same anxieties of making meaning through the material world. But it is luxurious indulgence nonetheless; call it what you will.

Going Dutch

Renaissance luxury, while the headwaters of modern opuluxe, was still too confined and private, albeit displayed in public spaces. Even in its final eruption in the seventeenth century, the baroque and rococo styles were fitted to objects far from common hands although in full view of common people. To find the real precursor to modern luxury one might look at objects painted with such passion in the Dutch Republic, 1585–1718. Here we see, really for the first time in the West, a joy in simply being aware of things, having things, showing them off, valuing them in terms of expense. The new bell tower on the Westerkirk in Amsterdam, the arrival of lapis lazuli from China, the fresh vegetables in the market, the carcass of an armadillo, all these were painstakingly rendered as things first, symbols later. While the Dutch memorialized common and everyday objects, they subtly implied the inner sanctification of these items.

Again, one asks the question: Why were these objects subjects for lux-urification? It is not entirely satisfying to contend that the painters chose these objects and chose to be so meticulous in painting them on their own. No, what seems more likely is that here was a culture that took joy in fine things, a joy in showing off these things, a joy in expanding an aesthetic cat-egory to include more things. In this sense the Dutch were the first to down-market luxury or to upmarket everyday things.

Looking at Dutch *pronck*, or still life painting, one has a sense of sheen and glitter that one now usually sees on the pages of those thudding ad-fat magazines coming from Condé Nast. As it does when you are paging through *Vogue* or *Vanity Fair,* this stuff comes at you with unremitting earnestness. Who cares what the objects are? The fantasy of having expen-sive things, things almost in your hand, things you recognize, things that fill the page and bleed over the margin, is almost palpable.

In many ways the Dutch Republic, not the Italian city-state like Siena or Florence, is most similar to modern America in its desire to luxurify the commonplace. On one hand, the Dutch economy was held together by a ruling oligarchy of business interests, of sustained economic growth pre-sided over by principles of hard work. On the other hand, here was a cul-ture that let loose the forces of spending and speculation, not by public au-thorities (such as the City Chamber of Marine Insurance or the Wisselbank) but private forces (such as the Dutch East India Company and the Dutch West India Company). Here was an entrepreneurial culture in the bud. The flood of money ebbed and flowed then as it does now, some of it making its way into collectible objects. And those objects, which could be classified, inventoried, priced, owned, and displayed, were memorial-ized by being painted. Those objects became deluxe objects. For the first time in the West luxury objects were not religious, but they were iconic: These were images of the good life, of personal salvation.°

°Look at the titles of scholarly books on the Dutch still life and you get a sense of what was happening to the empire of things: *A Prosperous Past: The Sumptuous Still-Life in The Netherlands, 1600–1700* (Sam Segal); *The Embarrassment of Riches: An Introduction to Dutch Culture* (Simon Schama); or *A Worldly Art: The Dutch Republic* (Mariet Westermann). You get the point. One has the feeling that even before scholars saw what was happening, the Dutch *pronck* painters would gather and complain about how to break through the clutter of compet-ing imagery, much like modern ad execs complaining about the density of commercialism, the very forest of images they have created.

The Luxury of Tulips

Very often some object of middling value broke loose, crossed the tipping point, entered opuluxe, and the market went bonkers. In the Florentine city-state the various church orders or entitled families bid up the prices of, who is it today? Giotto, Michelangelo, Da Vinci? In our world what is it today? A baguette handbag from Fendi? A Hermès scarf? A Porsche Boxster? An Armani suit? In the Dutch Republic, for the first time, individuals had the wherewithal to act alone or in concert to drive objects into the land of luxury. And did they ever.

Often the trigger for frenzied consumption was a new way of seeing an object, a new background, a re-siting. Open any glossy magazine today, and you will see the same process as we are presented with motor cars, handbags, designer clothing, or bottled water, again and again, in beautiful, positively *pronck* advertisements. Every once in a while the context fits and—ka-zam!—the object moves into a new aesthetic and economic category—ka-ching! The buzz starts, the object becomes hot, lines start to form.

For a few years in the early seventeenth century it was the now-humble tulip that let us have a peek at luxury fever in the modern world. Here for the first time in the West we can see the dynamics of consumption played out by the newly affluent and socially anxious. Although hundreds of objects have followed tulip trajectory since, the only previous analogy would be the art markets of the Greek, Roman, and Chinese cultures and then the explosive trade in relics during the Middle Ages. Forget aesthetics. What made a knucklebone of St. Francis an object of desire was not that it was ever proved to be said bone; it was valuable because other people desired it.

While the tulips' general journey into the Land of Manic Desire is well known, a few stops along the way are worth consideration. First, a little background. Tulips were introduced to western Europe from Turkey in the sixteenth century. The Austrian ambassador to Turkey gave some bulbs to Carolus Clusius, a scientist from Vienna who was in charge of the Dutch garden of medicinal plants. Clusius successfully propagated the bulbs in the sandy and humid soil that stretches along the North Sea between Leyden and Haarlem.

Tulips were already an extraordinary flower long before the Dutch had a go at rebreeding them. They had been cultivated in the garden of Sultan

Mehmed II in Constantinople since 1451, but botanists now made them meaningful by making them allusive, poetic, metaphoric. What made this possible was a congenital peculiarity that asserted itself when the bulbs were aggressively cross-pollinated. Some became susceptible to a virus that caused the pure colors of the original flower to break up, producing an unpredictable streaking effect. They became kaleidoscopic.

Today we think it strange that people could have fixated on this. Then we go down to the mall and have a serious conversation about the diamond we are considering. We talk about color, cut, weight, and clarity, forgetting that this is just a stone that, if market conditions were not obsessively manipulated by a cartel *and* our hunger for symbols, would go for about the cost of a car battery. Maybe a flashlight battery.

Horticulturists soon discovered that they could multiply the most eye-catching tulip blooms by taking offsets from their bulbs, a slow process that accounted for the rarity and price of their best specimens. In other words, horticulturists could tease streaking out of the flower almost as if it were a canvas to be brushed with oil paint. The problem of unpredictability only added to its value. And that, in a sense, was part of what made it luxurious.

To have the leisure to exploit this unpredictable beauty meant that the tulip soon became an accessory to class and a sign of wealth. Would your tulip "break" into coruscations of color? Would you find that your plain-colored tulip in the fall would emerge the next spring as a fabulous multicolored flower with petals feathered and flamed in intricate patterns? The tulip was both a lottery ticket and a diamond in a Tiffany box. It was precious; it might become more so. It was like having pre-IPO stock in an Internet firm. You wait for the pop when it goes public. But, of course, the tulip was better in one regard. It was beautiful, often startling, to look at.

Plus, just as luxury products often extend themselves from different home brands (you can buy a standard Cadillac, a Coup de Ville, an Eldorado, a limo, an Esplanade SUV . . .), it was perfectly possible that the seeds from an all-red tulip might suddenly produce bulbs with white streaks. Offsets from this next bulb would be streaked too. Like luxury car nameplates, those with red streaks on a yellow ground were called bizarres, those with carmine markings on a white ground were roses, those with near black, deep purple variegations on a white ground were bybloemens, and so on, creating a veritable explosion of brand extensions.

Dreary science would show that "breaking" results from a virus that affects the pigment in a tulip's petals. But not until the twentieth century was the scientific reason for this determined: Aphids spread the the virus. How common! From 1634 to 1637, though, the flowers were seen as valuable freaks of nature, freaks that could be taught to perform magic. Like all things luxurious, they were unpredictable. Holding them makes you somehow more special. And not being able to control them only emphasizes their dreamlike whimsy.

The tulip was the first luxury object in the nascent mass market. Although it shared much with the holy relic, the supply and demand for the tulip was genuinely democratic. Two other matters made it modern. First, gardening for show, rather than for subsistence or medicinal purposes, had only begun to catch on in the sixteenth century and was clearly a rich person's pastime. The Netherlands, then the hub of European commerce, had more than its fair share of wealthy planters. And, second, the very culture that focused on such flowers also lavished patronage and provided the robust market for still life painting.

These phenomena are related because the value of objects must be communicated, must be *ad-vert*-ized. People must *turn* their attention to the object. Remember that luxury is always socially constructed. Desire comes not from an isolated individual but is the act of unconscious collusion, of reaching the tipping point. The two fancies of planting and painting fed off each other, just as today manufacturing and marketing go hand in hand. Remember, when you are buying the luxury object, you are really buying the advertising. When you bought the tulip bulb, you were buying the painting.

Painters like Rachel Ruysch, Jan Brueghel the Elder, Ambrosius Bosschaert, Jan de Heem, Balthasar van der Ast, Dirck van Delen, and Jan van Huysum relished the tulips' bizarre patterns and colors. The painters found a ready market among the blooms' proud owners for memorializing their flowers' bounty. Needless to say, the prices they obtained for their paintings did not begin to match those of the most expensive bulbs. Not then, because the tulip was the real luxury. Now, of course, the paintings are the luxuries and their prices, ironically, perhaps, but tellingly, are every bit as tempestuous as those for the bulb had been. Do you think that someday people will collect advertising the way we collect paintings? It's already happening.

Dirck van Delen, Still Life with
Tulip in a Chinese Vase, *1637.*
John Brewer and Roy Porter, *Consumption
and the World of Goods* (New York:
Routledge, 1993), fig. 23.2.

Oil Paint Advertises the Value of Tulips

The paintings added value to the tulips, just as advertising adds value to otherwise interchangeable objects. When you hear ad execs talk about "adding
value" to objects, they are essentially arguing that by adding meaning to fungible objects, they can hype perceived value. Ad agencies were hardly the
first to understand that luxury resides not in the thing but in the language
that sites it. Church fathers and oil painters had been there before.

In a synergy weirdly predictive of Pop Art, the oil paint version of the
common object made the actual thing more alluring. And vice versa. Pictures increased in value, albeit at a much slower rate, in lockstep with the
tulips. Jan van Huysum, the great master of Dutch flower painting, could
rarely command more than 5,000 guilders for a canvas. But at an auction
in 1637, when tulipmania was in full flower, a trader paid 4,000 guilders,
the equivalent of a year's wages, for a single bulb (Dirkse 1999:12F).

It doesn't take much imagination to see the similarities between this
typical still life of a tulip and any number of modern ads. Take the object,

put it near another object of recognized value, and let the value flow from certified object of value to aspiring object. In fact, in ad lingo this is called borrowing value. The nautilus cone to the left of the flower signifying the complexities of nature, and the Chinese vase to the right, signifying, especially to a culture well versed in pottery, the handicraft of artisans, gives the tulip increased value.

Ever wonder why luxury cars are invariably pictured in ads next to artworks, country clubs, heroic vistas? Well, the Dutch knew why. In an interesting twist on this phenomenon of borrowed value we now place objects not inside the work of art but next to them. Proximity generates allure. Value leaks from the work of art to the mass-produced object.

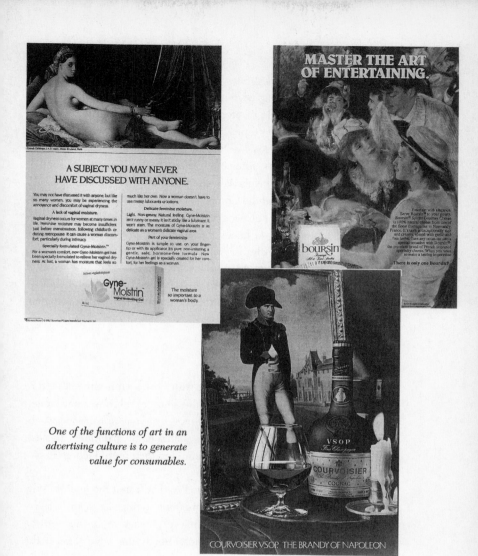

One of the functions of art in an
advertising culture is to generate
value for consumables.

Books for collectors, which were often illustrated with precise still lifes
of tulips, functioned like today's auction catalog. In much the same way
that the estates of, say, Jackie Onassis or the duke and duchess of Windsor
are sold to an eager public not by foregrounding the objects but rather according to the value of preceding ownership, so too these bulbs had value
based on who had already bought them. As well, Dutch burghers, unable
to afford individual bulbs, commissioned paintings by masters whose works

were considered cheap substitutes for the real flowers. Are teenage boys with Porsche ads and Ferrari posters on their bedroom walls any different? We who live in a world of eternal Ponzi schemes, trickle-down economics, state-supported lotteries, new improved Tide, diamond rings, Land Rovers in the city, designer clothing, Great Big Bertha golf clubs, bottled water from glaciers, filter tips, premium gas, and vitamin supplements are amazed by tulipmania. We who pshaw the Inquisition, the South Sea Bubble, witchcraft, and the Compagnie d'Occident always end up big-eyed in amazement at the behavior of the Dutch. That single bulbs of certain kinds of tulips changed hands for sums that would have secured a townhouse in the best quarter of Amsterdam or the equivalent of fifteen years' wages for the average Amsterdam bricklayer boggles our sense of proportion. Then we snap the cap on a $1.50 bottle of Evian water and call our broker to buy shares in an Internet company with a great-sounding name and no prospect of profits.

Tulipmania Was Not a Fluke

Often overlooked in our befuddlement with how such a rational culture could have been so hoodwinked is that the allure of tulips was not limited to the Netherlands. In the early 1600s almost everyone in Europe was obsessed with streaking tulips. After all, they had seen the paintings (the ads), if not the objects, and if not the actual paintings, then reproductions in picture books.

Still, one wonders why *this* luxury item so dominated the market. Why did people care so passionately about something so organic, so lowly, so reproductive? Historians are now beginning to put one more piece in the puzzle: Tulip madness occurred at almost exactly the same time as the onset of the bubonic plague.

The coincidence is not happenstance. From 1635 to 1637, just as the tulip market was coming to flower, the plague ravaged the Netherlands, killing 17,193 people in Amsterdam alone in 1636. One-seventh of the population died in a matter of months. The plague also caused 14,502 deaths in Leiden in 1635 (a third of the 1622 population), and it killed 14 percent of the population of Haarlem, the center of the tulip speculation, from August to November 1636 (N. Smith 2000:A27).

Little wonder people were caught in the fever of get rich quick. And little wonder that the tulip, a symbol of wildly unpredictable perfection and godly intervention, became such a harbinger of other-worldly peace and tranquility. Hold luxury, you hold meaning. Time slows down. That the plague anxiety reached its peak exactly as the market in tulip futures topped is informative. What's not to lose? Why not gamble? If life is a crap shoot, bet with the hot hand.

Who knows if the speculative fever was consciously tied to mortal anxiety? All we know is that when we look backward we see tulip imagery woven in tapestry, inlaid on furniture, glazed in tiles, and painted everywhere. The flower was totemic. One wonders why, if this loss of confidence in living took the form of a game centered around tulip affiliation, it did not recur in later plague outbreaks. Also, how to account for the fact that then-contemporary descriptions of the tulip craze fail to mention the plague?

But the key to the value of luxury is often in the unarticulated promise attached to undifferentiated objects. We never consciously contend that somehow this object will fill in the blank, that it will provide a temporary palliative, that even as a temporary stay it will tide us over some trauma. Luxury is an unconscious shortcut. Grace on the fly. Maybe what we see from the tulip fiasco is that we must consume lest we be consumed. This is never acknowledged, let alone even contemplated. Yet the history of human desires shows that, when anxious, we often give ourselves over as hostages to the material world. We die yet things endure, so we cling to things.

The tulip luxury is, in retrospect, typical of what we see happening throughout the nineteenth century and up through our own day. An object is isolated. It is imbued with magical powers. To begin with, only the rich have it, but then some market-driven energy makes it available to others. It gets advertised as part of a life made full of value and meaning—"short time's endless monument." Whether this compelling imagery is carried in oil paint, in pixels, or in ink, the allure is clearly not solely imposed from without but represents a deep yearning of a flummoxed audience. Yes, this is conspicuous consumption. And, yes, desire is being manipulated, at least for a while. But it is also a yearning for lasting meaning in a transitory world. Where would we be without fetishes?

Finally, after the ebb and flow of consumption, the object is reintegrated into the market at an affordable level. Ironically, in an inversion of desire, the breaking tulips are now too confusing for most consumers. We, who are accustomed to bursting colors, thanks to photography, find them only distracting. In an interesting turn of phrase the Dutch have a name for the monotonous, disease-free, nonstreaking tulips. They are called Rembrandts.

The result of the Dutch obsession for bulbs is that today Holland grows 90 percent of the world's supply. Although tulips come in thirty-five hundred varieties, most are simple red and yellow. The flower has now become such a staple of the mass market that the eccentric "breakers" are only still beloved by collectors and florists. We still seek floral luxury, however. Of all the flowers today the orchid behaves most like the seventeenth-century tulip.

Tulipmania still sounds maniacal and strange to us, unless, that is, you happen to remember the art market going over the top in the 1980s. Remember when *Irises,* a flower picture by a Dutchman, van Gogh, set a then-record price for a painting when it sold in 1987 for $53.7 million? Follow the price of any luxury collectible from antique autos to glitzy glassware and you will see the same mania expanding and contracting.

I have focused on the emotional effect of luxury (the Buchanan Moment) and on the seeming irrationality (via the Stendhal Syndrome) of the luxury object (shirts and tulips), because I want to counter the usual approach, which is to concentrate on the display of luxury. We'll get to that later. But first let's look at two other aspects of modern luxury, the entertainment and religious value of luxury, and to do that we need to pull up stakes and hit the road again. Tally-ho!

7.

Viva Las Vegas!

A STRIP OF LUXURY

> *"We came out here [Las Vegas] to find the American Dream, and now that we're right in the vortex you want to quit." I grabbed his biceps and squeezed. "You must realize," I said, "that we've found the main nerve."*
>
> *"I know," he said. "That's what gives me the Fear."*
>
> —Hunter Thompson, *Fear and Loathing in Las Vegas*

Sooner or later I knew I would have to go to Las Vegas. If luxury is a social construction, then this is the place to see it being built, one slab of Italian terra-cotta on one tube of neon on one ersatz Greek statue on one chromium light beam. I came with some fear and trepidation, for I had seen all the movies and read all the books. This is the place of the Fear all right. You can't play it safe any longer. After all, look how Vegas boiled the prose of Tom Wolfe and Hunter Thompson.

But I was also thrilled. All my life I had been taught to stay away. To make sure I was safe I had my fieldworker back on the payroll. Daughter Liz was to join me after the tears on Rodeo Drive. I promised her this time if she'd come, we would spend some *real* money. She was willing, nay, eager. She was even going to bring some friends from Stanford who think that Las Vegas is the place to go for a weekend of kitsch and glitz.

And they are not alone in wanting to come. For this is the place to go if you are following *one* of the two threads of American culture: the thread of make your own bundle, make it quick, make it count, and do it by being lucky. The other thread of American life, the one I understood, was cooperate, make it slow, get rewarded later, and do it by dint of labor. This is the classic battle of American culture, the battle between the fence-building farmers and the risk-taking cattlemen, between age and adolescence, substance and style, between savers and gamblers.

I knew I was an Eastern sodbuster saver. I have always known it. As a kid, I had paid attention to the story of the grasshopper and the ants. Grasshoppers who live in the carnival culture of chance get to the Land of Opuluxe. They want heaven on earth. Ants who live in the plodding culture of workaday repetition get to write about it. They have to die to find reward. Liz, who had done her time in Silicon Valley, must have known how I felt because her last words to me on the phone were, "Dad, don't be a downer, okay?"

I flew into Las Vegas in the dead of night beside two Florida grasshoppers from Ft. Lauderdale. They looked and behaved rather like the Pigeon sisters of *The Odd Couple*, chattering away next to me on the plane. What struck me was their unflappable enthusiasm. By the time we began our descent, they were positively furious with excitement. As we dropped lower over the city, I must admit that it was an apocalyptic sight. Total pitch darkness, then suddenly all that light, all bursting whiteness along the strip, pulsing beams from these now-visible signs, with one single great stream of light going straight up from the top of what was to be my hotel, the Luxor. All this glimmer against a black, almost forbidding, desert did seem like the light at the end of the tunnel. Dreary English teacher that I am, I kept thinking of the line from Yeats's *Sailing to Byzantium*: "And therefore I have sailed the seas and come to the holy city of Byzantium."

Las Vegas is a holy city all right and not just to the Pigeon sisters. Millions of people each year come here from all over the world. Almost half the population changes every three days. It's as if they were going to Chartres, or, better yet, to Lourdes. They come like pilgrims to Mecca, hoping not really to hit the jackpot as much as to, as I was repeatedly told, be near all the excitement, the lights, the luxury. Although they may say they come to strike it rich, they really come to spend.

The Pigeon sisters knew all the hotels, all the themes, all the entertainers, and had all the dreams. And what were their dreams? To make money. How? By luck. Why? So they could return and stay at the Bellagio or the Venetian and be "comped." They wanted to make it to spend it. One sister was a schoolteacher. The other was an interior decorator of yachts. Neither was married. Both were hard workers. They were more like moths than birds or grasshoppers, and the Calvinist in me thought how dangerous to be drawn to this flame.

Yet I knew what they were talking about. Like a dutiful ant I had done all my homework. But what they perhaps didn't realize was that all Las Vegas, and by extension Western culture, was moving toward these super-luxury hotels, these "themed destinations." Certainly, the rest of America is close behind, slouching toward Vegas to be born. All right, Vegas wasn't the City on the Hill, it was in the bottom of a desert. But it was doing the apocalyptic thing, it was harboring that bright, shining promise.

Vegas Is in the Out There

What you see of Las Vegas from the air is a strange glistening snake that seems to stretch from the McCarran International Airport down and around a slow corner until it peters out in downtown darkness along Fremont Street. This roadway is called the Las Vegas Strip, but it is really South Las Vegas Boulevard. What you don't see from the air but is clear from the history, is that, like a snake, this coruscating pattern of blinking excitement is continually shedding photons and picking up new ones. Every half-generation sees something new, not just a few new signs but an entirely new Strip.

"The Strip" is no haphazard characterization, for it is a strip of themed spangles, but it also is the result of peeling old imagery away layer by layer and then sliding on the new glimmer. If you want to see the syncretism of opuluxe in the modern world, you have to come here. Just as Christianity continually layered itself over the indigenous religion that it found, so too the mythos of Vegas gains strength by never attempting to change desire but always trying to get in the way of it. To use a painterly analogy what you see along the Strip is the pentimento of past dreams, each new one almost covering up the old.

If Las Vegas is all package and no content, it is a package continually being repackaged. Yes, it is the simulacrum of simulacra; yes, it is the omphalos, the snake with its tail in its mouth continually eating itself up. Not by happenstance is impersonation the favorite homegrown Vegas genre, second only to magic shows. For this place is all about the stagecraft of let's pretend. Yes, it is a world of skin-thin grandiosity, of populust extravagance, of cheap salvation, of democratic elegance, of sophist sophistication, of faux facades, but it is also the subconscious of American popular culture, theme park of the libido, the wet dream of consumption.

Vegas is all these things and more because, like all great cities, it sits on the edge of what's happening *now*. This is life in the limen, subliminal, materially sublime. It is beyond real life. As such it is filled with metaphors and ironies that are so impossibly juicy. For instance: Most of the new casinos have a $500-a-pull slot-machine salon; the lung-cancer death rate here is the second highest in the country (you see this the minute you arrive, for although the airport is filled with no smoking signs, the place reeks of tobacco); the suicide rate and cellular phone usage are the highest in the country; the place is in such flux that the phone books are updated twice a year. I was sure that a huge tuning fork is buried below the Strip, eternally vibrating.

A sense of isolation is crucial. For years the hotels on the Strip insisted that the coaxial cable carrying television into their hotel rooms drop CNN. Nor did these hotels provide minibars, room snacks, safes in the room, fax machines, and computer hookups. The whole idea was to deprive the guests of creature comforts but keep them cheery. Don't bring me down.

Or, better yet, don't let me get up. For in the subterranean guts of every Vegas hotel is the casino, a strangely inhospitable but eerily cheerful engine that sets the fork eternally pinging. The casino is always on the ground floor, but it feels like being deep in the earth. Up top, Las Vegas is contemporary America in concentrated form. It is a place aspiring to family values and looking for religion. But down below, in the factory, it worships money and is in thrall to vast, faceless corporations.

Great cities usually sit on the edge of something. They are on the ocean, beside a river, at the base of the mountains. But Las Vegas is out there at the edge of nowhere, smack in the middle of nothing. It began as a Mormon outpost, continued as a tiny railroad stop in nowheresville, and grew a little, though not much, as the initial bedroom boomtown for the men who built Hoover Dam. As we know from countless novels and movies, its very isolation made it attractive to some tough big-city gamblers. By all rights, *if* gambling were the only attraction, the city should be on the California border at Stateline, Nevada, but, no, it is about fifty miles to the east.

The allure of being *out there* is undeniable. And you pick up this sensation the minute you lift your head and look around. You are in the bottom of a bowl. People must like feeling this way, for not only is this the fastest-growing city in the United States, it is the largest American city founded in the twentieth century. The population grows by more than two thousand new residents each week. But, more important, Vegas is also the prototype for a new form of city, a city that is emerging all over the world, a city that now conducts most of its commerce on commercial strips, a city that all but worships the luxe life.

Perhaps Las Vegas may be the last great, mythic city that Western civilization will ever create. Over the centuries this civilization that we call *Western*, with its counterpoint between diverse influences and common roots, has birthed a slow, steady flow of cities whose very names have become symbolic of what they have offered newcomers: Baghdad, Babylon, Cairo, Athens; then Constantinople, Rome, Venice, Florence; then Paris, Vienna, Prague, Berlin, St. Petersburg; now London, New York, New Orleans, Los Angeles. Like it or not, Las Vegas has joined these mythic cities.

Ask anyone all around the world. Everyone knows Vegas. They want to see it. The style and texture of this place, so erotic yet antiromantic, so freakish, so much like a carnival world on speed, is like being caught in a lascivious dream. You keep wondering, like a modern Keats: Do I sleep or wake? Is this place for real? Of course, part of this is because the culture is built on the casino, and the casino has no clocks, no real light, no real human discourse, only dreams of El Dorado. Oxygen is pumped in. But part of the allure is that this is a place to go in order to get away from where you are from, to separate yourself from who you are.

The Strip: Survival of the Fittest Dream

There are six distinct periods in the development of the Vegas Strip, of which only the last is of interest to students of luxury. On a thumbnail, the protoStrip started in the 1930s, looking like something seen in any midwestern town, wooden buildings fronting hot dirt road. In 1936 Hoover Dam was finished. Electricity flowed into the desert, as did the water that spun the turbines. In 1939 the first casinos appeared on Fremont Street and then the first motor hotel, El Rancho. Soon these forms mutated into glorified motel-casinos like the Flamingo—modern, flat, and air-conditioned. Then, in 1958 the Stardust was built under a huge sign, then the Golden Nugget and the Horseshoe Club went up, each beneath a distinctive steeple of neon. You can see what is casting the allure of Vegas during the '50s, what is attracting the grasshoppers. It's in the names: It is the West, the American West, the land of freedom and plenty of luck. Strike it rich.

But then the world of themed luxury appeared in 1966 with the creation of the $19 million Caesars Palace and, two years later, the first family-oriented hotel and casino, Circus Circus. What had changed the motif from he-man tough to self-indulgent soft was a shift in ownership. In the late 1960s Nevada allowed corporations to own casinos, and people like Howard Hughes and his Mormon accountants made the mobsters take their tainted Teamsters-Central-States-Pension-Fund money and scram. The new moneymen with deep pockets and public rectitude made the world safe for opuluxe display as well as for the Hilton, Holiday Inn, and Ramada.

These CPAs were geniuses. They realized that because the money came from the casino, and because you could build straight up over the factory, you could essentially keep your clientele trapped in one shaft of living space, forever emptying into the casino. The new math: more rooms = more guests = more bettors = higher profits. With far greater resources than even mob-connected types, the new generation of corporate owners was able, as they say in Econ 101, to expand the physical plant, and, thanks to the elevator, they did—straight up.

Entertain and feed them cheap. Show them Dean and Jerry, Frank, Lena, Elvis, Liberace, Barbra, Siegfried & Roy. Plump them up, then harvest them below in the abattoir.

The Casino Is Where Opuluxe Is Funded

To get people to voluntarily enter these buildings, they had to build something so alluring that people would leave home for the desert and that, once inside, remain alluring enough to keep them from going home—or to the casino next door. The casino is where the money is—about half the casino profits are from slot machines—and it is all done automatically. Even the sound of the occasional jackpot is mechanical, the eerie dripping of coins in the phosphorescent half-light. The stories you hear about elderly women with gigantic cups of quarters sitting for hours at a slot machine are no joke. Half-sitting on a stool, one hand holding a plastic cup filled with coins, she feeds money to the machines for hours.

At four in the morning I saw the Pigeon sisters side by side, pumping coins into the maw of one of these tinkling machines. I asked them how they decided which place to go, and without batting an eye they said they go to the fanciest hotel. They were no longer smiling. Expressionless, joyless, they kept right on playing as we talked, shoveling their winnings back into the machine. Once you leave the theaters, Las Vegas is a place without laughter.

The theme that since the 1960s has proved the most alluring to the Pigeon sisters is l-u-x-u-r-y, pure and simple. Just as the Holy Roman Church learned how to fill the house with the rise of rococo and baroque, so too did the casino accountants learn. Fund the facade and the casino will take care of itself—the steeple theory of Renaissance churches. If the service is always the same, if the mass is always said the same way, if the slot machines and gaming tables are always rigged with the same payouts, then it's what you put around and above the altar/casino that draws the crowd, not what you actually offer for games of salvation.

This quid pro quo, the promise of magical redemption for giving up money, has always been the business of Vegas. Pay to play. But it was turbocharged in the last two decades as these games have been exported elsewhere. Legalized gambling, now sanitized as *gaming*, is all over. In 1978 New Jersey allowed the same machinery to be established in Atlantic City; governments have allowed lotteries, and Native Americans have cashed in with casinos on their reservations. There is riverboat gambling, cruise boat gambling, and the ever-present threat of some other city, like Miami or New Orleans, throwing craps and destroying Vegas. So the City of Lost Wages, the City of Sin, has to do them one better. They had better turn on the exterior lights and dim the casinos.

Sheds Become Ducks

When in the early 1970s the architects Robert Venturi, Denise Scott Brown, and Steven Izenour came here with their graduate students from Yale, the luxe explosion was just about to happen. Casinos were just at the edge of going into glimmer. The architects could still see Vegas in all its various early incarnations: ersatz Old West outpost in the 1930s and '40s, gangsters-meet-Hollywood high-life oasis in the '50s and '60s, and uncool polyester dump in the '70s. But the book they wrote, the book that turned the world of architecture upside down, the book that changed my life, is still just as true as when they wrote it.

The book was called *Learning from Las Vegas* and it was about learning about culture from reading facades, judging a book by its cover. Not only did they take this commercial strip seriously, they saw the Strip as the new form of suburban consumption. What they were really studying was the defining forms of modern American life: wide road, low building, huge sign. These are the primary elements in the symbolic landscape of our time, and Vegas had them in spades.

Venturi and his merry band put Vegas in context as a marketplace. They described the ancient markets in Europe with their narrow passageways, where communication takes place through direct contact, where you are persuaded to make your purchase because you can see and touch and smell and taste the things you are offered for sale. They pointed out that when the medieval market became Main Street, the products moved back behind windows, but you still had some direct contact. Commercial strips do not present the actual merchandise that is available, however. Here, information about the product comes from a sign, a sign that must make its point to the people who are moving along in a car at 50 miles an hour, twenty times faster than walking through a market.

The signs' primary role is to connect the driver to the product in a finger snap. The signs use words, pictures, and sculpture to make that connection. This system is perfectly logical for a population that moves around in cars. If the Strip is to Las Vegas what the piazza is to Rome, then the hotel is the miniature city-state.

One of the more compelling points made early in the book is that the commercial strip gave us an "architecture of persuasion," consisting almost entirely of photons on sticks. The buildings themselves, with the possible exception of some fast-food restaurants, tended to be almost invisible behind their vast parking lots and large roadside pylons. The graphic sign in front became the architecture, the dominant form, of this commercial landscape.

For the architects gambling was just a business like any other. If the suburb was the result of living by car, then the ubiquitous strip was the result of shopping by car. So what we see in Vegas is everything brought up to cheetah speed. These signs, those huge monsters of neon, were meant to be seen on the fly, but like the steeple of the church that betokens activity inside, the spectacular sign was essentially just a billboard built over the casino pit. In fact, Venturi, Brown, and Izenour call these early motel-cum-casinos *sheds*. For that is what they are; just sheds beneath signs.

West front of Amiens Cathedral (post-1250 in Picardy, France) and the street front of the Golden Nugget (post-1964 in Las Vegas, Nevada).

Signs as Steeples

Just as the Renaissance needed stone to make the signs of cathedrals, the Age of Opuluxe needs neon. Neon didn't just flourish in Vegas, it grew like kudzu. Since the English immigrant Thomas Young opened up his electric sign company in 1945 and began dazzling the inhabitants and visitors with his Technicolor neon "explosions," Vegas has been the evolutionary grid for a prolonged bout of sign one-upmanship among the city's casinos. While other cities began to lay down ordinances controlling the size and use of electric signs, Vegas gave the Young Electric Sign Company and the developers a free rein. Unfettered by space constraints, planning regulations, or a shortage of electricity, a whole citadel of light rose up from the barren desert in a unified chaos, a star chamber of competing supernovas.

As the signs grew, the sheds shrunk until they finally merged into one edifice. Venturi, Brown, and Izenour saw this coming. The architects called this new mutation a *duck*. A duck building is an edifice that looks like a sign, and they named it after a duck-as-restaurant building they had seen back east. But what they didn't realize was that the duck was about to grow even bigger than the early signs. In fact, far larger, for not just did the building become the sign but the building became a self-contained and unified cloister, a cathedral of sorts.

The Rise of Opuluxe as Thematic Destination

Take the building I stayed in. It was in the shape of a giant pyramid, bigger, I was told, than anything in Egypt. It's called the Luxor, is owned by the Circus Circus Company, and is clearly named not so much for the locale in Egypt—even the desk clerks didn't know what the name meant—but for the connotations with luxury. Lexus, the car; Luxor, the hotel.

The Luxor is drenched in frippery. There are fake oriental carpets, talking camels in the lobby, a Pharaoh's tomb, a sky-high Cleopatra's Needle, phony hieroglyphics everywhere, a lobby that can hold nine 747s piled one on top the other, a seven-story movie screen, and a "motion simulator" that purports to drag you from the bottom of the earth. You should wear sunglasses in the elevators because they gleam with a golden copper that signifies perpetual polishing. Shooting up from the top of the building-as-pyramid is a laser light, which the feds at the airport have dimmed a bit, fearing it might blind incoming pilots.

The Luxor sits across the road from the Excalibur, themed after King Arthur, with turrets and towers in pinks and purple, like a fairy-tale castle crafted from icing sugar. Here the search for the Grail is cast in terms of gambling, encapsulating dreams of glory and fears of bankruptcy in a fairy-tale blown up to the scale of a city. The Excalibur is interesting primarily because it is the low-rent path to paradise, a kind of poor man's claim on luxury, a kid's idea of grandeur.

To the other side of the Luxor, connected by a hermetically sealed tram, is Mandalay Bay, whose theme of luxury is just what it says. To prove it, there is a wet-and-wild wave machine so powerful that when it was first fired up, it destroyed the entire six-acre beach park. Here gambling is clearly part of the escape to a South Seas isle. But, as the desk clerk pointed out to me, the top four floors are set aside for the Four Seasons Hotel, a hotel within a hotel, the only hotel in Vegas that has no casino. Thus a cut above, literally and figuratively. The Four Seasons offers a different kind of luxe: a private entrance, private elevators, and *really* expensive rooms.

These hotels—Mandalay, Luxor, and Excalibur—anchor the southern part of the Strip and format luxury in nobrow pretensions lifted from Hollywood movies. Moving down Las Vegas Boulevard to the east is like being trapped in a modern multiplex. Each theater is playing a different show, yet each depends on the same concession stand a few steps down into the darkness. Ka-ching! Only the ticket taker in the box office knows which movie feature is pulling the larger audience.

In a sense the multiplex expands or contracts the theaters according to audience demand. Want more Romanesque? Then patronize Circus Circus and Caesars Palace. Want something for the kiddies? Then try Treasure Island. Want pure Renaissance luxury? Then go to the Bellagio and the Venetian.

Clearly, the one thing no one seems to want, at least on the Strip, is the one thing Vegas once produced, the myth of the rip-roaring West. No more great names like Old Rex, Boulder Club, El Dorado, Pioneer, Trader Bill's. Whatever *that* Vegas was, it's no longer on the Strip. It's downtown on the Fremont Street midway.

Or perhaps a more biological metaphor explains the tight thematic diversity, a Darwinian struggle to create the dreamy web in which the spider can pick the fly's pockets. Being on the Strip is like life in the Galapagos, where entire species are adapting differently on different islands but with one commonality: how to draw the sticky dollars out of the pockets of the passing lounge lizards. No matter the analogy, the principle is clearly the same. Create the imagery that humans will flock to see and will stay around long enough to be fleeced. Whatever that imagery is, whatever humans imagine as the good life, a life elevated from their own, a life they wish they could afford, is the imagery central to the reckless act of gambling. The connection between luxury and entertainment is intimate and necessary.

Hotels on Tropicana Boulevard form what has become known as the New Four Corners of the Strip. For my taste, however, the next four corners—at Las Vegas and Flamingo Boulevards, home to Caesars Palace, the Mirage, and Treasure Island—is where all the audience action is. Here the throngs were so thick that I could barely make my way from one city-state to the next. And here, of course, you see the real audience for Vegas, that same audience I saw on Rodeo Drive and Madison Avenue, the newly enfranchised young. How else to explain the Harley-Davidson Cafe, the Hard Rock Hotel, and the NASCAR cafe/museum? The dress code is egalitarian: T-shirts, baseball caps and jeans, just as it is across America, no matter the context. The average age in Vegas has been steadily dropping (it's now about forty), and here you see it in action.

What's on Top of the Casino

Between these corners are other attractions. For instance, as you leave the Luxor and head slightly north, you pass New York-New York, a mishmash that makes up in exclamatory image what it lacks (if that is the word) in size. It cuts a crisp silhouette of the Manhattan skyline, complete with replicas of the Chrysler and Empire State Buildings (but for some reason no World Trade Center), plus a roller coaster and the Brooklyn Bridge.

Across the street is the MGM Grand, complete with Studio 54 inside and a huge Leo the Lion out front. This thing—really, it doesn't look like anything—is simply *huge*, with more than five thousand rooms. For a while it was the largest hotel in the world. Its corridors are longer than a football field, and its swimming pool is so expansive that the health department classifies it as a swimming lagoon. It celebrates dreams just out of reach in a restaurant named after the patron saint of Vegas, Gatsby's. Next to the Grand is its opposite, another mishmash theme resort called Bally's Paris Resort and Casino. Like New York-New York, this place essentially recreates postcard landmarks: L'Arc de Triomphe, Champs-Élysées, Paris Opera House, Parc Monceau, and even the Seine. From the fifty-story Eiffel Tower you have a view of what? New York-New York, Luxor, Bellagio, the Venetian.

But what you really see from the faux Eiffel Tower is that Las Vegas is a place for people who want to see places they will never have to see. This is the new role of luxury: to transport just your senses but not your body. As the tourist is a traveler-lite, so this part of Vegas supplies the dehydrated culture, the context of going somewhere without ever leaving where you are; it's the "feelies" of Aldous Huxley's *Brave New World*.

If this is not clear by now, all you have to do is go on to Caesars Palace, which really started this mutation of luxury as entertainment, or luxurtainment. When it opened in 1966, Caesars Palace was a little, what? a little cheesy. But now that it has been remodeled, it is a lot cheesy. This is the Hollywood version of the grandeur that was Rome, complete with the gleaming marble reproductions of statuary (some of which talk), swimming pools inlaid with marble mosaics, accurate enough murals from movie scenes, and lots of cocktail waitresses in skimpy togas.

The achievement of Caesars Palace was that it was the first Mirage resort to create a coherent fantasy environment. Not only did it provide such diversions as shopping, dining, and show going at a level equal with gambling but it made them interactive. When in Rome act like the Romans, which means shop, eat, drink, and especially gamble as though the fall of the empire is at hand.

The Exploding Themed Resorts

Also on the Strip are mute reminders of Vegas's somewhat confused relationship with family life. On one hand, the casinos need to make a place for families to get rid of the kiddies, at least until they can come back at the age of Liz and her friends. On the other hand, the casino execs have come to realize that part of the allure of gambling is a kind of self-infantalization. And indeed, if you look at the reception areas of the exploding hotels, you will see that far more couples are checking in without the kids than with.

The two exploding hotels that we observed were the Mirage and Treasure Island. The Mirage has a volcano that "erupts" every fifteen minutes, courtesy of colored lights and a powerful sound system. The theme is the usual South Seas oasis in the desert, complete with tropical atrium filled with palm and banana trees, cascading water, and a huge aquarium with sharks. In the back are the big cats, courtesy of that indescribable duo Siegfried & Roy. Next door is Treasure Island, which stages a full-dress battle, between a pirate ship and the HMS *Britannia,* on a "sea" outside the hotel entrance. Two dozen actors on two full-size sailing ships exchange hokey dialogue—"Raise the gunpoints, my lads"—until the British (whaddayaexpect?) sink before your eyes. You enter this buccaneer world over a drawbridge and soon are funneled into a casino imitating a buried treasure. No one tells you that you are the booty. No one needs to.

I mention these themes—fake lore, pretend travel, movie versions of antiquity, explosions—because they have all been trumped by a new destination, the land of Italian luxury. It is as if the entire arc from south to north, from the Great Pyramid and Sphinx to turrets suggesting the castles of Europe to the classic American skyscrapers and Parisian delights to Pirate Land and Polynesia to the glory that was Circus Circus to the ancient memory of the Wild West, now preserved under glass on Fremont Street, all now converges on the last point of evolution—a Renaissance of Luxe. It's as if the entire evolution of Western civilization on the Las Vegas Strip ends in the pot o' gold: the Bellagio and the Venetian.

Et Tu, Bellagio?

If the history of marketing teaches us anything, it is that when you sell a fungible item—an item just like what is being sold by your competition—sooner or later ludicrous language will trump the judicious. So if you are selling something like, say, bottled water or denim or even T-shirts, you can predict that someone like Evian or Calvin Klein or Hugo Boss will appear to bump up the language of desire. Sooner or later, to maximize profits that language will invoke the aesthetic category of luxury.

The casino business is a perfect example of a totally interchangeable product. The slots are set by computer chip, the roulette wheel and dice are balanced by the state, the card games are "according to Hoyle," and the sports betting is controlled by the laws of supply and demand. The only thing that can change is the language, and that is why those neon signs grew to such Brobdingnagian proportions, why the giraffe has such a long neck, why the pufferfish can explode to twice its usual size when attacked. These are adaptive mechanisms and Las Vegas is nothing if not the most sensitive mechanism of adaptation to the yearning of its audience. The only other geographical locales so responsive to whim are Hollywood, Wall Street, and Washington, D.C.

You may not like what you see in advertising or on the Strip, but the one thing that it shows you is where the buried, and not so buried, desires of a culture currently reside. After all, the average gambler spends four hours a day in the casino. You have to show him something to get him to come inside before he goes down into that dark basement to be fleeced. And when he has to come out for air, if you can provide something for him to do before returning to the clipping room, so much the better. The key is not to let your competitor get to him first.

The two most extraordinary construction projects in Las Vegas in the last generation have been Steve Wynn's Bellagio and Sheldon Adelson's Venetian hotels. That both impresarios have constructed environments totally dedicated to the allure of Renaissance Italian luxury (not the Wild West, not Egypt, not ancient Greece, not Paris, not the Arthurian legends, not tropical islands . . .) tells us much about how close luxury is to the center of American materialism. These men know how to read profit-and-loss statements, the modern tea leaves of industry. And they are each betting more than a billion dollars that they are correct. The one thing they are not, and do not want to be, is gamblers.

Let's start with the Bellagio. When you realize that the ideal Vegas resort (at least from the owner's perspective) would be essentially a high-rise prison built over a casino pit, you can see what's going on here. First, the hotel is set way back from the Strip, divided from the hurly-burly by an almost nine-acre artificial lake, supposedly a bit of Lake Como. At regular in-

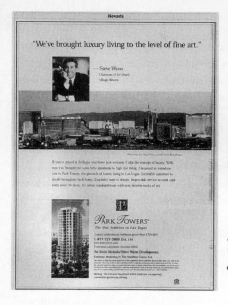

BELLAGIO

*Publicity photo of the Bellagio and Steve Wynn's
"We've brought luxury living to the level of art"
advertisement for high-rise condos.*

tervals twelve hundred synchronized fountainheads animate the water to the strains of an Italian aria or a Sinatra classic—water music à la Muzak. Framed through the falling mist and the twinkling lights decorating the lakeside foliage, the Bellagio appears every bit as enchanting, romantic, stately, and dignified as Sing-Sing.

What that lake is really doing is not just the work of a neon sign but the work of concertina wire, that razor-sharp barbed wire that spirals out around the prison yard, reminding the inmates to stay put. Once inside the Bellagio, it takes effort to get out. So this little Lake Como is really a bit of what San Francisco Bay is to Alcatraz. Sufficiently bankrolled, one could stay in here for days and never see a girlie show, never be tempted to indulge in a buffet pig-out, and never break out.

This hotel-cum-resort-supra-casino rises thirty-six stories above a glass-enclosed conservatory perpetually filled with flowers, an elegant shopping gallery filled with Rodeo Drive retailers, an art gallery filled with works by famous painters, restaurants filled with food prepared by chefs whose names I know that I'm supposed to know, and a water theater filled with a spectacular show with a French name. Each one of these sections resets the locks of luxury. You can almost hear the warden instructing the inmates, "There is no need to go outside." The moment you swoop up through the porte cochere, one thing is certain: You are not going to swoop away.

The Bellagio might have been designed to echo the imagined resorts of the Italian Lake District, but its room corridors are typical jailhouse. All the wings deadhead into a hub of central elevators that drop you into the casino. The design maximizes guest rooms with Strip views, to be sure, but can make for seemingly endless trudging, only to be forever dumped down into the fleecing pit.

Needless to say, the stores on the ground floor wings are all the ones we saw on Rodeo, Worth, and Madison Avenues: Armani, Prada, Chanel, Tiffany, Moschino, Hermès, Gucci, and other various Euroluxe franchises. And, needless to say, the restaurants continue the motif of franchised designer luxury. So Le Cirque and Osteria del Circo from New York are there, as well as versions of San Francisco's Aqua and Boston's Olives, plus undistinguished Chinese, Japanese, and Italian restaurants with fancy-sounding names. Liz and I liked the Picasso restaurant. The Picasso features not just Mediterranean cooking but also the real things, not only oils but also ceramic pieces. You enjoy, we were told, "the Picasso experience." Along with the artist's original paintings, drawings, and ceramics were some carpets and furniture designed by his son, Claude. All for sale. Nothing by sister Paloma.

You have to work to find the twenty-four-hour cafe that's not quite a coffee shop and the obligatory buffet that's not the usual buffet. But then again, the experience of experiencing high culture, not vulgar Vegas, is what the Bellagio is all about. As you are ushered inside by the wardens dressed in appropriate Gilbert and Sullivan garb, you pass works from contemporary artists in the vast lobby and arcades. It's a theme casino where the theme is luxury.

Flanking the registration desk are two Willem de Koonings. Over your head is a floral glass sculpture by Dale Chihuly, *Fiori di Como,* and it's massive—supposedly the largest glass piece ever blown. But what is really interesting is that this piece, which looks to me a bit too much like hundreds of multicolored sea anemones clinging to the ceiling, is one of the few original pieces in all of Las Vegas. 'Most everything else we saw was out-and-out imitative and proudly so. Or, get this, *really* real.

Show Me the Monet

What you don't see in this photograph of the Bellagio is what joins little Lake Como with the Strip, and that is the sign. This time not in neon, nor in an LED display, but in the old-time marquee plastic letters set against a white background surrounded by baroque decoration. Before Wynn, the erstwhile CEO of Mirage Resorts, Inc., cashed out, it used to say: "Now Appearing: van Gogh. Monet. Cezanne. Picasso." It looked just like other "now appearing" signs that announce Paul Anka, and Elvis look-alikes. The sign was a shock and, I must say, very effective.

Very effective because Wynn was exploiting one of the insights of modern advertising. The value of interchangeable objects is generated by association, not by intrinsic properties. And the association that Bellagio is claiming is—wouldn't you know it?—nothing less than the high culture of the Western world. It is easy to mock this association because it is so egregiously pursued. "*Now* Appearing," indeed!

On one hand, the marquee sign clearly sent up the endeavor, pimping the Impressionists as if they were Tom Jones and Wayne Newton. But on the other hand, once inside, the art was so in-your-face obvious that you were almost embarrassed to have it here. Before he fell on hard times and sold out to MGM and Kirk Kerkorian (the result of the Mirage corporation's trying to transport this kind of faux luxe to the Beau Rivage Casino in Mississippi), Wynn was the highest-salaried executive in this country for a reason. He knows marketing.

The real hoot was the gallery itself, the Bellagio Gallery of Fine Art. I was told by the ticket taker that the place keeps an art history Ph.D. "on retainer." He said it like it meant "on call." Everything about the gallery is miniaturized and compressed and a touch surreal. After skirting the casino and before you come to the wedding chapels, you see the quiet inmates penitentially standing in line to buy tickets to the "show." Savvy to the ways of the art world, Liz and I had dutifully bought our tickets earlier but, in truth, it made no difference. We waited to be herded into a little holding pen before being escorted into the gallery. It was just like waiting for the roller coaster at New York-New York, lined up to take the seats of those who had just passed through, and, who—"Whew! Now, that was something!"—were passing on to other entertainments deluxe.

For our $14 admission charge we were given an audio headset that looked like an old World War II field radio and were ushered into the inner sanctum. The guards were very serious and had little radio earplugs in their ears just like the Secret Service or the doormen at Gucci and Prada. Not a word was said. It was like being in church. It was dark and black, just like all Vegas casinos, no natural light permitted to filter in. I was told that this art was so valuable that before it made its way to this protected section of the hotel, it was kept in the special room reserved for the super-high rollers, the ones called whales. That, in Vegas, is what high security is all about. If *they* get to see it, it must be valuable.

On this audio device we heard the dulcet Wynn (who is all over the closed-circuit hotel television as well) hold forth on the *values* of art. I did not, alas, write it down, and when I asked for a transcription, I was told that none existed. Wise move. I can only give you the gist of what Wynn said by consulting his "Journal," which is provided to those pesky enough to ask for more. In his words:

> Attendance at museums in the past few years has exceeded attendance at professional sporting events throughout the United States. This surprising statistic seems to represent a popular and fundamental yearning in our diverse cultural souls for a glimpse of beauty, a desire to be near examples of singular creative energy.
>
> For me, the acknowledgement of art's deep attraction is not at all surprising. I believe that great art—whether in painting, sculpture, architecture, music, or dance has always had the power to deeply stimulate human consciousness.
>
> What really matters is that by offering our guests (and my fellow Las Vegas residents) the Bellagio Gallery of Fine Art, we acknowledge their capacity to appreciate beauty and elegance. When someone does that for me, I am pleased and grateful. I feel a kinship with people who demonstrate that level of sensitivity, and I believe it is a worthy aspiration in business and life in general. . . .
>
> All of these artists, regardless of chronology, share the most remarkable power to move us. I feel them and somehow am stimulated to think and feel more about the world around me than I did before. In a way it's habit-forming.
>
> I believe lots of people who share an affinity for things of beauty will join me in delighting in the experience of the Gallery, which just happens to be located in the Bellagio.

What Wynn didn't mention was that every painting was for sale and that he was, to some degree (at least for tax purposes), an art dealer. Not a big deal, but while he claimed he had to sneak into his own museum for the palliative powers of seeing his precious art, he was also trading it like the casinos he owns. Allowing the locals to see it for nothing meant that he was taxed as having a nonprofit museum, requiring his guests to pay to see it meant they were getting something of value. Recall that this is the same connoisseur who introduced white tigers and exploding volcanoes to the Strip at the Mirage Resort next door.

I certainly don't question Wynn on the salutary powers of art, but this art does not just happen to be here in the middle of the desert. It was here, perhaps ironically, for the same reason it was often in Renaissance churches—as a way to entice those in the street to come inside. As *Time* magazine's art critic, Robert Hughes, commented, such a collection is not bad for a city "where 'Art' is normally the name of someone's limo driver" (1998:76). But it is art with a purpose. Although Wynn's collection has been dismantled, the gallery still exists, most recently as the venue for the Steve Martin Collection (Glueck 2001).

The role of art in the Bellagio is to reinforce the connection between luxury, high culture, entertainment, and gambling. Just as this crowd will later in the day line up to see the Cirque du Soleil's "O," (pronounced *eau*, as in the French word for water) and think they will be seeing something Parisian (the show comes from Montreal), so too here with the real stuff. Not by happenstance does the Cirque's trademark aquabatics occur in a theater built to resemble a gilded European opera house.

Wynn's Bellagio collection was superb, what might be snootily said to be the best money could buy, and the visitors were duly impressed. It certainly was a collection of the greatest hits, one piece from every canonical big shot. Over and over we were told the price paid was $300 million and the value was appreciating even as we viewed it. Wynn's comments on the tape saw to this. He referred to the collection's prize pieces as "destination pieces," as in paintings so important that *real* art lovers might travel long distances to have a look. These included Cézanne's *Portrait of a Woman* (1900), Míro's *Dialogue of Insects* (1924–25), Picasso's *Portrait of Dora Maar* (1942), and van Gogh's *Peasant Woman Against a Background of Wheat* (1890). The concept of destination piece, like the entirety of the Bellagio as a "destination resort," is, as we will see in the next chapter, at the heart of Las Vegas Luxe. It's all about proximity, about being close-up, about certified value, about . . . redemption.

I have never been in museum rooms where there was such hushed reverie. This museum has only two rooms, both very small. Of course, we all had to have the audio devices pressed to our ears, but still, this group, a group that can just as easily visit the NASCAR museum next door, the Harley-Davidson collection across the street, or the Liberace Museum down the Strip (not a single book in the entire place, including the library), is here on its best behavior, "taking it in."

When the tape was over, we were led out as the next group that had been lining up was let in. As I was leaving, I heard someone coming in ask, "Are the paintings real?" and I was sympathetic. For in a town that thrives on fakery, magic, impersonation, and illusion, what's the advantage in importing real masterpieces of painting and sculpture? To what end would they function in a place known for pirates who nightly sink a British frigate, a volcano that erupts on cue, animated statues of Bacchus, Apollo, and Venus, or those talking camels at the Luxor?

As you leave the gallery, you are funneled into the museum store. Don't all real museums shunt you into the store before letting you back on the streets? After all, you need to buy some souvenir of your experience, and, rather amazingly, the Bellagio Gallery has almost exactly duplicated the museum experience, except that this store is about the same size as the galleries. Here are the wall posters in tubes for mailing, postcards of paintings, trinkets, shot glasses, and paraphernalia all duly embossed with the images you have just viewed. Plus, there are books on art! Real books on art for sale. But the best was the Catalog Raisonné of the Bellagio Collection, all done up exactly like what you would find at the Met or the National Gallery: glossy photos, learned text.

When you exit the museum store, you can either go back to the opulently planted conservatory or turn toward the wedding chapels. Along the way to the chapels you will see the Gauguin meeting room, the Degas meeting room, the Renoir meeting room, and so forth. We checked out the Deluxe Wedding Package. Never too early to plan, I told Liz. For $1,500 I could get her "one hour of chapel time," a Custom Bellagio Wedding Certificate, a Personal Bride Dressing Room (nothing for groom), a wedding coordinator, and express mailing of the photo package. For $1,000 more she could have the Luxury Bellagio Package. Included: Officiant Fee, Personalized Video, Rehearsal Time for Bride *and* Groom, and One-Day Spa Passes for Two (facility use only). We decided on the deluxe, when the time comes, of course. No pressure.

Venice, Anyone?

Across the street from the Bellagio is the Venetian. Same repressive Veterans Administration hospital/state penitentiary format, same long trip

Publicity photo for the Venetian, complete with learner's guide and interior canal scene with luxury shops on both sides.

from hotel room to central elevator, same dumping of passengers into the step-down casino, same difficult escape route to the street. Instead of Lake Como to box you in, Sheldon Adelson, a boy wonder who made his fortune from the Las Vegas Convention Center next door, settled for the island city of Venice. Take a look at what all $1.5 billion of the Venetian looks like.

The Venetian is a study in extraordinary mimicry, a paean to xerography. You can only appreciate it by having consumed countless Hollywood movies and too many trips to Disneyland. Forget Venice! This is way better. No stench, no lines, no surly Venetians in wife-beater T-shirts. This place makes craft the equal of art. In fact, it makes craftiness into art. We sometimes forget that decoration itself is at the heart of luxury. This is just a new art form, scenography, stagecraft, taken up a few clicks.

Everything from the Doges' Palace to the Campanile is built virtually to the scale of the original. Everything, and I mean every thing—Ca' d'Oro, Rialto Bridge, Contarini Palace—is jammed in together so that when you turn a corner, you are whipsawed the way you might be in a house of horrors. "Oh, my God, how did that get here!" is part of the frisson. The only thing missing is the Basilica of St. Mark. But that's because all spiritual imagery that might be offensive to religious gamblers has been excised. Only secular tourist attractions, please.

After New York-New York (the hotel-casino) opened, Adelson dismissed it as a fake, famously saying, "We are not going to build a faux Venice. We are going to build what is essentially the real Venice." Hoot if you must. This edifice may not be real Venice, but it is really something. In fact, being inside the Venetian is perpetually disconcerting. It's like being inside a compression chamber of all Vegas. It never quits.

As they say in faint praise about movie production costs, you can see every dollar on the screen. And here in the Venetian you can see every dollar—about one hundred million of them—spent on the walls. Luxury is all over. No gaps. Venice, we were told at the front desk, was the first city in Europe to open a public gaming house, accessible only to patrons wearing a mask. How appropriate. In this hotel slightly dazed gawkers and gamblers were wandering masked in amazement. Coming through the St. Mark and St. Theodore columns, which flank the pedestrian entrance into the domed and rounded lobby, is like stepping into a cold-water Jacuzzi. You pay attention. All above you is the gold-leafed Armillari Sphere, reminiscent of one found in the Doges' map room in Venice.

As you walk toward the casino, you find perfect reproductions of Tiepolo, Titian, and Veronese on the ceilings of the basilica-size hallways. Okay, okay, they were laid out on computers, transferred to canvases, and then hand-painted in with acrylics, or simply sprayed on, but they are . . . awesome. Working from photographs of the facades of the actual buildings, every column and capital, including cracks, effacements, defacements, and discolorations, has been perfectly reproduced. You cannot be blasé.

It's so easy in Vegas to howl in disbelief as you view faux-u-luxe used as a marketing device to sell you the idiocy of gambling. It's so well done that you forget that foam, plastic, Fiberglass, cast stone, or glass-reinforced concrete are really the marble and granite of our times. So what if it's going to be trashed in a decade? Then again, wasn't Michelangelo often doing the same thing? Frescoes were continually painted over, statuary rechiseled. Remember that Venice itself has miles of make-believe marble just out of reach. Recall that fooling the eye is part of the allure of in-your-face decoration. Trompe l'oeil is at the heart of deluxe, the essence of accessorizing, of making things appear slightly better than they are. Diamonds are cut to shine, gold polished, and copper plate laid on dull surfaces for the same reason.

Once past the casino, inside Venice proper as it were, the canals appear. The illusion of luxe dissipates, if only because it is now so hokey, so in the service of mallcondo commercialization. Drat! Real life intrudes. Having those Rodeo Drive stores face the canal, almost completely unaffected by the surrounding aura, makes the whole scene appear kitschy, as though you are in the Beverly Hills mall. And, of course, there they are, those same stores, same machine-made designer stuff, same clientele. Check out the slack-jawed guests sitting in the gondolas as they ply the eight-hundred-foot canal. Same people we saw coming out of NikeTown and the Hard Rock Cafe, same slingshots, baseball caps, shorts, and all.

There is something disconcerting about crossing the sixteenth-century Rialto Bridge through the Palazzo Contarini-Fasan (where Desdemona lived) and passing over the Bridge of Sighs to end up in a place selling sweatshirts with a happy face logo. Othello would have been dumbstruck. Although there are about 500,000 square feet of shopping space in the Grand Canal Shoppes, as they are called, it is really same-old, same-old. Here are the low-tone luxury retailers—Ann Taylor, Banana Republic, Kenneth Cole—slightly put off by being next to New Balance and Rockport shoe stores, but I guess this makes sense. I mean, isn't getting into sneakers how we know that real traveling/shopping is taking place?

Still, sneakers, sweatshirts, and all, coming out of a cigar store and basking in a perfect reproduction of the Piazza San Marco is a stunning experience. Under a seventy-foot cathedral-like ceiling painted in the tender hues of Venice's pink-dusted early evening sky, you forget for a second what is happening. Although management is working out the kinks, someday trained pigeons will appear hourly, their excretory clocks reset. But until then, the other kind of trained pigeons will fly their patterns, landing, the management hopes, in the casino or, if not, in these stores.

The same application of designer luxe to restaurant food that Liz and I saw at the Bellagio is happening here at the Venetian. What a tasty irony that a few years ago Las Vegas was the largest city in the country without a nationally known restaurant. Soon, if things continue, it will offer every nationally known restaurant. So here we have Eberhard Muller's Lutèce, Piero Selvaggio's Valentino, Stephan Pyles's Star Canyon, Joachim Splichanal's Pinot Brasserie, Kevin Wu's Royal Star, Wolfgang Puck's Postrio—all described in the literature complete with chef name/restaurant name, just as we have Giorgio Armani/Armani Exchange, Ralph Lauren/Polo Sport, or Donna Karan/DKNY. If the Venetian has an on-the-cheap Vegas buffet, we couldn't find it. Just like the "essentially real Venice."

Let the Bellagio have art in a room, the Venetian has art as a room. Baddaboom! Thomas Krens, impresario of the Guggenheim, is shuttling not only some of his collection but also some from the Hermitage out to the frontier. First show? The Art of the Motorcycle. The Venetian also has another touchstone of the luxe life, albeit righteous indulgence, a branch of the Canyon Ranch Spa. On the fourth floor is a nest of all that the old Wild West Vegas abhorred: a sixty-three-thousand-square-foot smoke- and alcohol-free warren of repentance. The Canyon Ranch is a kind of antidote to Vegas, a kind of glitz-free "miserabilisme de luxe," as Elsa Schiaparelli once accused Coco Chanel of inventing, the hair shirt of cashmere. Canyon Ranch is Calvin Klein to the Venetian Versace.

As we left the Venetian, we passed by Madame Tussaud's Celebrity Encounter franchise, portraying all the great stars who have entertained in Vegas. Somehow this is fitting. But, I wondered, would they mention that this "encounter" is occurring foursquare over the rubble of the old Sands Hotel, that celebrated haunt of Frank Sinatra and his rat pack? I doubted it. Just as there was no mention at the Bellagio that it was responsible for the "implosion" of the Dunes and its wonderful sign. Vegas doesn't go in for memory. It prefers its reality under a seventy-foot cathedral-like ceiling painted in the tender hues of Venice's pink-dusted early evening sky. And no wonder.

8.

Still Learning from Las Vegas
HOW LUXURY IS TURNING RELIGIOUS

> *Like so many Americans, she was trying to construct*
> *a life that made sense from things she found in*
> *gift shops.*
>
> —Kurt Vonnegut, *Slaughterhouse Five*

Back in my room at the Luxor I tried to figure out what it was that I had seen at the Bellagio and the Venetian and what, if anything, it all had to do with the current flood of luxury for the masses. Clearly, whatever this glittering stuff was, it was attracting hordes of people. They wanted to be near it, to see themselves in it, and would *spend* time and money to have at it.

Such an irony that glitz, on the surface at least, is made up of two of the first technoluxe products of the modern world: mass-produced glass and mirrors. Glass was the most magical of Victorian luxuries for, although fragile, it was to become the sturdy medium erasing distinctions between places, between indoors and outdoors, between people while giving the viewer an eerie sense of being able to penetrate the material world. And mirrors—"looking glass," really, glass in reverse—allowed everyone access to themselves. You could see yourself not just in the eyes of others but in your own eyes. You could have the most precious of luxuries—you could have self-knowledge *and* pretension. Nothing is more satisfying than solipsism and dreams of glory.

Luxury as Poshlost

But this stuff, glitz, has always attracted the young. Mass-marketed glitz is always on the edge of *poshlost*. Vladimir Nabokov coined this term to describe everything trite, banal, and commonplace in contemporary culture, albeit from the point of view of a curmudgeon. Clearly, he enjoyed the verbal play on *posh* and *lost*, elegance gone astray, thanks in part to mass production. To Humbert Humbert *poshlost* is the world surrounding his Lolita.

But Nabokov took this stuff seriously. In fact, he loved to catalog it. In his idiosyncratic and often simply weird study of Gogol in 1944, he forever linked *Dead Souls* to the actual Russian word *poshlost*. The Russian noun defies easy translation but suggests "the falsely important, the falsely beautiful, the falsely clever." He then devoted about twelve pages (out of 155) to defining and musing upon a single "pitiless" Russian coinage.

Nabokov claims the concept was invoked by Dostoyevsky to describe how his protagonist, Raskolnikov, is more upset to be thought common than to be considered a murderer. I think Nabokov focuses on this perversion, this turning inside out of traditional values, as a foreshadowing of what the material world wrought by mass production was producing. In a sense, if I read Nabokov correctly, he is predicting that we are exchanging traditional elegance for something more democratic and certainly more vulgar—the massification of finery, the trashing of taste. Machine-made luxe is oxymoronic.

Yet *poshlost* is everywhere. No culture is exempt. Go to Nabokov's own birth culture, go to Moscow. The Arbat, Moscow's half-mile pedestrian mall, is filled with this glitzy stuff. It's the umpteenth set of matryoshki, the wooden nesting dolls shaped like bowling pins, with a vacant "happy face" on each. It is the imitation Palekh box, the black-lacquered papier-mâché knick-knack with a fairy tale painted on the top. It is fake preciousness done in glass and mirrors. If you have been to Russia recently, you will see that this is just the preparation for the surging attraction for the stuff seen on Rodeo Drive and Madison Avenue—Euroluxe made *poshlost*.

The Farouk Conundrum

I like the term *poshlost* because it implies that this is where posh is lost, in unappreciated parody, in meaningless display. To be sure, it tends toward the grotesque, like the countless designer shoes of Imelda Marcos. Contemplating it boggles the mind, literally. It stymies us. Why do we consume not just unnecessary things but unaesthetic things? If Imelda Marcos changed her shoes three times a day, and never wore the same pair twice, it would take her more than two years and five months to work through her shoe supply. And, assuming she was laying away new shoes at her peak rate, it is possible she would never finish, a Zeno's paradox of consumption (Morrow 1986:80). Little wonder that Imelda has recently opened the Footwear Museum in Manila to display her extravagance—her obsession—now in the service of boosting tourism.

This is parodic display of luxury: comic, sad, awful, and weirdly alluring. There is something childish about the delusional aspect of such focused consumption and, by extension, of all opuluxe, something exhibitionistic and omnipotent. It's magical, dreamlike, childlike. Indeed, *pissing* it away does seem the appropriate trope.

And what of Egypt's King Farouk, the Donald Trump of my childhood, who drained much of the value from luxury by brute force, by furious consumption? He always had more oysters than he could eat. He was always getting sick and vomiting. His conundrum was prefigured by his grandfather, who died in 1895 while trying to guzzle two bottles of champagne in one draft. The senior Farouk kept a harem of three thousand women. But why? This is luxury not at the point of not enough but of way too much. Perhaps in his last days he was drinking to forget the harem. Perhaps the road of excess does indeed lead to the Palace of Wisdom. More likely, it leads to the Palace of Exhaustion.

The Experiencing of Fantasy Luxe

When an individual achieves such wretched excess, we say it is avarice, but when an entire city like Las Vegas does it, it is not so easy to categorize. In fact, a Canadian sociologist, John Hannigan, has coined the term *fantasy city* to describe this new mutation in urban creation—a place to go to consume, to give in to the urge to splurge. Cities used to be based on manufacturing, or hog butchering, or the shouted trading of stocks, or the exchange of goods, or putting things on ships. Now a new kind of urban economy, rooted in tourism, sports, gambling, entertainment, and spending, is reworking the landscape. You go there to spend, just to spend—time and money. T&A is almost an afterthought.

For students of luxury consumption the fantasy city is every bit as prescient a concept as Joel Garreau's relentlessly cited 1991 *Edge City*. The edge city was the suburban minicity that arose outside the urban core. And before that, of course, the *suburb*, the city set off to the side. The fantasy city is exactly what was being created on Rodeo Drive, Worth Avenue, or upper Madison. It just hadn't gone as far as Vegas. The fantasy city is, in a sense, the Trump Tower squashed and made horizontal—the mallcondo city. And what holds it together is not production but consumption.

Still, Vegas does more. It also swallows up concepts like the Mall of America, complete with Camp Snoopy; it jumbles bars and wedding chapels; it has the spectacular signage of Times Square, the ordered routines of Disneyland, the never-ending chaos of conventioneering, and the relentless gambling. The fantasy city takes a central theme—in this case the luxe life, the life better than the one you have at home—and spreads it through an infrastructure of megaplex malls, themed restaurants, interchangeable casinos, designer stores, musical extravaganzas, and other large-scale complexes, all of which adapt to one impulse: spending *on* entertainment, spending *as* entertainment; pleasure is consumption and consumption is pleasurable.

In this sense gambling has become almost secondary in Vegas. In fact, what gambling now seems to do is set the tone of vague licentiousness. What I thought I saw in Vegas is how much we enjoy escape into dreamland and how much we are willing to pay to get there. Although more than half of all Americans older than eighteen have been in a darkened casino, less than a third have been to Vegas. If demographic projections are correct, before long, they will go. The population of the country will flit through Vegas like cards through a shuffler. And, once there, chances are they will end up somewhere like the Bellagio, the Venetian, Caesars Palace, or the Luxor.

And this is not to gamble but to just *be* there, to participate in something indulgent and sumptuous. In the last few years the spending habits of Las Vegas's thirty million annual visitors have been shifting dramatically away from gambling to spending on hotels, shopping, dining, shows, shows, shows. In the 1990s nongambling revenue often accounted for more than 50 percent of the annual $12 billion take. It is estimated that by 2025 it may reach as high as 75 percent (Mirabella 1998:1D). Clearly, what is happening is that shopping/eating/gambling/shows is becoming not just a vacation experience but a coherent themed lifelong experience.

Clearly, those shops, the same shops I had seen on Rodeo Drive and Worth Avenue, selling the same stuff I had seen advertised in *Vanity Fair* and *GQ*, were an integral part of being in the fantasy city. And when you realize that the stuff itself—that designer purse, that logo-encrusted tie, those fancy shoes, the embossed sunglasses—is rapidly becoming susceptible to e-commerce, where price points will trump locale, you can see that maybe Vegas is the future after all. We will travel somewhere to buy the experience of being somewhere—anywhere but in front of our keyboard!—to buy something.

Caesars Palace

Of all the places I visited in Vegas, Caesars Palace seemed to understand best how to make luxury consumption into a free-standing experience linked by one-way moving sidewalks. Consider the Forum Shops, for instance. This mall, next to the casino inside the hotel, displays its distinctive theme—an ancient Roman marketplace—in every detail. The Simon DeBartolo Group, which is better known for developing innumerable boring shopping centers off numerous interstate cloverleafs, developed this shopping "experience," right down to the mosaics in the men's room. Let's face it: You don't often enter a mall through a 150-foot-high re-creation of the Pantheon.

It has marble floors, stark white pillars, hermetically sealed "outdoor" cafes, living trees, flowing fountains, and even a painted blue sky with fluffy white clouds that burst into simulated storms, complete with lightning and thunder. Every entrance to the Forum Shops and every storefront is an elaborate re-creation of a Roman portal. Inside the main entrance animatronic statues of Caesar and other Roman luminaries come to life every hour and speak. "Hail, Caesar!" is as frequent a cry as is "Yo, dude," as Roman centurions periodically march through crowds of hoi polloi on their way to the adjacent Caesars Palace casino. I must admit that the casino-anchored mall is a little much. But still, it's like nothing anything I have ever seen.

The Roman theme even extends into the shops. A jewelry store's interior, for instance, features scrolls, tablets, Roman numerals, and gold draperies. The theme doesn't imply opulence, it shouts it. And the mall's sales repeatedly record the fact. This mall consistently earns more than $1,200 per square foot per year, compared with a typical mall's sales of less than $300. Clearly, people with a lot of money to spend and not much to do are walking back and forth from hotel to hotel, just like kids attending the same movie over and over. Clearly, they have seen these stores before. Same-old, same-old: Armani, Versace, or Louis Vuitton at the top; Gap, Victoria's Secret, and Ann Taylor in the middle, and then the ubiquitous multilevel superstores like NikeTown and Virgin Megastore at the bottom. While no other shopping space comes close to generating such excitement, as you approach the cash register, it is just been-there, bought-that.

What I found astonishing was that these were the same stores selling the same stuff that I saw down the road at the Bellagio and the Venetian. In other words, this was the same audience, consuming the same stuff, at each of the hotels. Clearly, it was the experience of buying something *in Vegas*, not just buying something, that was exciting. As well, there is also the feeling that all this luxury is close at hand—not the result of hard work but of luck. An hour throwing craps and *you* could buy those Gucci slippers. In other words, what I was seeing was perhaps the future of luxury in the Western world. It is not buying stuff but buying the sensation of buying. When you've got enough of everything, what do you buy? You buy buying.

Vegas Has Its Roots in the Themed Exposition

As I've already argued, while a fruitful analogy can be had with the Holy Roman Catholic Church in the Renaissance, the themed exposition is the proximate inspiration for Vegas. Not by happenstance did it originate in the church square. But from the 1850s on, the great expositions created large public places for the display of goods and the celebration of secular materialism. What was progress but better things? The concept of salvation was always close at hand, *Deo volente*. First, at the Crystal Palace in London (1851), followed by the Universal Exposition Park in Paris (1855), the movement of perfectability and self-congratulations through consumption exploded. The United States put in its two cents' worth at the Centennial Exposition in Philadelphia (1876), and the World's Columbian Exposition in Chicago (1893). You traveled, you saw, you bought stuff, you brought it home, it made you feel better.

The amusement component broke loose from the exposition. And, as Gregory Beck of the Harvard Graduate School of Design tells us,

> by the turn of the century, amusement parks in Europe and the U.S. were in full bloom. The beaches of Coney Island, N.Y., overflowed with immigrants

anxious to forget the trials of urban life and pursue new forms of pleasure and fantasy. Here, at last, was tangible evidence that the American Dream could pay off. Amusement-park architecture leapt from the pages of story books and pulp science fiction into the American experience. A visit to Coney Island's Dreamland attraction (1904) immersed guests in an unforgettable world of palaces and rides that were both lyrical and surreal. (1999:132)

It was as if escape to the market had been replaced by escape into sensation. Even the World's Fairs of the twentieth century could not compete with the visceral call of leisure parks. You pick and choose sensations to buy.

While we may think that "themed escape" is a licensed thrill for the kiddies and a debasement of sobriety for adults, it has become the default behavior of almost every modern social, educational, and political endeavor. Entertainment is not just at the heart of almost all American culture, it *is* American culture. When you hear museum directors talking about the "guest experience," retail merchandisers speaking about "store immersion," "brand narratives," and "length of stay," or even college professors talking about "servicing needs" and "demand-based education," you know something has happened.

Borrowing a phrase from the computer industry, the *new,* new thing is not about the content, not about hardware, it's about the sensation of use. Intel chairman Andrew Grove was not far off when he declared at the November 1996 COMDEX computer trade show (in Vegas, incidentally), "We need to look at our business as more than simply the building and selling of personal computers. Our business is the delivery of information and lifelike interactive experiences" (in Gilmore 1998:102). That luxury would be consumed as a "lifelike" experience, not just as a pattern of objects, was inevitable.

Look at the worldwide explosion of consumption *as* entertainment and you will see not just the context of Vegas but the future of luxe. Consider these hybrids built in the 1990s: the World of Coca-Cola, Atlanta; Universal Studios, Orlando, Florida; Planet Hollywood, New York; NikeTown, Chicago; Mall of America, Minnesota; Expo '92, Seville, Spain; Disneyland, Paris; Luxor and Caesars Forum Shops, Las Vegas; SonyWonder, New York; Liberty Science Center, Jersey City, New Jersey; Universal CityWalk, Los Angeles; BMW Visitors Center, Spartenberg, Tenn.; Trocadero, London; Sony IMAX Theater, New York; House of Blues, Boston; Fremont Street Experience, Las Vegas; Port Aventura, Spain; All-Star Sports Cafe, New York;

AT&T Pavilion, Atlanta; Mohegan Sun Casino, Mystic, Connecticut; Sega-World, London; Canal City Hakata, Japan; Cirque du Soleil, Orlando, Florida; Virgin Megastore, New York; GameWorks, Seattle; ESPN Zone, Baltimore; Animal Kingdom, Walt Disney World, Florida; Navy Pier, Chicago; DisneyQuest, Chicago; NBA City, Orlando; NBC Access Store, New York; Universal Islands, Orlando, Florida; Sony Metreon, San Francisco; Estacao Plaza, Curitiba, Brazil (Beck 1999:132).

The Franchising of Luxury as Experience

That this list has a disproportionate number of sites created by the Walt Disney Company is not happenstance. After all, the two most important *fantasy* cities for the future are Celebration, the Disney city near Orlando, and the Strip in Las Vegas. The genius of Disney—or, specifically, Walt Disney Imagineering, the in-house design group—was in seeing that the themed experience, in which the "host" corporation gives up exchanging an *object* for money and instead embarks on the more rewarding exchanging of a *story* for money, was the wave of the future. Not by happenstance has the U.S. government stopped supporting the World's Fair with an exhibit. Many companies have followed suit. Why give away what people will come here and pay to experience?

While you may think that Vegas and Disneyland/World are separate and distinct from the rest of Western culture, such is clearly not the case. As Joseph Pine and James H. Gilmore make clear in *The Experience Economy,* the selling of *experience,* especially the fantasy experience of luxury, is the future of top-end transactions. After all, that is exactly what advertising attempts to do; it's the value advertising adds to an object. In ad lingo, if they will buy the brand, why not make that the product? As the authors point out, saleable experiences come in four varieties: entertaining, educational, aesthetic, and escapist. Clearly, the last one is becoming dominant as leisure time becomes an exploitable luxury.

Look at it this way, says Gilmore in his *Harvard Business Review* article on this subject:

> The entire history of economic progress can be recapitulated in the four-stage evolution of the birthday cake. As a vestige of the agrarian economy, mothers made birthday cakes from scratch, mixing farm commodities (flour, sugar, butter, and eggs) that together cost mere dimes. As the goods-based in-

dustrial economy advanced, moms paid a dollar or two to Betty Crocker for premixed ingredients. Later, when the service economy took hold, busy parents ordered cakes from the bakery or grocery store, which, at $10 or $15, cost ten times as much as the packaged ingredients. Now, in the time-starved 1990s, parents neither make the birthday cake nor even throw the party. Instead, they spend $100 or more to "outsource" the entire event to Chuck E. Cheese's, the Discovery Zone, the Mining Company, or some other business that stages a memorable event for the kids—and often throws in the cake for free. Welcome to the emerging experience economy. (97)

This phenomenon helps explain Las Vegas. It's just like such establishments as Sony Style, Microsoft SF, and PlayStation stores. Enter, look, be entertained, buy. Houston's Momentum Motor Cars has a miniature racetrack complete with a retired race car driver to command it. You race the luxury car. Then you buy the street version. In Seattle you go to the Recreational Equipment store to climb a wall, descend into a cave, enter a bubble to live "at altitude." Then buy a parka. In NikeTown, inside New York's Trump Tower, there is a gymnasium where shoppers can shoot a few hoops and test the merchandise. What do they sell? Sneakers? This is not just "shoppertainment" or "entertailing"—it's a mimic of the actual experience: the "feelies."

The prime example, of course, of how to succeed at embedding goods into a total experience is Harley-Davidson. The first Harley Cafe opened in New York City in 1993. The second opened in Las Vegas in 1997, right across the street from the Bellagio. These stores cater to the idea that a Harley-Davidson motorcycle is not just a mode of transportation, it is a lifestyle that can be bought. The attractions inside include real bikes, celebrity Harley memorabilia, and, by the way, pretty dreadful food. Say what you want, any product that encourages customers to have a likeness tattooed on their bodies is doing something like the luxury experience. The customer literally brands himself with your logo.

Why Go Anywhere If What You Really Want Is the Comforts of Home?

I had been seeing the edges of this phenomenon of marketing luxe as experience, not object, in all those earlier venues of New York, Palm Beach, and Los Angeles. The convergence of luxury as a mode of understanding where we are in life, and in the world, seems to be defining modern cultures.

Thinking again about Las Vegas, this might explain the importance of the travel motif in Vegas. You have to go to Vegas. From there you go to the worlds of faraway luxe (Luxor, Caesars Palace, Bellagio, Venetian); to standard tourist destinations (New York-New York, Paris, MGM Grand Hotel, Mandalay Bay Resort), or else to an out-and-out fantasy world (Mirage, Treasure Island, Excalibur). It's just like Disney World. You have your choice of Main Street USA, Fantasyland, Frontier-Land, Tomorrowland, Adventureland, Exhaustionland. Little wonder these magic kingdoms are called "destination resorts." After a few days there, all you want to do is lie down.

But travel in Vegas is different in that it's not for the kiddies and thus there is always the sense of wink-wink irony. The kids have to take it seriously; we don't. We know where we are. Yet the repeated motif of getting away is omnipresent. For instance, I'm holding in my hands the information packet that the Venetian sends to prospective guests. In the company's own words but with my italics, the "Venetian Experience" is explained:

> The Venetian *transports* you to another place and time by providing a sense of being surrounded by the festivity and splendor of Venice's architecture, music, art and history.
>
> Your *sojourn* will provide an extraordinary *journey* to the most unforgettable vacation resort ever.
>
> Visitors will be *transported* to another place and time. Upon entering the Venetian, guests will feel they've actually been *transported* to Venice. The Venetian *recreates* the famous landmarks that make Venice the most loved romantic city in the world. In fact, two historians are on retainer to ensure the integrity of the design and architecture.
>
> The Grand Canal Shoppes is an extensive 500,000-square-foot themed, indoor retail mall. Shoppers will be *transported* to another time and place in a festival-like atmosphere, including serenading gondoliers, artisans, glass blowers and masque makers.
>
> A one-quarter mile Venetian streetscape filled with authentically designed neighborhoods will *transport* shoppers to the festival-like atmosphere of old world Venice. Shoppers can enjoy a cappuccino at one of the waterside cafes while being entertained by Venetian performing artists, bringing to life legendary Italian characters. Shoppers will be *enchanted* by the tales of world-explorer Marco Polo, *succumb* to the charms of beguiling Marianne and *fall in love* with irresistible Casanova. The vibrant sense of an open-air experi-

ence culminates at St. Mark's Square, the centerpiece of the mall, set beneath a cathedral-style ceiling painted in the beautiful colors of the Venetian sky.

Some years ago Dean MacCannell, a landscape architect-turned pop-cult-scholar, wrote a book, *The Tourist: A New Theory of a Leisure Class,* in which he argued that midcult travel was slowly transforming into a kind of entertainment characterized by consumption, seeing designated sights, and then buying mementos of it. His point: Because where we now go is almost the same as where we left, it might be more provocative to ask not what do you want to see but why you want to leave where you are.

Face it . . . literally. If you go down the Champs-Élysées in Paris, you find the same stores, the same use of public space, the same tourist post-card sights (albeit in different scale), and the same hotels that you'd find on any square in any major city in the world. Well, almost. So it does leave the question of the motivation for this kind of sightseeing rather open. Essentially, sights have been set up to "see," surrounded by places to buy images of what you have "seen." Thus the paradox of tourism is that no matter how different the place is that one wants to go, when you get there you will find that it's pretty well set up to be seen, that it will look pretty much like any other destination, and that, now seen, it's time to leave. The Oregon bumper sticker is no joke: "Welcome to Oregon, now go home." *Veni, vidi, ivi domum.*

Tourism and travel do have a lot in common, which is why it's not hard for us confuse them. Both are mechanisms of escape—from the daily grind, the job, the boss, even the parents or the kids. But in their common quest for "authenticity," resemblances between tourism and real travel peter out. Travel derives from *travail* and is less like vacationing and more like a quest. It is laborious. One of the traveler's ailments is homesickness, and another is loneliness. And a customary, if not always admitted, companion is panic—of strangers, of embarrassment, of violence or madness appearing in unaccustomed forms. In fact, as Paul Fussell (1991) has said, real travel tends to be sickening, literally, at least temporarily. As Sandy Pittman found out on her ill-fated jaunt up Everest in 1996, this may be the *real* luxury of modern life, and it can be profoundly upsetting (Krakauer 1997).

Tourism, however, is travel without labor. In the fauxluxe version, you are transported there, you see what is there, you photograph it, buy something, and come straight back home. It is comfortable and consoling. You move in a bubble of known language, food, and services. Ever wonder why cruises are the fastest-growing segment of the travel industry? What makes it a common form of modern luxury is that the experience of being somewhere else is analogous to dreaming. You are transported, magically. Look at any cruise ad and you see this again and again. My favorite? "Cruises to Nowhere" from SeaEscape in Miami. This $500 million-a-year business has thirteen ships that take you out to sea, let you gamble and buy duty-free stuff, and then, six hours later, bring you back to port.

But, of course, the promise of Vegas is that you experience none of the hassle, all of the dreams. Who wants to really go anywhere when the very act has been made hopelessly tedious? Even Eugene Fodor, whose guidebooks have been among the most effective stimulators of international tourism, is now almost contrite about the damage he has wrought. In his guidebook to Rome he ruefully notes that partly as a result of his own efforts, eleven thousand tourists per day now swamp the Sistine Chapel, making a visit to it "an equal blend of pleasure and torture" (Fussell 1991:26). Better go to the Bellagio Gallery of Fine Art or the Doges Palace at the Venetian.°

Have you ever been to Venice? What a chore! How much easier to experience the mimicry of Vegas. Plus, if mass tourism has Disney-fied the planet, Coca-Colonized cultures, unbalancing ecosystems and degrading both holiday makers and hosts, ecosalvation may sit atop these casinos. Replicas, simulations, impersonations, and heritage "experiences" are now an integral part of tourism, and Vegas just gathers them up and sells them to us as souvenirs of experience. Such tourism simply becomes an extension of the great cultural expression of the late twentieth century: shopping for stuff, buying experiences.

The Tourism of Indulgence

It may be an irony of note that the farther away from home we travel, the closer we get to our home selves. Free from prying eyes, our yearning for

---

°Access to the Parthenon is restricted because of damage caused by visitors. Stonehenge has been so trampled that there are plans to build an exact replica next door. The floor of Canterbury Cathedral has been worn down by human feet. More than a hundred visitors enter Notre Dame in Paris each minute. Buses idle their engines outside, their fumes corroding the stonework. At Lascaux in the Dordogne, the bacteria from the breath of visitors left a mold that degraded the paintings. The prehistoric cave paintings are better seen in replica, much acclaimed for its exactness.

luxury, in soothing the self, consuming passion, and passionately consuming, becomes more obvious. This is the opposite of what Veblen saw in the Gilded Age, and, strangely enough, this kind of privatization of conspicuous consumption is just too obvious to miss in Vegas. It's everywhere.

Of all the sights I marveled at in Vegas, none was more marvelous than my bathroom at the Luxor. First, it was huge. It was easily a third of the size of the bedroom. And it was fit for a king. Everything done in regal splendor, every inch on fire with shine, a tub you could languish in, a shower stall with two shower heads, a commode that gleamed, flanked by *two* toilet paper dispensers, the requisite two sinks, and a mirrored wall complete with a magnifying makeup mirror on accordion suspension that came halfway across the room. This place was surreal. And it was all mine. I felt like Stendhal in Florence, like Daisy Buchanan in the closet, like stout Cortés staring into the Pacific.

What was the connection between this private luxury that no one could see but me and the garish display of the Strip, which couldn't be missed? This room was the essence of private indulgence on the inside, and it must have something to do with the business of this place, namely, getting me into that casino.

Selling Indulgence: The Economic Power of Luxury

Las Vegas, the modern Rome, lives by selling indulgences. Indulgence was once a religious concept. Now it has come to mean individual satisfaction. Essentially, the religious argument supporting indulgence was that "good work" (prayers, fasting, almsgiving) could be used to shorten the length of penance demanded for sin. By the Middle Ages the emphasis on almsgiving had become an institutionalized method of raising funds. Most of the great cathedrals and universities of Western Europe were created by the gathering of indulgences, the bounties of the greatest protection racket the world has ever seen.

Two kinds of indulgences developed: plenary, or remission from all punishment for a sin, and partial, or remission for part of a specific sin. Prices were negotiable, but what was being transferred for money was the sense of palpable relief, the sense of lifted weight. Such a powerful means of anxiety control was hardly neglected by early modern man. And such a powerful means of capital creation was hardly neglected by the popes. In the sixteenth century Pope Julius II offered vast indulgences in exchange

The democratizing of indulgence as a way to sell watches, soap, cereal, hotel rooms, towels, dresses, and you name it.

for contributions to build St. Peter's Basilica in Rome. Until Martin Luther, no one much cared that the industry selling forgiveness was the same one creating the sin.

The institution is still alive and well in the Vatican. It clearly still meets parishioners' needs. In 1985 Pope John Paul II allowed Catholics to receive partial indulgences by watching television. Believers who follow a church service on television or radio are granted a reprieve from punishment so long as they fulfill the same conditions as those physically present, including confession, communion, and prayer. Next time you pass through the Rome airport, notice the concessionary chapel. You can purchase an indulgence on a stopover, much to the embarrassment of the government, which has tried to move the chapel out of public space. Good luck. There is always a line out front. And, as I write this, the pope has announced that

in celebration of entering the third millennium of Christianity—the Jubilee Year—penitents who do a charitable deed or give up cigarettes or alcohol for a day can earn a partial indulgence. Church officials are quick to emphasize that such indulgences are not a loophole for sinners. Still, some liberal Catholics are embarrassed by a practice that seems to offer a shortcut to salvation. The protection racket aspect is just too obvious to miss, no matter how it is disguised.

But what is important is that the illusion of the *remission* of sin is so powerful to humans. As one might imagine, any exchange this powerful is not to be neglected on Madison Avenue. In advertising everyday items, the promise of reciprocal salvation for minor indulgence—partial indulgences, as it were—is at the heart of many a pitch. Often, thanksgiving is directed to the producer, as in the rhetoric of penitential religiosity: "Thank you, Paine-Webber." "Thank you, Tasty-Cakes." "I love what you do for me." "Thanks, DelCo." "Thanks, Crest."

But more often it is the promise of what the object will *do* for your sense of self-esteem that is important. If you wonder about the allure of indulgence, the sense of providing relief, simply pay attention to advertising. How else to understand the claim of such otherwise outrageous slogans as "You deserve a break today," "You are worth it," "You only go 'round once," "Treat yourself." Such affirmation is at the heart of the invocation to *self*-indulgence.

Sometimes this subtle affirmation of value is expressed as totally private. The argument is couched thusly: You may be the only one who knows you are wearing cashmere socks, but you still get a boost in self-worth from the sumptuous softness. A silver key ring may be one of Tiffany's most budget-minded treasures, but you'll appreciate what it says about you every time you unlock your back door. Gucci puts its logo inside the man's wallet so only he can see it as he reaches for his bills. L'Oréal hair coloring is done in private. But what's the pitch? "I'm worth it."

As one might expect, the selling of personal products often relies on this level of deserved indulgence. In fact, there is a magazine, mostly for men, called *Indulgence: The Art of Fine Living*, which is loaded with display items like boats, cars, ghastly wall hangings called Works of Art, and paperweights. As I've mentioned, there is even a Web site that sells beauty products, mostly to women, called indulge.com. But the invocation of self-indulgence is so common in modern culture as to be unremarkable.

If the appeal to indulgence is muted in selling everyday luxury items, when it comes to hawking top-of-the-line products, it can be like banging a spoon on a kettle. Look at how this expensive watch exploits the concept of self-reward via consumption. We are invited to "be late" by Concord watch. Why? Because "Time is a luxury" for someone like yourself who can afford such an expensive timepiece. Presumably, "Time is a necessity" for the rest of us. If you can afford this watch, you don't need to tell time, don't need a watch, so having it is special precisely because you don't need it.

Does "Be Late. Time is a luxury" really mean "Be Rude. You're special"?

Back to the Bathroom

Could this be the explanation for the almost furious luxurification of the bathroom? Is there a connection between regal self-splendor that leads to increased confidence in self-worth and the final goal of such confidence, namely, to gamble away money? You are special. You are a winner. Now go lose your money. I became so intrigued by the role of bathroom as contrived pardon, as proof not just of worth to others but remission of sin, that I decided to inspect what this private space looked like at the Bellagio and the Venetian.

I was not disappointed. If the euphemism "master bedroom" works for sleeping space and "king-sized" is invoked for bedding, then surely the most heraldic aspect of the Vegas hotel room is the most private. A tour of the upstairs accommodations reveals that the Bellagio's just-for-folks guest rooms, which carry a publicized nightly rate ranging from $159 to $459, make the Luxor look like Ho-Jo's. The Bellagio's standard-issue bathroom has a marble floor and oversized soaking pool (hardly a *tub*) with Jacuzzi jets. And across the street at the Venetian, where I was repeatedly told that every room is a *suite*, the situation is simply ridiculous. First, every room features a marble foyer entrance complete with crown molding and base-boards. Every room (whoops, suite) has a private "bedchamber" with draped canopies and recessed lighting. And every suite has a sunken living room, separated from the rest of the space by a wrought-iron railing. The bathroom is a simply massive 130-square-foot extravaganza finished top-to-toe in Italian marble. You could almost swim laps in this lagoon. The whole bathroom is about the size of my Luxor bedroom.

When I went downstairs to check the bathrooms for commoners off the street—not the guests—I saw the same phenomenon. In the public men's room of the Bellagio everything is done in faux gold: gold urinals, gold handles, golden-framed pictures on the wall of aspirational ancestors, marble floors, comfy sitting chairs, golden mosaic molding, and in the stalls golden paper dispensers and private reading lights. Whatever is happening here in Vegas is simply the big-print version of what is happening to the rest of American culture: the voluptu-izing of private space with intense ornamentation, the absolution of ablution. "Look upon my works, ye mighty, and then get to the casino," this room seems to say. "You are good for it. Now go!"

*Publicity photo of bathroom in suite at
the Venetian.*

The Aura of Vegas

Somehow these disparate aspects of public and private luxury are coming together in postmodern Vegas: the importance of textured experience, manipulated indulgence, isolation, increasing levels of private affirmation, and, most of all, a dream world where some kind of subtle reaffirmation and redemption occurs just by being there. The one thing Vegas luxury is not is simple. It is layering itself down over other experiences.°

I should have listened more closely to the Pigeon sisters. They understood what Vegas was all about. I now realized that their yearly trip here had all the characteristics of pilgrimage. They planned it, they knew where they wanted to go, what to see, they moved out into the temples at night, and at the end they were exhausted and ready to go home. They had come to spend what they had saved, to gamble, to get rich, to be saved in a money culture in which luck is as good as any other redemptive device. Amazing grace, how sweet the sound. Ka-ching.

And the place they had picked did have eerie similarities to the cathedral towns of the medieval period. It's "out there," literally and figuratively. Could the same reason that Florence has so many churches, so many over-the-top ornamented churches, be the same reason that Las Vegas has so many casinos, so many over-the-top ornamented sheds? Bear in mind that the essential product, the mass and the casino, are so tightly controlled that distinguishing marks can appear only on the interior walls and on the external facades. Only the faces of the waferlike betting chips were different. This place, for all its devil-may-care attitude, is regulated by the state, the secular Vatican. I don't mean to say that Chartres is Caesars Palace but only that the similarities may be instructive.

Vegas as Modern Florence

Look at Vegas from an art historical point of view. Why was there so much art in Tuscan Italy in the late sixteenth century? Why is there so much luxury in Las Vegas at the end of the twentieth? Florence was a magnet in the

---

°I couldn't get the religiosity of luxury out of my mind. Later, leafing through a catalog of bathroom accessories for the home, I came upon the next new, new thing. You can buy a shower stall with head-to-toe Jacuzzi jets surrounded by stained-glass wall panels. You walk into this stall and it's like going to church, except that you are now both priest and center of adoration.

sixteenth century; people flooded in. Vegas was the fastest-growing city of the 1990s. People were flooding in.

To see low-culture Vegas and high-culture Florence as similar in any meaningful way is an academic sacrilege. After all, separating them has been the major goal of the modern educational enterprise. One is so good for you; the other so bad. So, for now, let us only concentrate on whatever it was that filled, say, Florence during what we call the Renaissance. This luxurious stuff, which was only later called "art," was everywhere. It covered churches both inside and out. New churches and chapels were being built continuously just to showcase these things. Architecture was a Florentine obsession, and much of what was being discovered about the natural world (mathematics, civil engineering, perspective, to name a few) went into their construction. As with modern skyscrapers, occupancy rates ebbed and flowed and many of these churches went bankrupt, their goods disbursed and their spaces reformatted for the next owners.

Corporate alignments were formed to distinguish individual churches from each other. A network of, say, the affiliates of St. Francis allowed liaisons in which the sharing of technology and objects could occur. Certainly, one of the most interesting aspects of this corporate culture was the use of relics. Not only were reliquaries constructed to house items of dubious provenance in order to swell a crowd but these objects separated this church cluster from all others. The showcasing of the relic, be it a piece of hair, straw from the manger, or a patch of swaddling clothes, resembled the modern logo, a blinking sign announcing a specific culture.

If you really wanted to see the glut of luxury objects, however, you had to go inside the churches. Florentine churches were as cluttered with this iconic stuff as the public spaces of these casinos. If ever you wanted to observe the phenomenon of brand extension, here it is.

The Holy Roman Catholic Church is unique in its organization around things, to begin with, and the magic of transubstantiation almost demands an elaborate panoply of objects. As with no other religion, the Catholic mass is filled with display items necessary to conducting the mass. Priests celebrated more than a hundred masses a day in certain Florentine churches during the sixteenth century. They needed more space for all their stuff.

The city-state church became a vast plasma, an ever-expanding medium dedicated to the production and display of early opuluxe articles. These casino-states competed with each other to amass more and more decoration. For instance, Florence went toe to toe with Siena in much the same way that Vegas competes with Atlantic City, the Bellagio with the Venetian.

The main cathedral, the Duomo, was corporate headquarters, fitted out with Ozymandian glee. Surely, the Catholic hierarchy was servicing a demand so prevalent and powerful that it was willing to countenance what we might consider outrageous waste. Not all these edifices survived. For the most part those that did had one thing in common: intense decoration.

One of the reasons there was such abundant supply of this opuluxe stuff is, as the Johns Hopkins economic historian Richard Goldthwaite argues in *Wealth and the Demand for Art in Italy 1300–1600,* because there was so much *demand*. There was intense competition for stuffing those spaces full of eye-catching objects because those spaces could be used to sell services. Opulence was advertising. The mendicant orders, like the Franciscans, Dominicans, Carmelites, Servites, and Augustinian (or Austin) Friars, all established by the midthirteenth century, were organizing massive fundraising drives by providing memorial opportunities and indulgences for large contributors. So successful were they that new orders like the Theatines, Barnabites, Jesuits, Oratorians of St. Philip, and Neri Somaschi joined the fray, all competing for the luxury displays by which they could attract attention for their organizations. So-called second orders for nuns and third orders for laity (Tertiaries) joined other confraternaties (of which there were more than a hundred in Florence alone) in needing their own apparatus, their own display, their own billboards.

The privatization of liturgical space, called laicization, only increased the competition for attention. Florentine churches essentially franchised space, renting walls along the aisles, in the transcepts, and even along the chancel rails. In addition, entire vestries, porches, oratories, altars, sacristies, chapter rooms, and, most lucratively, inner chapels were sold to what was essentially the highest bidder. This bidding was intense. It was not uncommon for corporate families like the Medici, the Strozzi, or the Riccardi to have their own chapels inside the Duomo, buy space in smaller churches around Florence, and then have private chapels inside their houses. The guilds also wanted a piece of this space. Weavers, smithies, traders, and a host of other confederations of workers wanted recognition.

What makes Florence so important is that the real art of the Renaissance was not confined to objects. Donald Trump did not perfect the art of the deal, no matter what he claims. Little wonder that double-entry bookkeeping, the adoption of the florin as international currency, and the colonization of ecclesiastical space all happened in the same place at the same time.

Much of what these artists produced was not what church fathers wanted as much as what the congregation demanded. If a crowd grew in front of a certain wall panel, then similar panels were produced. If an altar proved popular, soon imitations appeared. "I need a fresco like Giotto's," says the Benedictine superior as he watches the crowd thinning out in his church. "I need another Donatello but bigger," says the Steve Wynn of earlier times.

The Renaissance concern—nay, obsession—with opuluxe ended not because of surfeit, not because there was no more space to fill, not because the baroque took clutter to the nth degree. Nor did the Renaissance end because the melancholy northerners had had it with a church that was not holy, Roman, or even very Catholic. Nor did supply dry up because there were no new artists. Renaissance luxury ended because there was no more frantic demand to fill *these* spaces. The weird confluence that had so overheated the market cooled. Ecclesiastical images were no longer so important. The rise of print (the graphic revolution), the interest in the natural sciences, the market reward for producing objects of practical use, left nonutilitarian "art" to be produced by the few for the pleasure of the fewer. Graven images, the stock-in-trade of thousands of guildsmen, would become progressively less important until finally, by the nineteenth century, they became such anomalies that they were hoarded by very wealthy collectors or housed in special institutions called museums. Only then did they really become *works of art*.

The process of the embourgeoisement of opuluxe, or the down-marketing of the signifiers of value, is clearly at the heart of the industrial revolution. Individuals could now hold in private what the church had held in quasi-public. The magical allure of the material world, of things that shone and excited, remained. The promise of indulgence had simply been moved across the street to the marketplace.

The Epiphany: Getting to Bingo

Let's continue the infelicitous comparison of the religious promise of salvation and the gambling luck of hitting the jackpot because inside these systems we may see the powerful allure of material luxury. As I've argued, although we don't usually think of them this way, they are both entertainment cultures. Entertainment cultures have one thing in common. They efficiently exchange some kind of experience for money, and most often the experience has a high affective component. By that I mean a physical sensation is at the heart of the transaction. You *feel* different.

First, some analogies. Because of my training in romanticism, the commercial exchange I know best is horror. The great gothic myths of the vampire (*Dracula*), the manmade monster (*Frankenstein*), and the transformation monster (*Dr. Jekyll and Mr. Hyde*) were all nineteenth-century creations. The way you judge a scary tale is by how successfully it has lifted the hairs on your neck. That sensation, called *horripilation*, is still what you pay for when you buy such entertainments as a roller coaster, a Stephen King novel, or whatever new summer movie is making its way from Hollywood.

Certainly, this observation is not new. Of course, buying sensation is central to human pastimes. What did Aristotle say was the attraction of tragedy? You feel pity and terror. Comedy comes close: You are paying to be made to laugh. In the nineteenth century the marketplace opened up to sell the ersatz tragedy as melodrama and the sentimental novel, both of which exploited the sensation of lacrimation, of bursting into tears, of weeping. And what of the purest entertainment culture, pornography, where the transaction is judged solely in terms of glandular arousal?

So what is the trade-off in religion? What does it offer at the *affective* level? And why does it need so many *things* to accomplish it? At one level, the macro level, the answer seems clear. Religion provides an organized system of meaning that appears to be coming from the top down, from the priests to the parishioners, from the producers to the consumers, from God to man. It lets us know where we are and what to do about it. At the micro level, however, it offers something quite unique. It offers peace of mind, tranquility, rest, surcease, quiescence. To do this, of course, it has to generate unease.

The term at the heart of Christian exchange is *epiphany*. It comes quite directly from a central act, namely, the witnessing of the Christ child by the wise men. As he lay in a manger, his holiness "showed forth" and was witnessed. By extension, this sensation is experienced by the penitent during the mass. In the twentieth century the term has picked up a secular meaning that privileges art by promising the same sensation, the same quick flash of recognition, followed by the slow surge of understanding. James Joyce famously said that in experiencing art, "the soul, its whatness, leaps to us from the vestment of appearance." This sudden insight is the secular epiphany.

In a magical sense this ah-ha sensation is the product marketed by religion, just as horripilation is the product of horror, sexual arousal is the product of pornography, and tears the product of melodrama. There may be more complexity, to be sure. In fact, there is an entire moral and ethical sociosphere in religion missing in popular entertainment. But at the heart of the system is the affective promise. Yes, you will be saved in the future, but you will feel better *right now,* in the present. In the Roman Church the transaction takes literal form, as a palpable sacrament. The Eucharist, the promise of epiphany, is offered the penitent. The wafer and wine are not metaphoric but actual, and the experience is not analogous but real.

The Sacred and Profane in Consumer Behavior

In 1989 Russell W. Belk, the Tanner Professor of Business Administration at the University of Utah; Melanie Wallendorf, a professor of business and public administration at the University of Arizona; and John Sherry, a professor of marketing at Northwestern's Kellogg School spent the summer traveling across America. They had an outrageous idea. They would do "ethnography" on wheels, as it were, going to places where people gathered to exchange things and see if they could figure out exactly what the process was by which certain objects became more valuable than others. Could they find another system of exchange that lurked below the simple money exchange? Was there a reverential level below the experiential level in the commercial world?

The result of their groundbreaking work was the lead article in the *Journal of Consumer Research* entitled "The Sacred and the Profane in Consumer Behavior: Theodicy on the Odyssey." Their conceptual basis was the work of Émile Durkheim and Max Weber, but Belk, Wallendorf, and Sherry gathered their data in interviews at such places as swap meets, flea markets, and yard sales. They pieced together a taxonomy of consumption in which the attribution of top-end value is eerily close to equating the luxurious with the holy. In other words, the attribution of religious value to objects, the idea that certain named objects have redemptive values unseen in common exchange, is at the very heart of materialism.

According to the professors, the properties of sacred consumption, of luxury consumption, are these (couched in religious terminology):

- *Hierophany:* The manifestation of the sacred, the attribution of aura around certain objects in the luxury class, logo as halo, how the Guggenheim can title its Armani show as "An Exhibition of Visionary Works" or the Victoria and Albert Museum can do a show called "Salvatore Ferragamo: The Art of the Shoe, 1927–1960."

- *Kratophany:* The fascination and fear of certain objects, some too luxurious to consume, are made taboo by the community; the basis of sumptuary laws.

- *Opposition to the profane:* Certain goods have their value in not mixing with others; the concept of luxury goods includes mandates to exclude.

- *Contamination:* The veneration of certain objects means they must be separated from other similar objects. Certain relics cannot be grouped together, nor can certain designer goods, or they will lose value.

- *Sacrifice:* To hold these objects we often violate rational pricing structures and willingly submit to what looks irrational—the Veblen effect.

- *Commitment:* Focused attachment, confused identity between the object and the holder; I am my logos.

- *Objectification:* The luxury object means something tangible. It is not just a thing *standing* for value, it is value; the brand has value as an independent thing.

- *Ritual:* Rules of conduct, don't touch, how to handle, how to display; again, rules of ensemble.

- *Myth:* Stories surrounding who else uses the object, celebrity value, affiliation of others.

- *Mystery:* A sense of the ineffable meaning, a belief that the luxury object cannot be understood by the uninitiated, the dog-whistle aspect of luxe.

- *Communitas:* Holders of the object are linked into a community; consumers cluster toward a destination; sometimes invokes the pilgrimage motif.

- *Ecstasy and flow:* Possession of object is to enter a liminal state of shifted consciousness—the sensation is . . . joy, salvation, a peak experience, epiphany.

As opposed to our usual thinking, materialism is not the opposite of spiritualism. Materialism is what you spiritualize when you have plenty of stuff. But if you have a dearth of things, you spiritualize the next world, the world after death. You develop a populated and fully furnished heaven. If you have a surfeit of stuff, you spiritualize the here and now. You deserve a break today. Not tomorrow. Heaven on earth. Now.

As the marketing professors observed, we seem to spiritualize objects as a necessary way of consuming them. Essentially, we cook them and season to taste. Thus the use of luxury is close to the use of sacred objects, namely, a way to make distinctions not just between and among other objects but between parts of experience. Consuming tells you not just who you are but *where* you are. So, for instance, in church the sacred objects are used to punctuate the times of day. Certain objects are part of morning prayers, part of midday meals, part of evening vespers. Ditto the objects of human maturation. Take cars as an example. You get a used jalopy at sixteen, a sports car at twenty-two, a sedan at marriage, a stationwagon with kids, an SUV for midlife independence, a Porsche for midlife crisis, *then* the Lincoln Town Car.

The Consumption of Holidays

One can see this microecology on holy days—holidays—where special objects are displayed, used, and even exchanged. Just recall the special luxuries of Christmas, a wedding anniversary, Valentine's Day, or even Mother's Day. We sacramentalize certain passages with gifts *only* from the luxury category. The gift becomes totemic and mixing them up—as, for instance, giving money instead of a present—is taboo.

Consider Christmas. Giving—though it can hardly be called *giving* in any traditional sense of the word—is the essence of this secularized festival of consumption. What is given is usually of low utility. In fact, economists call such objects deadweight gifts. "Deadweight" is short for "deadweight loss," which is the difference between what the gift giver has spent and the value the recipient places on it. Joel Waldfogel, a Yale economist, has estimated that up to a third of the gifts given during Christmas are in this category. Billions of dollars are "wasted" each Christmas as Uncle Louie receives an unwearable Countess Mara necktie from his niece to whom he has sent an unusable Fendi purse. Both parties would be better off exchanging cash. But they don't, and that is what makes the transaction so interesting to economists and students of luxury.

Or what of wedding presents? Look at how weddings have exploded with gifts in the last half-century as they have become ritualized ceremonies of payback and acquisition. Before World War II no one had heard of such things as the bridal registry, nonrecyclable wedding garments, an industry of how-to manuals ("on the wedding day they give one another a piece of wedding jewelry—tiny diamond earrings or a pearl necklace for her, priced anywhere from $35 to $60,000, and cufflinks or a wrist watch for him . . . "), elaborate ring exchanges, and even now, as I write this, the development of wedding-day jewelry exchanges between the participants and their in-laws. Spend an hour reading a bride's magazine, or look at the ubiquitous newspaper supplements, and you will see what was once a communal or civil or religious ceremony is shifting into a holiday of luxury exchanges.

Note that whenever we come close to these exchanges, we tend to become quiet and reverential. Not by happenstance does this reverentiality happen elsewhere. For instance, we are quiet inside an art gallery, a museum, or a library. And then, of course, there are special places where the codes of silence are unambiguous, such as a church, temple, or shrine. In the nineteenth century shoppers were hushed inside department stores. In fact, they were called dream palaces and lands of enchantment for a reason. The chaos of Filene's Basement was an eruption of no-longer-controlled excitement. It happened in the basement for a reason.

Think as well of the almost religious awe generated in theater lobbies or entrances to grand hotels. Cathedrals, palaces, department stores, and casino hotels share architectural similarities for a reason. The key to the sacred and the luxe is always the same: Being in them, being where they are, allows us to momentarily transcend the here and now. In short, to experience epiphany.

Transubstantiation of Luxury Into Feeling

So the next question is *how* do ordinary things get to be sacred? By what mental magic do identical machine-made objects escape the real world and enter the sacred? Here the three marketing professors act as if they have spent the weekend in Vegas, for they observed what I found so startling as I wandered up and down the Strip. Sacralization occurs through

- Travel to a particular place to consume—a concept in religious history known as external sanction.

- Metonymic consumption, having a part for a whole (i.e., buying a designer T-shirt as part of an ensemble of goods).

- What they call *quintessence,* or consuming something "top of line" beyond which nothing else is—the Holy Grail is the overarching image.

- The process of gifting, or the special value attributed to the object by place or time and donor (holiday gift, graduation gift from grandfather).

- Sacralization through collecting, in other words, the concept of an assemblage that is a dim analog with an impossible-to-complete series, as with the piecing-together of relics.

- The value of magical passage as with inheritance, or simply heirloomness, where the value of patina, say, represents time passage while high shine represents freshness.

In each case the professors had the temerity to ask exactly what this object "does" for the holder. Again and again they heard the refrain that having this luxury thing allows the holder to cross some boundary. At the topmost, the experience is sublime, out of the body, but more usually it was simply that the object was "performing as advertised." In other words, it was changing my social place in much the same way that proximity to the sacred object changes the place of the penitent. Want to see it? Look at the often blissed-out faces in luxury ads. "I've got it. I'm there," they seem to say.

Luxury in the Chain of Being

Observe the process in macrocosm through economic history. Look at the Great Chain of Being, one of the central organizing principles of early modern life. All one has to do to see how deep this system runs is to study English culture before, during, and after the industrial revolution. On the eve of the transformation of machine-made luxury, Samuel Johnson could visualize English society as a graded hierarchy in which every subject had a God-given place. The Great Chain of Being is based on the concept of *copia.* God made the system and it was already full. Know your place and keep to it. Don't overreach. The sin is hubris, pride. Luxury is prideful.

With the application of steam to the instruments of production, we still hear the British poet laureate Robert Southey (1774–1884) invoking, "That appointed chain,/Which when in cohesion it unites/Order to order, rank to rank,/In mutual benefit." But not for long. As industrial machinery started to produce much of the items of social place, from colored buttons to Wedgwood pottery to calico, the late nineteenth-century Darwinists were still claiming hierarchical order as God given, yes, but things were shifting. Your place was being determined by what you owned. Having certain things meant you had social position. The status panic of the rising middle class was soon resolved by the language of the market: Buy me, buy place. The reward of consumption is social elevation. Forget the old luxuries of ancestry, club, town house, country estate, marriage partner. The game's been changed. Patina is replaced by shine. Inheritance is replaced by inventory.

The new luxury objects are high in what marketers call involvement and loyalty. Other terms reassert the role: *positional goods, bridge goods, induction goods.* Back in religious terminology, they are essentially sacralized commodities, shortcuts to redemption, analogs of the sacred, secular salvation. Thus the centrality of indulgence, which in religious terms is a form of forgiveness but in marketing terms becomes a form of consumption. If the late twentieth century saw the transformation from object-based shopping (*telic*) to recreational shopping (*paratelic*), the next step may be from recreational shopping to devotional shopping (*teleotelic*).

In such a context luxury is, you could say, a form of cheap grace, epiphany on the fly, a momentary stay against existential confusion. Little wonder that the wrath raised by Martin Luther about the selling of indulgences is mimicked by the censure of top-end consumption by social reformers today. Although there are other concerns as well, at the center of both reformations is the assertion that redemption should be a matter of good faith, not good bargaining. Far more telling, however, is that both moralistic assertions have done so little to curb our desire to have what we supposedly don't need. Could it be that in the way we live now we *do* need a little luxury?

Conclusion

A (Mild) Defense of Luxury

Who but fools, toadies, and hacks have ever come to the defense of modern American luxury? No one, not even bulk consumers of the stuff, will ever *really* defend it. And why should they? The very idea that what we have defines who we are is repulsive to many of us. The irrationality of overvaluing certain rocks, fabrics, logos, textures, wines, bottles, appliances, nameplates, tassels, zip codes, T-shirts, monograms, hotel rooms, purses, and the like is insulting to our intellect. At one level this kind of luxury is indefensible. The "good life" seems so blatantly unnecessary, even evil, especially when millions of people around the globe are living without the bare necessities. Plus, after all, it's just cake, a sugar high. Empty calories.

And few of us truly admire those who have amassed vast quantities of this stuff. If Donald Trump has his defenders, it is primarily those who are entertained, not edified, by his obstreperousness. Imelda Marcos is a pathetic character. Ditto Leona Helmsley. It's hard to be on Rodeo Drive and see a man wearing a pinkie ring, a flashy Rolex, decked out like Regis Philbin, getting into a Lincoln Navigator, and not feel a kind of smug self-satisfaction with one's own life. And let's face it, the Vegas Strip is an exciting place to visit, but most of us wouldn't want to live there.

Generations ago the market for luxury goods consisted of a few people who lived in majestic houses with a full complement of servants, in some time-honored enclave of the privileged. As Holly Brubach (1998) has wittily observed, they ordered their trunks from Louis Vuitton, their trousseaus from Christian Dior, their Dom Perignon by the case, and spent lots of time looking out over water. Their taste, like their politics, was determined largely by considerations of safeguarding wealth and perpetuating the social conventions that affirmed their sense of superiority. They stayed put. We watched them from afar. We stayed put. Maybe they had money to burn. We had to buy coal.

The very unassailability of old luxe made it safe, like old name, old blood, old land, old pew, old coat of arms, or old service to the crown. Primogeniture, the cautious passage and consolidation of wealth to the firstborn male, made the anxiety of exclusion somehow bearable. After all, you knew your place from the moment of birth and had plenty of time to make your peace. If you drew a short straw, not to worry. A comfortable life as a vicar would await the you. Or the officer corps. For females marriage became the defining act of social place.

The application of steam, and then electricity, to the engines of production brought a new market of status, an industrial market, one made up of people who essentially bought their way into having a blood line. These were the people who so disturbed Veblen, and from them this new generation of consumer has descended. First the industrial rich, then the inherited rich, and now the incidentally rich, the accidentally rich. Call them yuppies, yippies, bobos, nobrows, or whatever; although they can't afford a house in Paris's Sixteenth Arrondissement or an apartment on Park Avenue, they have enough disposable income to buy a Vuitton handbag (if not a trunk), a bottle of Dior perfume (if not a flagon), a Bombay martini (if not quite a few), and a timeshare vacation on the water (if not a second home). The consumers of the new luxury have a sense of entitlement that transcends social class, a conviction that the finer things are their birthright—never mind that they were born into a family whose ancestral home is a tract house in the suburbs, near the mall, not paid for, and the family crest comes downloaded from the Internet.

These new *customers* for luxury are younger than *clients* of the old luxe used to be, they are far more numerous, they make their money far sooner, and they are far more flexible in financing and fickle in choice. They do not stay put. They now have money to burn. The competition for their attention is intense, and their consumption patterns—if you haven't noticed—is changing life for the rest of us. How concerned should we be? I say, not very. Let them eat cake.

The Economic Defense of Opuluxe

While making status distinctions on the basis of luxury consumption seems silly, even incompatible with common sense, contemporary economists and sociologists are not so sure. Economists like Martin Feldstein at Harvard and Paul David at Stanford have been arguing that certain acts of consumption mimic a kind of equitable savings, a kind of universal investment in a mythic bank of communal value (Lewis 1998:B7). After all, it may be more efficient—not to mention, more fun—to spend your money buying a badge good like a fancy car or an Armani wardrobe to announce your social place than to do it the old-fashioned way and join the country club. Plus, you don't have to play golf.

Although it is not pictured this way in popular culture, the consumption of high-end goods is rarely impulsive, emotional, or extravagant. Instead it may more often be thoughtful, clever, and sensible. *Pretty Woman* makes a point worth considering. In a sense modern luxury is insurance against misunderstanding, a momentary stay against panic and confusion. If you can't tell where you are in life by consulting the *Social Register,* then check your car nameplate, your zip code, the amount of stainless steel wrapped around your barbecue.

That such "peace of mind" can be bought may seem shallow until you realize that the transformation is dependent *only* on money, and the color of money is always the same. This is a far more equitable currency than the capriciousness of ancestry and the whimsy of gender and birth order. Well into the nineteenth century the placement of your family pew was a marker of status. The higher your birth and the larger your bank account, the closer you were to the front—the closer, by implication, to God. Given a choice between a lucky-sperm culture in which birth decides social place or a lucky-stock-option culture in which market whimsy decides social place, I think I prefer the latter.

What's Happiness Got to Do with It?

Now, mind you, this has *nothing* to do with happiness. As Freud famously said of consuming another product—psychotherapy—high-end consumption will not make you happier, only less anxious. While the poor, loveless, ever-anxious crowd may think that individual satisfaction tracks closely with luxury consumption, such is not the case. Numerous studies show that as society grows richer over time, the average level of happiness—as measured by the percentage of people who rate themselves "happy" or "very happy" in national surveys—doesn't budge. In fact, sometimes it falls.

Does this mean consumption is a treadmill going nowhere? Well-tenured and -tended economists like Robert Frank and Juliet Schor certainly argue that it does. But one might suggest that at least the treadmills get more comfortable and more people have more access to them. That's got to mean something.

Economists have known about this perplexity for a while. In a famous 1972 essay titled "Is Growth Obsolete?" the Yale University economists William Nordhaus and James Tobin pointed out that the growing gross domestic product doesn't account for such important factors as leisure, household labor, pollution, and unsnarling traffic jams. In fact, in many categories quality of life may even decline as high-end consumption increases.

On the heels of this study Richard Easterlin, now an economic historian at the University of Southern California, argued that there was no clear trend in surveys of Americans' reported happiness. Average happiness rose from the 1940s to the late 1950s, then gradually sank again until the early 1970s, even as personal income grew sharply. Returning to the subject a few years ago, Easterlin cited an annual U.S. survey that showed a slight downward trend in the percentage of Americans saying they were "very happy" from 1972 to 1991—even though per capita income, adjusted for inflation and taxes, rose by a third. In fact, this perplexity has become so established that it is known as the "Easterlin paradox" (Marshall 1998:B1).

Even when you move away from material consumption as an index, the contradiction remains. William Bennett's leading economic indicators, as well as the environmental indicators from quality-of-life groups like Redefining Progress or from lobbying groups from individual cities, like Sustainable Seattle or Livable Tucson, show that happiness may be beside the point (Stille 2000:A17). Some groups throw into the mix such concerns as legal fees, medical bills, divorce rates, affordable housing, and levels of trust.

Other groups foreground such matters as SAT scores, charitable giving, clean-air days, or commuting time. No matter how you slice it, chances are if a group makes an index, the one thing it is sure to show is that there is no correlation between affluence and what the group considers happiness. In addition, this disconnect between consumption and happiness seems not to depend on cultural differences. For instance, during the so-called Asian miracle from the late 1950s to the late 1980s, real per-capita income soared nearly fivefold, taking Japan from a developing country to an industrial superpower in a generation, yet average levels of reported satisfaction didn't change an iota.

So let's forget any argument that happiness correlates with buying stuff, let alone luxurious stuff. Lottery winners don't stay happier than other people for long (about two weeks), and accident victims who become paraplegics typically return over time to pretrauma levels (Marshall 1998). So if happiness is not related to consumption, why not tamp down luxury consumption by taxing it—or shaming it—into oblivion?

The answer is not rocket science; in fact, it's simple. While being on the treadmill to the Land of Opuluxe may not provide happiness, *not* being on the treadmill almost certainly guarantees unhappiness. And discomfort. Instead of asking the haves how they are feeling, ask the have-nots. Their answer is existentially simple. Forget where we're going, and since there is nowhere else to go, why not get there in comfort? All aboard. Ironically, the problem is not how to get some people off the treadmill but how to get other people on. If goods are what carry meaning in this world (and, alas, they do, and have always) then the poor are doubly disenfranchised: They don't have stuff and they don't have the meanings that stuff carries.

Are We Happy Yet? Not So Fast

While the happiness as be-all-and-end-all argument has the whiff of a red herring, it is not entirely dismissible. Before you denounce (or applaud) happiness research as leftist propaganda, be aware that it also cuts the other way. For example, if happiness doesn't equate with income, why worry about minimum wages or distributions to the poor? Or to move it up a notch, if you don't want a society in which everyone is desperately trying to get ahead, you might advocate government policies that slow down consumption: high tax rates, generous health and unemployment benefits, long mandatory paid vacations, maybe even a limit on individual working hours. In other words, you might want to turn the United States into France. But are the French happier? Nope. France has an unemployment rate more than twice as high as that of the United States, largely because of those same government policies. And unemployment makes some people very unhappy (Krugman 2000:A15).

Professor Stanley Lebergott, an economist at Wesleyan University, has ventured into this moral and economic quicksand. A few years ago he argued in *Pursuing Happiness: American Consumers in the Twentieth Century* that Americans have "spent their way to happiness." Lest this sound overly Panglossian, what Lebergott means is that while consumption by the rich has remained relatively steady, the rest of us have certainly had a good go of it. If we think that the rich are different from you and me, and that the difference is that the rich have longer shopping lists, then we have, in the last fifty years, substantially caught up.

The most interesting part of *Pursuing Happiness* is the second half of the book. Here Lebergott unloads reams of government statistics and calculations to chart the path that American consumption has taken through a wide range of products and services—food, tobacco, clothing, fuel, domestic service, and medicine, to name only a few. Two themes emerge strongly from this data. The first, not surprisingly, is that Americans were far better off in 1990 than they were in 1900.

For example, real consumer spending rose in seventy of the eighty-four years between 1900 and 1984. In 1990 an hour's work earned six times as much as in 1900. Most Americans walked to work at the start of the century, but by 1990 none did, in part because nearly 90 percent of families had a car. By 1987 all households had one-time luxuries: a fridge, a radio, nearly all had a TV, and about three-quarters had a washing machine. Per-capita spending on food rose by more than 75 percent between 1900 and 1990, with a marked increase in meat consumption. "Wants" became "necessities" because, ironically, the pushing and shoving of other consumers was lowering the price. Your consumption of luxury has made life easier for me.

And the second theme emerging from Lebergott's data is that old-line, Left-leaning academic critics such as Robert Heilbroner, Tibor Scitovsky, Robert and Helen Lynd, Christopher Lasch (and legions of others now teaching American studies), who have censured the waste and tastelessness of much of American consumerism, may have simply missed the big point. Ditto the Voluntary Simplifiers with all their self-help books, their how-to-buy-less magazines, and their cut-excess-consumption videos. Okay, okay, money can't buy happiness, but you stand a better chance than with penury.

Lebergott poses a simple question for such critics: Would they want to return to 1900? Even if they say yes, in a democratic society would they be justified in forcing their aesthetic and moral judgments on other consumers? And if they say yes, they should carefully watch the recent BBC/PBS show called *1900 House*. As a modern family found by trying it, life at the turn of the nineteenth century was hard, very hard indeed. The idea that it was easy is one of our most cherished luxuries.

The Sociological Defense of Opuluxe

Economists aren't the only ones to crook an eyebrow at consumption scolds. Social scientists like Mary Douglas, Baron Isherwood, Mihaly Csikszentmihalyi, and Eugene Rochberg-Halton have put forward what are called the "good life definitions" of "positive sociology" (Ruark 1999). While studies may show that people who purchase luxuries are not happier than those who cannot, they also show that being able to consume these positional objects seems to be a driving force in most large social groups today. Call these goods whatever you want—bridge goods, heraldic goods, demonstration goods—the ability to have them seems to be restructuring communities. Happiness may not be improved by having luxe, but unhappiness is increased by not being able to get into the supposed community of supposed peers.

It is now clear why modern transgenerational poverty is so debilitating. If who you are is increasingly what you have, then the have-nots are doubly distressed. For not only do the poor miss out on creature comforts, they miss out on community meanings. Whatever these meanings may be, they are superpotent and no longer culturally specific. No Berlin Wall can keep them out for long. This new definition of must-have luxury is spreading around the globe at the speed of, first, the television and now the Internet. As the last two decades of the twentieth century have shown, governments, religions, and cultures neglect this unnecessary stuff at their peril.

We need to be reminded that luxury has a bright side as well as a dark side. Yes, luxury is a one-dimensional status and hierarchy marker. Yes, pecuniary emulation is still key for shallow social distinctions and contrived position. And, yes, such positional power is transitory. Opuluxe *is* one dimensional, shallow, ahistorical, without memory, and expendable. But it is also strangely democratic and unifying. If what you want is peace on earth, a unifying system that transcends religious, cultural, and caste differences, well, whoops! here it is. The Global Village is not quite the City on the Hill, not quite the Emerald City, and certainly not quite what millennial utopians had in mind, but it is closer to equitable distribution of rank than what other systems have provided.

Why Academics Criticize the New Luxury

Remember in *King Lear* when the two nasty daughters want to strip Lear of his last remaining trappings of majesty? He has moved in with them, and they don't think he needs so many expensive guards. They convince themselves by saying that their dad, who is used to having everything he has ever wanted, doesn't need a hundred or even a dozen soldiers around him. They whittle away at his retinue until only one is left. "What needs one?" they say.

Rather like governments attempting to redistribute wealth or like academics criticizing the consumption habits of others, they conclude that his needs are excessive. They are false needs: sumptuous, wasteful, luxurious. Lear, however, knows otherwise. Terrified and suddenly bereft of purpose, he bellows from his innermost soul, "Reason not the need."

True, Lear doesn't need these soldiers any more than Scrooge needed silver, Midas needed gold, the characters on *Friends* need stuff from Crate & Barrel, those shoppers on Rodeo/Worth/Madison Avenues need handbags, or I need to spend the night at the Luxor. But not needing doesn't stop the desiring. Lear knows that possessions are definitions—superficial meanings, perhaps, but meanings nonetheless. Without soldiers he is no king. Without a BMW there can be no yuppie, without tattoos no adolescent rebel, without big hair no southwestern glamourpuss, without Volvos no academic intellectuals, without cake no Marie Antoinette.

Professor Robert Frank tells a revealing story in his *Luxury Fever: Why Money Fails to Satisfy in an Era of Excess*. It seems a relative of his bought a red Porsche in France. When the relative returned to California, he found that the German car couldn't be retrofitted to meet the state's rigorous pollution regulations. He offered it to the professor at a fraction of its market value. Now, in Professor Frank's words,

I was sorely tempted. Yet my small upstate college town has a strong, if usually unstated, social norm against conspicuous consumption. People here are far more likely to drive Volvos than Jaguars, and although ours is a cold climate, we almost never see anyone wearing a fur coat. At that time, a red Porsche convertible really would have been seen as an in-your-face car in a community like ours. Although I have never thought of myself as someone unusually sensitive to social pressure, I realized that unless I could put a sign on the car that explained how I happened to acquire it, I would never really feel comfortable driving it. (168)

Professor Frank knows exactly what goods to buy and exactly what goods *not* to buy. He doesn't want to keep up with the Joneses or ditch the Joneses. He wants to fit in with the Joneses. He knows who the Joneses are. It's pretty much bow ties, Volvos, and horn-rimmed glasses, thank you very much.

My point is simple: This is a social decision, not an moral one or even an economic one. He has decided not to define himself in terms of a red Porsche convertible. He wants what his consumption community wants. But this opens up such an interesting question, at least to me. Why have academics proved such myopic observers of the consumerist world? Why so universally dour and critical? And why can't they see that their own buying habits are more a matter of taste than degree?

Here, for instance, is Frank talking in *Luxury Fever* not about consumption per se but about the anxieties of relative position. He is using his sons' behavior to illustrate the childish nature of competitive consumption. Read just a bit between the lines:

Having been raised as an only child, I have always observed the sibling rivalries among my own children with great interest. On returning from a friend's house, my 8-year-old son immediately asks, "Where's Chris?" if his 11-year-old brother is not in sight. When Chris is at his violin lesson, or at the orthodontist's office, we have no problem. But let him be at a movie, or just visiting a friend, the next thing we'll hear is Hayden's angry shout of "That's not fair!"—the inevitable prelude to an anguished outburst about the injustice of life. (1999:109–10)

Now, I don't know either Professor Frank or his sons, but I'll make a prediction. Here's what the boys can look forward to: straight teeth, plenty of soccer (not football) equipment, music lessons galore (preferably piano and violin), summer camp at Duke, magnet school or maybe a year or two at Deerfield, trips to Europe, four years at a private college or university or at one of the public Ivys (celebrated on the rear windscreen of the professor's BMW—not Volvo; remember he's in the B-school, not arts and sciences), and then postgraduate polishing. Nothing extraordinary about this expenditure of—what?—about $400,000 a kid.

What's extraordinary is that rarely, if ever, will Frank roll over at night and think he is spending foolishly. Never will he see himself as a luxury consumer, deeply embedded in a consumption community. No, to bobos like the professor (and me, I hasten to add), these choices have nothing to do with taste. They are *needs,* goddammit! Educational affiliations for academic offspring have nothing to do with the lawyer next door who drives an S-class Mercedes or the software designer I play tennis with who sports a Patek Philippe wristwatch. Nothing! We're talking education here, not tail fins!

I think one reason we academics have been so unappreciative of the material world, often so downright snotty about it, is that we don't need it. Academics say they don't need it because they have the life of the mind, they have art, they contemplate the best that has been thought and said. (Plus, not a whole lot of disposable income.)

But that's not the entire story. I think that another reason most academics don't need store-bought affiliation is because the school world, like the church world it mimics, is a cosseted world, a world in which rank and order are well known and trusted and stable. In fact, buying stuff is more likely to confuse status than illuminate it.

Let me tell you who I am in this context. I am a professor in the English department at the University of Florida; I teach romanticism. Here's what that sentence looks like when I explode it to show how each part marks me on the academic totem pole.

Now, of course, if you are an academic, you will immediately disagree with how I have arranged the hierarchies. But you can't disagree with the depth of the description. Nor when you think about it, how deep the academic system is relative to others. If you are an academic, I instantly know about you from just a few words. Just say something like "I am a visiting assistant professor of sociology at Podunk U" and I can pretty accurately spin a description of what your life has been like. Give me a bit more, like a publication cite (not the subject, but where it appears), and you are flying right into my radar. This system of social place is so stable that you wear it like a pair of Gucci sunglasses or an old school tie. Little wonder academ-

	named professor		philosophy
I am a	*professor*		mathematics
	associate professor	in the	*English* department
	assistant professor		history
	instructor		sociology
	teaching assistant		

			medieval lit
	Ivy League		Renaissance lit
	public Ivy		postmodern litcrit
	good big school		eighteenth-century lit
at the	*University of Florida*;	I teach	*romanticism*
	not so good big school		modern lit
	community college		American lit
			film
			popcult

ics are so perplexed by an outside world that seems preoccupied with social place via consumption. Little wonder we misunderstand it. I can't imagine what it would be like to tell someone I was a CFO of a pre-IPO dot-com. I'd much rather just have them check out my nifty chunky loafers from Prada and my Coach edition of Lexus out in the driveway.

Future Disappearance of Luxe? Maybe

Most of us, yes, even academics, are living in a time of intense *extro*personal relationships (in Latin *extro* means outward), in which the focus on things, on people as things, on relationships as things, defines modern meanings. Look at how we define relationships in economic terms:

Is he/she *worth* the trouble?
being *invested* in a relationship
This relationship is *costing* me too much.
Is he/she marriage *material*?
Where's the *payoff*?

*Is every car
a luxury car?
It seems so.*

Cost-benefit analysis is second nature to our language because it is second nature to our perceptions, regardless of how far we are from the market-place. However, we may be reaching the point where the center of such a system will not hold, things fall apart, and, like it or not, we find ourselves moving away from defining the self via goods, because positional goods have become too plentiful and thus not meaningful enough.

As so many luxuries become necessities, maybe the concept of luxury is

being drained of meaning. As the standard of living has risen, erstwhile luxury is becoming the norm. Since the 1970s we have been defining luxury downward into ordinary goods and services even as we have increased our ability to consume objects and sensations hitherto beyond our reach. Perhaps the social construction of luxury is deconstructing. Maybe we are indeed slouching toward Utopia.

The differences between top-of-the-line luxury objects, and the differences among various midrange objects, have in many cases ceased to be observable. Perhaps we have overluxurified the commonplace. Remember the problem that Volvo was having in positioning its car as a luxury item? a problem so pressing that the company had to take the desperate measure of consulting an English professor? Well, take a look at some car ads; it's easy to see why.

When I mentioned the possible disappearance of luxury as a distinction to a friend who is the creative director of a large midwestern advertising agency, his eyes lit up. One of his clients is a manufacturer of specialty faucets. When the agency tested images of kitchens that women felt reflected their sense of comfort and ease, the deluxe kitchen, complete with all the yuppie appliances, tested surprisingly low. What was high? The old-fashioned Kenmore-type kitchen in which the appliances looked like what they were instead of pieces of commercialized built-in elegance. It was, he said, as if the women were tired of seeing themselves as perfectionists and yearned for the more relaxed life of their mothers or grandmothers. Restoration Hardware may really be on to something more than nostalgia.

A more temperate view of luxury?

Perhaps the mass class of consumers has been living in the lap of luxury for too long. We used to be outside looking in. Now millions of us are on the inside looking out. Who knows? Maybe the very ubiquity of luxury will cause us to recharge human relationships and deflate material values. Have a look at some more ads for the luxe life. While the insurance ad makes its case by separating itself from the crass world of commodities, and the car ads (including Lincoln) now make luxury a mark of personal choice, the Saturn ad is a masterpiece of equilibration. Here's what it says,

There is a point where luxury becomes somewhat silly. It becomes overdone. Absurd. And obscenely expensive. Parked a few miles from that point is the L-series from Saturn. True, the L-series has more room, more power, more everything than other Saturn models. Some might even say they're bordering on luxurious. But the difference is, the L-series costs thousands less than cars with the same features.

Luxurious, yes. Silly, no.

American Luxe Moves Elsewhere

Look at public display for a hint of what is happening. Just as luxury may have ebbed from the private sphere because positional goods have been so furiously down-marketed, so too has it evaporated from urban works. Adam Gopnik, a staff writer for the *New Yorker,* has pointed out that the very act of trying to display communal luxury has become so bizarre as to render the concept of conspicuous consumption into something resembling both *Field of Dreams* and Russian roulette. Build it, no one may come, and it may self-destruct.

Gopnik divides the twentieth century into five distinct styles of public display. The first, from the turn of the twentieth century to the Depression, is pure show-off. If you've got it, flaunt it. Gopnik points to the Metropolitan Museum as an apt image of look-at-me consumption. It makes an unambiguous statement. This is industrial-strength wealth. In the second stage, from 1930 to the end of World War II, a form of counterdisplay sets in. Here the Manhattan site is the Museum of Modern Art, restrained and almost embarrassed to be calling this stuff *art*. That the Rockefellers, who footed the bill, were reviled is not happenstance. This is a kind of redemptive luxury: payback for the sins of the father. Then, from 1950 to 1960 *counter*-counterdisplay is the mode and Frank Lloyd Wright's Guggenheim is the perfect monument. Gopnik calls it "an advertisement of natural values" (182).

But then comes the parody display of the next burst of Veblenism. The rise of populuxe in the late 1970s, the wink-wink grandiosity of old-style Las Vegas and Miami Beach, designer jeans from Gloria Vanderbilt, or the almost-built (but thank God not) Michael Graves extension to the Whitney Museum of American Art. Gopnik brings us up to date by proclaiming the rise of "new sincerity," reformed Veblenism, the *really* meaningful consumption proclaimed by nothing *in* Manhattan but by something *of* Manhattan, the Frank Gehry–Thomas Krens Guggenheim in Bilbao, Spain. Here we have the perfect embodiment of symbolic consumption and sincere extravagance. Want to see postmodern American luxury? You'll have to go elsewhere.

Gopnik's tongue may be in his cheek, but his eye is prescient. What he sees on the macrolevel of exhibitionism is also true of individual show. Luxury is being removed from the world around us because the only thing out of American reach is the world *outside* America. Gopnik points to Sandy

Pittman's ultimate leisure-class Mount Everest expedition as the apt individual analogy. Pittman had no business on that mountain, and that's just the point. It was elaborate, expensive, dangerous to everyone, stupid, and undertaken as an exercise in self-indulgence for all to see. She was, in fact, broadcasting her exploits via cell phone and the Internet. That she almost died, and that others did, is exactly the point. This is real serious luxury, not symbolic but strangely invidious luxury.

Was It Worth It?

The question then becomes: Are we better off for living in a culture in which luxuries are turned into necessities, in which mild addictions are made into expected tastes, in which elegancies are made niceties, expectancies are made into entitlements, in which opulence is made into populence?

And the answer, from the point of view of those historically excluded, is yes. Absolutely, yes. Ironically, just as the very stuff that I often find unaesthetic and others may find contemptible has ameliorated the condition of life for many, many millions of people, the very act of getting to this stuff promises a better life for others. I don't mean to belittle the value of religion, politics, law, education, and all the other patterns of meaning making in the modern world but only to state the obvious. Forget happiness; if decreasing pain and discomfort is a goal, consumption of the "finer things" has indeed done what governments, churches, schools, and even laws have promised. Far more than these other systems, betterment through consumption has delivered the goods. Paul Krugman is certainly correct when he writes, "On sheer material grounds one would almost surely prefer to be poor today than upper middle class a century ago" (2000:A15).

But is it fair? Do some of us suffer inordinately for the excesses of others? What are we going to do when all this stuff we have shopped for becomes junk? What about the environment? How close is the connection between the accumulation of the new luxury and the fact that the United States also leads the industrialized world in rates of murder, violent crime, juvenile violent crime, imprisonment, divorce, abortion, single-parent households, obesity, teen suicide, cocaine consumption, per-capita consumption of all drugs, pornography production, and pornography consumption? What are we going to do about the lower sixth of our population that seems mired in transgenerational poverty?

These are important questions but ones I will leave to others. Entire academic, governmental, and commercial industries are dedicated to each of them. One of the more redemptive aspects of cultures that produce the concept of luxury is that they also produce the real luxury of having time and energy to discuss it. Who knows? Perhaps the luxury of reflection will help resolve at least some of the shortcomings of consumption.

Consuming Goods and the Good of Consuming

Remember my dad from the first chapter? Episcopal choirboy, fourth-generation Vermonter, Harvard-trained doctor? We lived in a city on a hill next to a lake. We lived near the top of the hill, right next to his parents, who were just down from my great-grandparents. One day when I was about ten, Dr. Slavin came driving up the hill. He always drove a new black Cadillac, probably a Fleetwood. He stopped and chatted with my dad. Dr. Slavin was a prosperous obstetrician; in fact, he delivered me. He came from a small town in Vermont, had attended the local university, and was, in that perplexing term to me, a "self-made man."

In order to talk with my dad, Dr. Slavin pushed a button and the window automatically descended. I looked inside. Xanadu. Before he drove off, he opened and closed all the windows for me, automatically. I was amazed, it was a Daisy Buchanan Moment, a frisson of the Stendhal Syndrome. I remember asking my dad if we could have a car like that instead of the stupid green Plymouth. He said we could but that we didn't need to.

My dad always knew where he was. He was never haughty, just confident. He was an atheist in midlife, but, my mother later told me, when he went into the hospital to die, he asked for the bishop to come by for a chat.

Of course, I regret the passing of that world. It had much I miss. I go for months now without hearing "noblesse oblige." Still, all in all, I like this new world better. I know to some it's the joyless economy but not to me. I think it's quite joyful and, moreover, I think it's far more fair than the world I grew up in.

Bowling alone is not a lot of fun. It's a lot more fun, however, than not being able to bowl at all. And given a choice, I'd rather be in the Prada league than the Junior League.

I don't mean to belittle current inequities. I don't mean to overlook racial profiling, sexual stereotypes, job discrimination, glass ceilings, unemployment, hunger. I only mean to say that romanticism, my erstwhile field of study, still informs much of the academic interpretation of commercialism. I am often reminded of something my mother told me. Her father ran a country store in the small town of Shelburne, Vermont. During the Depression he sold on credit. And how did he know to whom to extend credit? He did it by smell, aroma profiling. Smell of horses, good; cows not so good, pigs and sheep bad. Shelburne is such a pretty little town: church, library, town hall, and community green. After the war she and her siblings couldn't wait to get the hell out of there.

Let's face it: The idea that consumerism creates artificial desires rests on a wistful ignorance of history and human nature, on the hazy, romantic feeling that there existed some halcyon era of noble savages with purely natural needs. Close your Rousseau, open your Darwin. Once fed and sheltered, our needs have always been cultural, not natural. Until there is some other system to codify and satisfy those needs and yearnings, capitalism—and the promise of the better life it carries with it—will continue not just to thrive but to triumph, Muslim extremists notwithstanding.

While you don't have to like needless consumption, let alone participate in it, it doesn't hurt to understand it and our part in it. We have not been led astray by marketers of unnecessary goods. It would be nice to think that this eternally encouraging market for top-of-the-line products will result in the cosmopolitanism envisioned by the Enlightenment *philosophes,* that a universalism of the new luxury will end in a crescendo of hosannas. It would be nice to think that more and more of the poor and disenfranchised will find their ways into the cycle of increased affluence without contracting the dreaded affluenza or, worse, luxury fever. It would be nice to think that commercialism could be heroic, self-abnegating, and redemptive. It would be nice to think that greater material comforts—more and more luxuries—will release us from racism, sexism, terrorism, and ethnocentrism and that the apocalypse will come as it did at the end of romanticism in Shelley's *Prometheus Unbound,* leaving us, "Sceptreless, free, uncircumscribed . . . Equal, unclassed, tribeless, and nationless . . . Pinnacled dim in the intense inane."

But the globalization of the new luxury is more likely to result in the banalities of an ever-increasing, worldwide consumerist culture. Recall that Athens ceased to be a world power around 400 B.C., yet for the next three hundred years Greek culture was the culture of the world. The age of European exposition ended in the midtwentieth century; the age of luxury markets may be losing steam in North America, but it is just starting to gather force elsewhere. Academic Marxists love to refer to this as "late capitalism." *Early* capitalism is probably more like it.

We have been in this lap of luxury a short time, and it is an often scary and melancholy place. This is a world not driven by the caprices of the rich, as was the first Gilded Age. Nor is it being whipsawed by marketers eager to sell crapular products. They contribute, to be sure. But our world is being driven primarily by the often crafty and seemingly irrational desires of the mass class of consumers, most of them young. In many ways this is more frightening. A butterfly flapping its wings in China may not cause storm clouds over Miami, but a few lines of computer code written by some kid on his Palm Pilot in Palo Alto or Calcutta may indeed change life for all the inhabitants of Prague. Worse still, a Fendi purse or a Lexus automobile or a weekend at the Bellagio may be better understood by more people than the plight of the homeless, a Keats ode, or the desecration of the rain forest. Whatever it becomes, the mass-mediated and mass-marketed world of the increasingly powerful information age is drawing us ever closer together. The act of wanting what we don't need is indeed doing the work of a generations of idealists. Terrorism is a perverse tribute to its power.

We have not been led into this world of material closeness and shared desires against our better judgment. For many of us, especially when young, consumerism *is* our better judgment. Getting to luxury is a goal. And this is true regardless of class or culture. We have not just asked to go this way, we have demanded. Now most of the world is lining up, pushing and shoving, eager to elbow into the mall to buy what no one needs. Woe to the government or religion that says no. They don't seem to last for long.

Getting and *spending* have been the most passionate, and often the most imaginative, endeavors of modern life. We have done more than acknowledge that the good life starts with the material life, as the ancients did. We have made consuming stuff, most of it unnecessary stuff, the dominant prerequisite of organized society. Consumption has become production, especially at the high end in the category of luxury. That we should be unified by sharing this material and the brand stories they tell is dreary and depressing to some, as doubtless it should be. Remember Oscar Wilde's observation that "the brotherhood of man is not a mere poet's dream: it is a most depressing and humiliating reality"? But one should not forget that the often vulgar, sensational, immediate, trashy, tribalizing, wasteful, equitable, sometimes transcendent, and unifying force of consuming is liberating and democratic to many more.

Selected Bibliography

Agins, Terry. "How Fallen Gucci Got Its Glamour Back." *Wall Street Journal*, January, 27, 1999, p. B1.

Akst, Daniel. "The Indulgence Police." *Wall Street Journal*, October 29, 1999, p. W17.

Appadurai, Arjun. *The Social Life of Things*. New York: Cambridge University Press, 1986.

Apter. Michael J. *The Experience of Motivation: The Theory of Psychological Reversals*. New York: Academic, 1982.

Babin, Barry J., William R. Darden, Mitch Griffin. "Work and/or Fun: Measuring Hedonic and Utilitarian Shopping Value." *Journal of Consumer Research* 20, no. 4 (March 1994): 644–68.

Baudrillard, Jean. *The Mirror of Production*. Translated by Mark Poster. St. Louis, Mo.: Telos, 1983.

———. *Simulacra and Simulation*. Translated by Sheila Glaser. Ann Arbor: University of Michigan Press, 1994.

Beck, Gregory. "Form in the Era of Fun." *Architectural Record* 187 (December 1999): 132.

Belk, Russell. "Hyperreality and Gobalization: Culture in the Age of Ronald McDonald." *Journal of International Consumer Marketing* 8, no. 3 (1996): 23–38.

Belk, Russell, Melanie Wallendorf, and John Sherry. "The Sacred and the Profane in Consumer Behavior: Theodicy on the Odyssey." *Journal of Consumer Research* 16 (June 1989): 1–38.

Bell, Daniel. *The Cultural Contradictions of Capitalism*. New York: Basic, 1976.

Benjamin, Walter. *The Arcades Project*. Cambridge, Mass.: Harvard University Press, 1999.

Berg, Maxine and Helen Clifford. *Consumers and Luxury: Consumer Culture in Europe, 1650–1850*. New York: Manchester University Press, 1999.

Berry, Christopher J. *The Idea of Luxury: A Conceptual and Historical Investigation*. New York: Cambridge University Press, 1994.

Blake, William. "Proverbs of Hell." *The Marriage of Heaven and Hell*. New York: Chelsea House, 1987.

Bourdieu, Pierre. *Distinction: A Social Critique of the Judgment of Taste*. Translated by Richard Nice. Cambridge, Mass.: Harvard University Press, 1984.

Bowlby, Rachel. *Carried Away: The Invention of Modern Shopping*. New York: Columbia University Press, 2001.

Brady, James. "Brady's Bunch." *Advertising Age*, August 16, 1999, p. 33.

Brancaccio, David. *Squandering Aimlessly: My Adventures in the American Marketplace*. New York: Simon and Schuster, 2000.

Brant, John. "Rethinking the Fast Lane: Simple Life; Materialism Fails to Ensure Happiness." *Buffalo News*, September 17, 1995, p. 6F.

Breathnach, Sarah Ban. *Simple Abundance: A Daybook of Comfort and Joy*. New York: Warner, 1995.

Brewer, John and Roy Porter, eds. *Consumption and the World of Goods*. New York: Routledge, 1994.

Bronner, Simon J., ed. *Consuming Visions: Accumulation and Display of Goods in America, 1880–1920*. New York: Norton, 1989.

Brooks, David. *Bobos in Paradise: The New Upper Class and How They Got There*. New York: Simon and Schuster, 2000.

Brubach, Holly. "And Luxury for All." *New York Times Magazine*, July 12, 1998, p. 24.

Calder, Lendol. *Financing the American Dream: A Cultural History of Consumer Credit in America*. Princeton N.J.: Princeton University Press, 1999.

Campbell, Colin. *The Romantic Ethic and the Spirit of Modern Consumerism*. New York: Blackwell, 1987.

Cowan, Tyler. *In Praise of Commercial Culture*. Cambridge, Mass.: Harvard University Press, 1998.

Cox, Michael W. and Richard Alm. "Defining Poverty Up." *Wall Street Journal*, November 2, 1999, p. A26.

——. *Myths of Rich and Poor: Why We're Better off Than We Think*. New York: Basic, 1999.

Cross, Gary. *An All-Consuming Century: Why Commercialism Won in Modern America*. New York: Columbia University Press, 2000.

Csikszentmihalyi, Mihaly and Eugene Rochberg-Halton. *The Meaning of Things: Domestic Symbols and the Self*. New York: Cambridge University Press, 1981.

Cushman, Philip. "Why the Self Is Empty." *American Psychologist*, May 1990, pp. 599–611.

D'Souza, Dinesh. *The Virtue of Prosperity: Finding Values in an Age of Techno-Affluence*. New York: Free Press, 2000.

David, Paul, ed. *Nations and Households in Economic Growth: Essays in Honor of Moses Abramovitz*. New York: Academic, 1974.

Diderot, Denis. "Regrets on Parting with My Old Dressing Gown." *Rameau's Nephew and Other Works by Denis Diderot*, pp. 309–17. Translated by Jacques Barzun. New York: Bobbs-Merrill, 1964.

Dirkse, Linda. "Tulipmania." *Rocky Mountain News*, January 31, 1999, p. 12F.

Douglas, Mary and Baron Isherwood. *The World of Goods: Toward an Anthropology of Consumption*. New York: Basic, 1979.

Drucker, Peter. *The Age of Discontinuity: Guidelines to Our Changing Society*. New York: Harper and Row, 1969.

Dubois, Bernard and Claire Paternault. "Observations: Understanding the World of International Luxury Brands: The 'Dream Formula.'" *Journal of Advertising Research* (August 1995): 69–76.

Durkheim, Émile. *The Elementary Forms of the Religious Life*. New York: Free Press, 1965.

Durning, Alan. *How Much Is Enough: The Consumer Society and the Future of the Earth*. New York: Norton, 1992.

Easterlin, Richard. "Does Economic Growth Improve the Human Lot?" In Paul David and Melvin W. Reder, eds., *Nations and Households in Economic Growth*, pp 98–125. Stanford, Calif: Stanford University Press, 1974.

Elgin, Duane. *Voluntary Simplicity*. New York: Morrow, 1981.

Ellis, Bret Easton. *American Psycho*. New York: Vintage, 1991.

Englis, Basil and Michael Solomon. "To Be and Not to Be: Lifestyle Imagery, Reference Groups, and the Clustering of America. *Journal of Advertising* (March 22, 1955): 13–27.

Evans, Bergen. *Dictionary of Quotations*. New York:Delacorte, 1968.

Falk, Pasi and Colin Campbell, eds. *The Shopping Experience (Theory, Culture, and Society)*. London: Sage, 1997.

Featherstone, Mike. *Consumer Culture and Postmodernism*. Newberry Park, Calif: Sage, 1991.

Fine, Ben. *The World of Consumption*. New York: Routledge, 1993.

Finnerty, Amy. "Shop Till You Pop." *New York Times Magazine*, April 6, 1997, p. 30.

Firat, A. Fuat and Alladi Venkatesh. "Liberatory Postmodernism and the Reenchantment of Shopping." *Journal of Consumer Research* 22, no. 3 (December 1995): 239–67.

Fitzgerald, F. Scott. *The Great Gatsby*. New York: Scribner's, 1925.

Flahive, Gerry. "Europe Says 'Non.'" *New York Times*, April 12, 2000, p. A31.

Forty, Adrian. *Objects of Desire: Design and Society from Wedgwood to IBM*. New York: Pantheon, 1986.

Fowles, Jib. *Mass Advertising as Social Forecast: A Method for Futures Research*. Westport, Conn.: Greenwood, 1976.

Fox, Richard Wightman and T. J. Jackson Lears, eds. *The Culture of Consumption: Critical Essays in American History, 1880–1980*. New York: Pantheon, 1983.

Frank, Robert. *Luxury Fever: Why Money Fails to Satisfy in an Era of Excess*. New York: Free Press, 1999.

——. "Which Do We Need More, Bigger Cars or Better Schools?" *New York Times*, July 31, 1999, p. A11.

——. *The Winner-Take-All Society: How More and More Americans Compete for Fewer and Bigger Prizes*. New York: Free Press, 1995.

Frum, David. *How We Got Here: The '70's, the Decade That Brought You Modern Life*. New York: Basic, 2000.

Fussell, Paul. *Class: A Guide Through the American Status System*. New York: Simon and Schuster, 1992.

——. "The Lost Art of Travel." *Los Angeles Times Magazine*, June 2, 1991, p. 26.

Galbraith, John Kenneth. *The Affluent Society*. New York: Houghton Mifflin, 1958.

Garreau, Joel. *Edge City: Life on the New Frontier*. New York: Doubleday, 1991.

Gertner, Jon. "What Is Wealth?" *Money*, December 2000, pp. 94–107.

Gilmore, James H. "Welcome to the Experience Economy." *Harvard Business Review*, July 1998, p. 97–104.

Gladwell, Malcolm. "Listening to Khakis." *New Yorker*, January 28, 1999, pp. 53–65.

——. "The Science of Shopping." *New Yorker*, November 4, 1996, pp. 27–32.

——. *The Tipping Point: How Little Things Can Make a Big Difference*. New York: Little, Brown, 2000.

Glueck, Grace. "In Vegas, Steve Martin Tries a Different Kind of Show." *New York Times*, April 24, 2001, p. E1.

Goldthwaite, Richard. *Wealth and the Demand for Art in Italy, 1300–1600*. Baltimore, Md.: Johns Hopkins University Press, 1993.

Goodis, Jerry. *Have I Ever Lied to You Before?* Toronto: McClelland and Stewart, 1972.

Goodman, Walter. "Let Them Eat Microchips." *New York Times*, March 4, 2001, sec. 4, p. 3.

Gopnik, Adam. "Display Cases." *New Yorker,* April 26, 1999, pp. 175–84.

Grant, Elizabeth. *Memoirs of a Highland Lady.* 2 vols. 1797. Reprint, London: J. Murray, 1911.

Hacking, Ian. *The Social Construction of What?* Cambridge, Mass.: Harvard University Press, 1999.

Halter, Marilyn. *Shopping for Identity: The Marketing of Ethnicity.* New York: Schocken, 2000.

Hannigan, John. *Fantasy City: Pleasure and Profit in the Postmodern Metropolis.* New York: Routledge, 1998.

Harrison, Molly. *People and Shopping: A Social Background.* Totowa, N.J.: Rowan and Littlefield, 1975.

Hayek, Friedrich. *The Road to Serfdom.* Chicago: University of Chicago Press, 1976.

Hays, Constance. "PepsiCo Calls on J. Walter Thompson." *New York Times,* March 2, 2000, p. C10.

Heilbroner, Robert. *The Worldly Philosophers.* New York: Simon and Schuster, 1961.

Hine, Thomas. *Populuxe.* New York: Knopf, 1986.

——. *The Total Package: The Evolution and Secret Meanings of Boxes, Bottles, Cans, and Tubes.* New York: Little, Brown, 1995.

Hirsch, E. D. *Cultural Literacy: What Every American Needs to Know.* New York: Houghton Mifflin, 1987.

Holbrook, Morris. *Daytime Television Game Shows and the Celebration of Merchandise.* Bowling Green, Ohio: Bowling Green University Popular Press, 1993.

Hughes, Robert. "Wynn? (Steve Wynn Opens Sophisticated Bellagio Resort in Las Vegas)." *Time,* October, 26, 1998, p. 76.

Jardine, Lisa. *Worldly Goods: A New History of the Renaissance.* New York: Doubleday, 1996.

Katz, Jane. "The Joy of Consumption." *Regional Review of the Federal Reserve Bank of Boston* 7, no. 1 (1997): 12–17.

Kaufman, Leslie. "Retail Boom Isn't Reliant Only on Rich." *New York Times,* May 7, 1999, p. A1.

Klebnikov, Paul. "Museums Inc." *Forbes,* January 8, 2001, p. 68.

Kleinfield, N. R. "The Cost of Really Living Versus Just Living." *New York Times,* March 20, 1991, p. D8.

Klepp, Lawrence. "Voltaire for the Defense." *House and Garden,* September 1998, pp. 140–44.

Kowinski, William Severini. *The Malling of America: An Insider Look at the Great Consumer Paradise.* New York: Morrow, 1985.

Krakauer, Jon. *Into Thin Air: A Personal Account of the Mount Everest Disaster.* New York: Villard, 1997.

Krantz, Judith. *Scruples.* New York: Bantam, 1989.

Krier, Beth Ann. "Hot to Shop: Can Retail Therapy Cure the Blues?" *Los Angeles Times,* November 1, 1991, p. 1.

Kristol, Irving. "The Emerging American Imperium." *Wall Street Journal,* August 18, 1997, p. A14.

Krugman, Paul. "Turn of the Century." *New York Times,* June 18, 2000, p. A15.

Lapham, Lewis. "Caesar's Wives." *Harper's,* October 1, 2000, p. 8.

Lasch, Christopher. *The Culture of Narcissism: American Life in an Age of Diminished Expectations.* New York: Norton, 1978.

Lebergott, Stanley. *Pursuing Happiness: American Consumers in the Twentieth Century*. Princeton, N.J.: Princeton University Press, 1999.

Lehmann-Haupt, Christopher. "When Economic Theory Fails, Consult an Insect." *New York Times*, January 10, 2000, p. E9.

Leiby, Richard. "Yuppies: An Aging Trend," *Washington Post*, September 2, 1994, p. D1.

Leiss, William. *The Limits to Satisfaction: An Essay on the Problem of Needs and Commodities*. Toronto: University of Toronto Press, 1976.

Levere, Jane. "BBDO New York Breaks Down Why, When, Where, and How Young Adults Get Their Information." *New York Times*, December, 9, 1999, p. C12.

Levine, Joshua. "Liberté, Fraternité—but to Hell with Egalité." *Forbes*, June 2, 1997, pp. 80–89.

Levy, Sidney. *Marketing, Society, and Conflict*. Englewood Cliffs, N.J.: Prentice-Hall, 1975.

Lewis, Paul. "In Buying We Trust: The Foundation of U.S. Consumerism." *New York Times*, May 30, 1998, p. B7.

Linden, Eugene, *Affluence and Discontent: The Anatomy of Consumer Societies*. New York: Viking, 1979.

Lobrano, Alexander. "The Fine Art of Shopping." *International Herald Tribune*, February 28, 1995, feature sec.

Longinotti-Buitoni, Gian Luigi. *Selling Dreams: How to Make Any Product Irresistible*. New York: Simon and Schuster, 1999.

Lynd, Robert and Helen Lynd. *Middletown: A Study in Contemporary American Culture*. New York: Harcourt, Brace, 1937.

Lynes, Russell. "High Brow, Middle Brow, Low Brow." *Life*, April 11, 1949, pp. 100–3.

MacCannell, Dean. *The Tourist: A New Theory of the Leisure Class*. New York: Schocken, 1976.

Maffesoli, Michel. *The Time of Tribes: The Decline of Individualism in Mass Society*. London: Sage, 1996.

Malloy, John. *Dress for Success*. New York: Warner, 1975.

Mandeville, Bernard. *The Fable of the Bees*. 1714. Reprint, London: Penguin, 1989.

Marks, Marjorie. "Stopping the Shopping Juggernaut." *Los Angeles Times*, December 3, 1987, pt. 5, p. 1.

Marshall, Jonathan. "Rich in Cash, But Not in Happiness." *San Francisco Chronicle*, March 23, 1998, p, B1.

Marx, Karl and Friedrich Engels. *The Communist Manifesto*. 1872. Reprint, New York: Oxford University Press, 1992.

Mason, Roger. *Conspicuous Consumption: A Study of Exceptional Consumer Behavior*. New York: St. Martin's, 1981.

——. *The Economics of Conspicuous Consumption: Theory and Thought Since 1700*. Northampton, Mass.: Edward Elgar, 1998.

McCracken, Grant. *Culture and Consumption: New Approaches to the Symbolic Character of Consumer Goods and Activities*. Bloomington: Indiana University Press, 1988.

McDonald, William J. "Time Use in Shopping: The Role of Personal Characteristics." *Journal of Retailing* 70, no. 4 (1994): 345–72.

McDowell, Colin. "Spend, Spend, Spend." Review of *Fashioning the Bourgeoisie*, by Philippe Perrot. *Sunday Times* (London), July 17, 1994, p. 12.

Miller, Daniel. *Acknowledging Consumption: A Review of New Studies*. New York: Routledge, 1996.

——. *A Theory of Shopping*. Ithaca, NY: Cornell University Press, 1998.

Miller, Daniel, ed. *Shopping, Place, and Identity.* New York: Routledge, 1998.

Mirabella, Lorraine. "Vegas Tries for Mall Jackpot." *Baltimore Sun,* July 19, 1998, p. 1D.

Morrow, Lance. "The Shoes of Imelda Marcos." *Time,* March 31, 1986, p. 80.

Morton, Andrew. *Monica's Story.* New York: St Martin's, 1999.

Mui, Nelson. "Talkin' 'Bout a Luxe Revolution: *Esquire* Study Reveals the Democratization of Luxury." *Daily (New York City) News Record,* March 22, 2000, p. 30.

Mukerji, Chandra. *From Graven Images: Patterns of Modern Materialism.* New York: Columbia University Press, 1983.

Nabokov, Vladimir. *Nikolai Gogol.* New York: New Directions, 1944.

Nader, Ralph. *The Big Boys: Power and Position in American Business.* New York: Pantheon, 1986.

Nelson, Emily. "'90s Getaway: Drive to Hotel, Shop." *Wall Street Journal,* November 14, 1997, p. B1.

Nordhaus, William and James Tobin. "Is Growth Obsolete?" In Victor R. Fuchs, ed., *Policy Issues and Research Opportunities in Industrial Organization.* Fiftieth Anniversary Colloquium, University of Chicago, 1970. National Bureau of Economic Research, General Series No. 96. New York: NBER/Columbia University Press, 1972.

Ode, Kim. "It's a Mall, Mall World: But Is It a Shopper's Safe Haven?" *(Minneapolis) Star Tribune,* August 2, 1992, p. 6.

Offer, Avner. *In Pursuit of the Quality of Life.* New York: Oxford University Press, 1997.

Ormerod, Paul. *Butterfly Economics: A New General Theory of Social and Economic Behavior.* New York: Pantheon, 2000.

Packard, Vance. *The Hidden Persuaders.* New York: D. McKay, 1957.

——. *The Pyramid Climbers.* New York: McGraw-Hill, 1962.

——. *The Status Seekers.* New York: D. McKay, 1959.

Pavord, Anna. *The Tulip: The Story of a Flower That Has Made Men Mad.* London: Bloomsbury, 1999.

Pine, Joseph and James H. Gilmore. *The Experience Economy: Work Is Theater and Every Business a Stage.* Cambridge, Mass.: Harvard Business School, 1999.

Postrel, Virginia. "The Rich May Get Richer, but Numbers Suggest the Poor Are Doing Better, Too." *New York Times,* August 10, 2000, p. C2.

Quimby, Ian, ed. *Material Culture and the Study of Material Life.* New York: Norton, 1978.

Rainwater, Lee. *Social Standing in America: New Dimensions of Class.* New York: Basic, 1978.

Randazzo, Sal. *Mythmaking on Madison Avenue: How Advertisers Apply the Power of Myth.* Chicago: Probus, 1993.

Rosenblatt, Roger. *Consuming Desires: Consumption, Culture, and the Pursuit of Happiness.* Washington, D.C.: Island Press, 1999.

Ruark, Jennifer K. "Redefining the Good Life: A New Focus in the Social Sciences." *Chronicle of Higher Education,* February 12, 1999, pp. A13–15.

Safire, William. "Jeremiah Speaks." *New York Times,* November 29, 1999, p. A25.

Samuelson, Paul. *Economics.* New York: McGraw-Hill, 1962.

Schama, Simon. *Embarrassment of Riches: An Interpretation of Dutch Culture in the Golden Age.* New York: Knopf, 1987.

Schor, Juliet B. *The Overspent American: Why We Want What We Don't Need.* New York: Basic, 1998.

——. *The Overworked American: The Unexpected Decline of Leisure.* New York: Basic, 1991.

Schudson, Michael. "Delectable Materialism: Were the Critics of Consumer Culture Wrong All Along?" *American Prospect* 3 (1991): 26–35.

Scitovsky, Tibor. *The Joyless Economy: An Inquiry into Human Satisfaction and Consumer Dissatisfaction.* New York: Oxford University Press, 1976.

Seabrook, John. *Nobrow: The Culture of Marketing and the Marketing of Culture.* New York: Knopf, 2000.

Segal, Sam. *A Prosperous Past: The Sumptuous Still-Life in The Netherlands, 1600–1700.* Cambridge, Mass.: Fogg Art Museum, 1988.

Sekora, John. *Luxury: The Concept in Western Thought.* Baltimore, Md.: Johns Hopkins University Press, 1977.

Shorris, Earl. *A Nation of Salesmen: The Tyranny of the Market and the Subversion of Culture.* New York: Norton, 1994.

Silverman, Debora. *Selling Culture: Bloomingdale's, Diana Vreeland, and the New Aristocracy of Taste in Reagan's America.* New York: Pantheon, 1986.

Singer, Peter. "Famine, Affluence, and Morality." *Philosophy and Public Affairs* 1 (spring 1972): 229–43.

——. "The Singer Solution to World Poverty." *New York Times Magazine,* September 5, 1999, pp. 60–63.

Smith, Nancy deWolf. "All's Well That Ends Like the Tulip Mania." *New York Times,* April 4, 2000, p. A27.

Smith, Paul. "Welcome to High Street, Beverly Hills." *(London) Evening Standard,* December 9, 1996, p. 25.

Solomon, Michael R. and Bruce Buchanan. "Product Symbolism: Mapping a Consumption Community." *Journal of Business Research* 22, no. 2 (March 1991): 95–109.

Sombart, Werner. *Luxury and Capitalism.* 1938. Reprint, Ann Arbor: University of Michigan Press, 1965.

Springen, Karen. "It's a Feel-Good Millennium: Putting the Mass into Massage." *Newsweek,* January 18, 1999, p. 12.

Stevenson, Richard W. "Fed Says Economy Increased Net Worth of Most Families." *New York Times,* January 19, 2000, p. A1.

Stille, Alexander. "A Happiness Index with a Long Reach." *New York Times,* May 20, 2000, p. A17.

Tagliabue, John and Cathy Horyn. "Suddenly, at LVMH, Money *Is* an Object." *New York Times,* March 25, 2001, sec. 3, p. 1.

Thompson, Hunter. *Fear and Loathing in Las Vegas.* New York: Modern Library, 1996.

Thoreau, Henry David. *Walden.* Princeton, N.J.: Princeton University Press, 1971.

"Thoughts." *Forbes,* January 22, 2001, p. 160.

Todd, Richard. "Spending It: The New American High." *Worth,* October 1998, pp. 64–146.

Tolstoy, Lev Nikolayevich. "The Kreutzer Sonata." *Short Stories.* Translated by David McDuff. New York: Penguin, 1985.

Upmarket. "Upmarket Philosophy." *Economist,* December 26, 1992, p. 95.

Vaillant, George. *Adaptation to Life.* Boston: Little, Brown, 1977.

Veblen, Thorstein. *The Theory of the Leisure Class.* 1899. Reprint, Boston: Houghton Mifflin, 1973.

Venturi, Robert, Denise Scott Brown, and Steven Izenour. *Learning from Las Vegas: The Forgotten Symbolism of Architectural Form.* Cambridge, Mass.: MIT Press, 1977.

Voltaire. *Philosophical Dictionary.* Translated by Peter Gay. Vol 2. 1764. Reprint, New York: Basic, 1962.

Warhol, Andy. *The Philosophy of Andy Warhol: From A to B and Back Again*. New York: Harcourt Brace Jovanovich, 1975.

Weber, Max. *The Protestant Ethic and the Spirit of Capitalism*. 1905. Reprint, New York: Scribner's, 1958.

Weiner, Sue and Fran Michelman. *Shopping Bag Secrets*. New York: Universe, 1999.

Westermann, Mariet. *A Worldly Art: The Dutch Republic*. New York: Harry Abrams, 1996.

Williams, Raymond. "The Magic System." *New Left Review* 4 (1960): 27–32.

Zachary, Pascal G. "Obscured by the Roar of the World's Battles, Peace Is Advancing." *Wall Street Journal*, March 27, 2000, p. A1.

Zola, Émile. *The Ladies' Paradise*. Translated by Brian Nelson. New York: Oxford University Press, 1995.

Index

Page numbers in *italics* indicate illustrations.

Abercrombie & Fitch, 10, 95
Adcult, 154
Adelson, Sheldon, 228, 235
Advertising, *42*, 58–62; for cars, 20–23; and future of luxury, 280–82, *280*, *281*, *282–83*; and high art, 198–200, 208–11, *210*, *211*; history in media, 135–37; how it works, 68, 157–59; and luxury, 14–20, 65–68, 134–52, 154–73 *passim*; in Manhattan newspapers, 136; and religion, 156–57
Advertising Age, 83
Affluenza, 36–38, 287
Agins, Terry, 119
Akst, Daniel, 55
Alajalov, Constantin, 50
Alm, Richard, 28
American Express, 2; "People and Their Stuff" advertisement, 51–54, *52*
Antoinette, Marie, xi
Apter, Michael, 7
Aquafina (bottled water), 158n
Architectural Digest, 140, 146
Armani (store), xv, 9, 64, 86, 90, 91, 96, 106, 115, 121, 127, 128, 156, 230, 238, 244

Armani, Giorgio, 73
Arnault, Bernard, 129–34, 187; insight of, 129
Arnold, Matthew, 6
Arrow shirt advertisement, *184*
Art Brilliant (Rodeo Drive gallery), 91, 94, 111
Art of Simple Living (magazine), 151
Artemis (holding company), 131
Ast, Balthasar van der, 208
Aston Martin, 192
Auchincloss, Louis, 118
Ayer, N. W., and Son (advertising agency), 107

B. Altman & Co (store), 114, 170
Balenciaga (designer), 65, 125
Bally's Paris Resort and Casino, 226
Barberini, Antonio, 201
Barney's (store), 101, 113, 138
Barton, Bruce, 153
Baudrillard, Jean, 53
BBDO New York (advertising agency), 134–35
Beck, Gregory, 244–45
Beer, Thomas, 25
Belk, Russell, 28, 167, 262–64
Bellagio Gallery of Fine Art, 230–34, 250; art as "destination," 233;

297